IN LANDS NOT MY OWN

IN LANDS
NOT MY OWN

A WARTIME JOURNEY

Reuben Ainsztein

RANDOM HOUSE

NEW YORK

All rights reserved under International and Pan-American Copyright Conventions.
Published in the United States by Random House, Inc., New York,
and simultaneously in Canada by Random House of Canada Limited, Toronto.

RANDOM HOUSE and colophon are registered trademarks of Random House, Inc.

Photo p. ii courtesy of Brian and Frances Friedman

ISBN 0-375-50757-4

Random House website address: www.atrandom.com

Printed in the United States of America on acid-free paper

24689753

First Edition

Book design by Casey Hampton

The Jew, like the timid or scrupulous person, is not content merely to act or to think: he sees himself acting, he sees himself thinking. . . . It is not the man but the Jew that the Jews seek to know within themselves and through introspection.

—Jean-Paul Sartre, *Portrait of the Anti-Semite*

© 2002 Jeffrey L. Ward

CONTENTS

In Lands Not My Own

WILNO:
A ROMANTIC PRELUDE

O N ONE OF THE LAST DAYS of March 1940, I got up late enough to
save myself the expense of breakfasting. The weather was bleak,
rainy, and hopeless. So was my mood. There was no hope in the war, and
there was no hope for myself. As I came downstairs from my attic and
reached the lobby, with its air of departed splendor, I found an official letter
waiting for me on the marble table. The envelope had the words ON HIS
MAJESTY'S SERVICE on its front, but I was not anxious to open it, for I
had had many such letters before, and they all commenced with "We
regret . . ." When I did open it, neatly and without haste, there it was! The
impossible had happened: I was allowed to join the Royal Air Force Volunteer Reserve as an aircrew.

As I read the letter from the Air Ministry, sent as a result of Sir Samuel
Hoare's personal intervention, I knew that I had been given the chance to
take part in the struggle against Nazism, and I could not help thinking how
strange it was that a letter from an unknown ministry in an unknown city
should end one and open another chapter in the life of a twenty-two-year-
old Polish Jew living in Brussels.

I was born in Wilno on November 30, 1917, while the Germans were still
occupying the city and people were dying in the streets from hunger and

typhus. From my earliest childhood I was enthralled by its two rivers, the castle, the hill of the Three White Crosses with its pagan traditions, the woods covering the gentle heights that surround the amphitheater in which Wilno lies. As I grew up, my love for my native city grew as well, and I was proud to know that many well-traveled foreigners called Wilno "the Florence of the North."

My father and mother spoke Yiddish between themselves and to their children—the Yiddish of Wilno, clear and agreeable to the ear. When I was very young, my sisters mostly spoke Russian. Later they spoke Polish, so I learned to understand and speak all three languages almost simultaneously. The first language I learned to read and write was, however, Hebrew, followed soon by French.

My mother was a woman of old virtues and prejudices, with an iron will that spared nobody—least of all herself. Intensely religious, she followed every command of Israel. She would spend the long winter evenings and nights in darkness if there was nobody at home on Friday or Saturday to turn on the electric light, and she was scrupulously honest. It was my mother who first introduced me to England. She told me that after two thousand years of wanderings, persecution, and abasement, a great noble people called the English, who lived on an island where it always rained and the sun was hidden by a constant fog, had given us back Judea, in an agreement drawn up in 1917.

My father, as far as I can make him out, was predominately a skeptic. He never protested against my mother's bigotry but did not encourage it. He certainly had more respect for the wise atheist than for the foolish devotee. Nor did he believe in the Jews being a chosen people. Very early in my life he began to explain the Bible to me. He never dwelt on the ritual laws and the historical record it contains but drew my attention instead to the perpetual search after justice and truth to be found in its pages.

At home the atmosphere was very Jewish, but once I was outside, my environment was entirely Christian. Very soon I found myself facing the problem of having to achieve a synthesis between the two. This I did quickly and without much pain once I had started my studies in a Polish school. I became an enthusiastic student of Polish history and literature, so much so that I became the pride of my school in both and forgot my Hebrew entirely—a loss I now feel acutely. It was easy for me to achieve this synthesis, because the history of Poland appeared to me to have a moral sense, to have been the story of a struggle between good and evil, a constant fight against oppression, slavery, and injustice.

Yes, it seemed to me that Poland really was my country and the Poles really were my brothers; that no people in the world could better understand our misfortunes or sympathize with them more deeply. But very soon I learned how different reality was.

In the first place, it was the Poles themselves as individuals who caused my ideas to change. I had been led to believe that Poland was a nation of heroes and gentlemen, always practicing fair play, ready to help and protect women and the weak. Instead, my young Christian contemporaries did not think twice of attacking an outnumbered Jew without any provocation. As for the older Poles, who, having been brought up under the oppression of three empires, should have known better than their offspring, they only laughed at their sons' exploits and never hesitated to lie in their defense if a policeman appeared. For a time this ungentlemanly behavior seemed to be confined to the uneducated lower classes. But as I grew up I saw university students attacking Jewish women and old men with heavy sticks.

The ruling class of Poland was bent on destroying the economic basis of Jewish existence. Through heavy and unfair taxation they ruined Jewish businessmen, shopkeepers, and artisans; by applying discriminatory laws they prevented Jewish youths from obtaining a technical or university education and closed all government, army, state, and municipal careers to them; and finally, just before I left Poland, ruthless and brutal pogroms of Jewish shops occurred. During the last czar's reign, Pobedonostev, the Supreme Procurator of the Holy Synod of the Greek Orthodox Church, had candidly admitted that he hoped Russian anti-Semitism and pogroms would have this effect on Russian Jewry: "One third will die out, one third will leave the country, and one third will be completely dissolved in the surrounding population." The new Poland endeavored to carry out his plans to the letter. I finally understood why my parents, who had known the rule of the czar, nevertheless considered the Poles to be worse anti-Semites than the Russians, because they were better educated and because the worst among them were not illiterate peasants and workers but the so-called intelligentsia itself.

. . .

As I grew up, rejecting my mother's Zionism, slowly coming to terms with
the anti-Semitism of the Poles among whom we lived, I realized that what I
needed was a hero, a model to follow, and in this my guide was literature.
The first thinking hero I had come across had been Robinson Crusoe, an
Englishman, and as I grew up and the range of my reading widened, the
choice of an Englishman as hero became strengthened by Joseph Conrad's
writing. Somewhere between the ages of sixteen and twenty I also realized
that the English intellect was the one that satisfied my requirements best.
Of course, when we learn about a foreign country from books, we are
always behind the times. I was very much behind the times, because the
England I fell in love with was Victorian, and so was my English hero—
Faraday, Owen, Darwin, Livingstone, and Stanley all combined to produce him for me.

Yet how strange that I should have gone to England for an ideal. I could
have gone to Russia, lying so near, so well known, so exciting because of
the experiment that was taking place within her borders, and so appealing
to me as a Jew because of her proscription of anti-Semitism. I could have
gone to France, whose language and culture were admired by all around
me; whose ideals of freedom were so near to my heart; whom to love and
cherish I had been taught at school; whose serene, incisive reason, stopping
at nothing, appealed to my Jewish intellect. I could have gone to Germany,
whose learning and organization were admired by my father; whose language, thanks to Yiddish, seemed to be my own. Yet I chose a country
about which I knew nothing and whose ideals, because of my Polish
Catholic background, I ought to have hated. I was guided in my choice
mainly by my belief that, however powerful and attractive a nation may
seem, the real criterion of its greatness can be only the individuals who
compose it.

Natural sciences taught me that in nature there is an unbreakable sequence
of cause and effect. I believed that the same existed in human affairs and
that its results were evolution and progress. But at the age of sixteen doubts
came, and my bewilderment reached its climax when I came to the history
of the French Revolution. Here the same men who had brought about a
revolution because of certain logical principles they held in common fin-

ished by murdering one another. Why? And why was it that the Christian friends of my boyhood, who as children were as much at home in my house as I was in theirs, had become my enemies? Is there a way of finding out the causes that lie behind human actions, or do human actions depend on uncontrollable things in our souls known as "good" and "evil"?

At first there seemed to be no answer to these questions. And then the solution came in the shape of a small booklet called *The Communist Manifesto*. Today, whenever I reread it, I find its style a little too declamatory for my taste, although its truth remains unchallenged. But when I first read it, at the age of sixteen, every word seemed to bear thunder and lightning. Historical materialism explained to me why Antek, the friend of my childhood, was now a rabid anti-Semite; why the Jacobins murdered the Girondins; why those who had persecuted the Jews—in Spain or czarist Russia—came to ruin. To me Marxism was, and has remained, a magic key with which it is possible to unlock the mystery of motives and reasons that cause human actions. By using it we might get anywhere; by ignoring it we remain the prisoners of our passions and appetites, bound for catastrophe and frustration.

Having become a Marxist, I was forced to adjust my previous ideas, ideals, and plans. Communism appeared to me to be the only possible way in which Marxism could be applied in practice. Communism also attracted me because of its ruthless battle against all forms of racial hatred and its solution of national problems. Theoretically there was nothing in communism that I could find fault with. But whenever I met communists my enthusiasm for the idea disappeared. Their fanaticism and burning hate frightened me.

We had as neighbors a well-to-do Jewish family. The parents, quiet and mild, owned a tannery and were both liberals and Zionists. Two of their sons were Zionists, the third was sentenced to six years' imprisonment for spreading communist ideas and had to flee Poland. The daughter, a thin, breastless girl, was as ardent a communist as there ever could be. She spent five years in prison, contracted tuberculosis there, and was released just at the time when I was searching for an answer to my difficulties. I was then seventeen years old; she was about twenty-four but looked thirty-four. We used to talk quite often, and every time I was awed by the fury of her hatred for the capitalist world, by her fanatical faith in the Communist

Party. I could not help thinking of some Spanish inquisitor, with thin, cruel lips, burning eyes, and hollow cheeks, as I looked at her face lit with the glow of tuberculosis. Finally, I decided that she was a religious fanatic—just like any Catholic inquisitor or Jesuit I had read about—with the only difference that her religion was communism. And the moment I saw in communism a religion I was lost to it. Religion and fanaticism had been throughout history the cause of my people's sufferings. I refused to trust them even if they seemed to favor my people.

After three months of freedom she was arrested again. I later learned that she died in prison before the entry of Soviet troops into Wilno in 1939. Of course, I could not blame her for her fanaticism. Capitalism to her meant arrest for daring to proclaim her beliefs, torture at the police headquarters, and spitting her life away in a damp and sunless prison cell.

But, to be honest, I must admit that it was not on philosophical grounds alone that I refused to become a communist. Becoming a communist in pre-1939 Poland meant belonging to a secret cell and sharing, sooner or later, a fate similar to my neighbors'. Although I felt quite ready to fight in a revolution and, if need be, to die for its ideals, I was not prepared to become a martyr languishing behind bars. There was too much on the earth to be seen and experienced.

The kind of hero I wanted to become was a traveler or explorer. I had arrived at the conclusion that a traveler is a man who combines the personal pleasure of experiencing all sorts of adventures with usefulness to others. One day an overheard conversation between my mother and a friend of hers showed me that my aspirations were not completely fantastic. My mother's friend was telling her about her son, who had left Wilno to study medicine in Belgium and was now a doctor in the forests of the Belgian Congo. Suddenly everything seemed clear and possible to me. Somehow or other I, too, would find the means to study medicine in Belgium and then go to Africa. As a Marxist, I had had misgivings about becoming the average traveler, who only helps to spread imperialism and exploitation. But going to Africa as a doctor—although well paid and working for a big capitalist concern—did not seem objectionable to me.

I now became seriously interested in Africa and African travels. Of course, this made me want to read the works of Livingstone, Stanley, Baker,

Burton, and Speke. But I could not find their books in Polish or in any of the languages I knew, so my vague desire to learn English now became a firm resolve. I could not afford a teacher, and besides there were not many in Wilno whose knowledge and pronunciation I trusted. So I began to look for self-instruction books, only to find that they never agreed with one another when explaining the intricacies of English phonetics, and that they were full of omissions. At last I found a work whose bulk and thoroughness convinced me of its worth: the German *Toussaint-Langenscheidt Method*. The book cost almost two pounds, and I had to pay them out of my own pocket. I also had to pay most of my school fees at that time. However, because I was pretty popular as a tutor in Polish literature and history, I somehow managed to earn enough money to pay for both. Nevertheless, in order to get the *Langenscheidt* I had to give up going to the dentist and consequently lost two molars.

For almost eight centuries of our history in Poland, we had been sitting on a volcano. It erupted many times, but what prevented an explosion on the Spanish scale was not a greater amount of sympathy for the Jews than had been the case in other Christian countries, which had expelled us or tried to exterminate us in the course of the last ten centuries. It was self-interest or the realization of our indispensability that made the Polish ruling classes tolerate our presence in their country. Since the First World War, however, we had lost the guarantee provided by our economic indispensability. Laissez-faire capitalism was finished, state capitalism was crushing us, and a new Polish middle class could see a place for itself only by dislodging us. Most of us young Polish Jews were only too ready to give up our position in Poland's national economy if we could just find another country to go to. But the frontiers of the world were closed. So our enemies, thinking at first of expelling us, got used to the idea of having to liquidate us.

They dared not do it on their own. Poland was too weak; she had too many enemies and could not lose face with the West. But when, in 1933, Germany boldly recalled the Middle Ages and staged an auto-da-fé of books in the main squares of all German cities, we knew that the beast had been set free and would soon be at large in Poland.

The situation of the educated Jewish youth in Poland was tragic. There we were, with matriculation diplomas in our pockets and unable to go on

with our studies in Polish universities; or with university degrees yet finding most professions and all civil service and army careers closed to us.
Most of us did not want to go into business; besides, even in business there
was no future for us. Many were therefore ready to give up all our diplomas
and become humble peasants and laborers in Palestine. As for me, I was
still determined to become a pioneer, so when, in the summer of 1936, I
found myself despite the matriculation papers in my pocket with no hope of
being able to continue my studies in a Polish university, and with the
prospect of having to wait many years before being granted an immigration certificate to Palestine, I allowed my egotism to get the upper hand.

I had managed to save some money by acting as a tutor to my fellow
students. In the same year, the house my mother and a host of uncles and
aunts had inherited from my grandfather was sold. The little money that
became my mother's share was needed to give her security in her old age.
Nevertheless, I had no scruples in availing myself of my mother's generous
offer to pay my traveling expenses to Brussels and the fees for my first
year's studies in the University Libré there.

My mother did not see me off at the train. She turned back on the steps
leading to the railway station and did not even cry. She simply said in an
unusually quiet voice that she would never see me again.

BRUSSELS:
THE PAINFUL INTERLUDE

I ARRIVED IN BRUSSELS at the end of October and walked out of the Gare du Nord to be greeted by scores of steel-helmeted gendarmes armed with rifles. The same night I was given another taste by my cousin and her husband of the difficulties to come. But none of this mattered. At last I was breathing the air of the West and moving among civilized people. For nothing in the world was I going to give that up!

How could I possibly describe the feeling of safety and freedom that I enjoyed during my first weeks in Brussels? To be able to walk all the streets of the city at any time of the day and night; not to have to struggle between my pride and my instinct for self-defense every time I walked along a pavement and saw coming toward me a bunch of young Christians who might, being of superior numbers, assault me with impunity; to know that the policemen would not use their batons on me without the slightest provocation; to receive polite answers from everyone—all this made me feel almost as if I were living among my own people.

In the Bibliotheque Royale I was at last able to find all the books by Stanley, Livingstone, Speke, Burton, and Baker I had read about in Wilno but had not been able to obtain there. I also passed my entrance examination in French and began to attend lectures at the university, only to realize that the basis of my whole undertaking was nonexistent.

On leaving Wilno I had known that I could not count on receiving more than the equivalent of twenty-five shillings per month from home. This sum I expected to be sufficient to cover my rent. And so it was. As for other expenses, like transport, having an occasional haircut, visiting the cobbler, and once in a while going to the cinema, I had not given them much thought. Having lived in a small city, where I had a ten-minute walk to school and would have had no farther to go to the university, I never thought that transportation would be a problem. As for food, never having paid for it at home, having often forgotten to eat when immersed in books at the public library, having been used to eating at my school friends' homes or having them eat at my own without any ceremony, I assumed that my wealthy cousin could not refuse me one hot meal and a few sandwiches a day. Of course, I should have tried to find out while still in Wilno whether she and her husband would want to provide me with food, but it never occurred to me that any well-to-do Jew of East European origin would refuse to help a young and capable but impecunious Jewish student.

Having left Eastern Europe, however, and finding a niche in the liberal-bourgeois society of Belgium, my cousin and her husband promptly forgot all the essential traditions of East European Jewry. My cousin's husband found the whole idea of studying medicine sheer madness. The course lasted seven years—much too long for any man, let alone one without a steady income. Even if I managed to go through with my studies, he reasoned, I would find a stone wall awaiting me, for being a foreigner I would not be allowed to practice in Belgium, and my degree would not be recognized in Poland. My duty, he told me, was to make money and not to spend it on useless studies. We all had to make sacrifices at times; he, for instance, had sacrificed his youthful ambition to become a lawyer and had gone into business instead. To this I could, of course, reply that I failed to see what kind of sacrifice he had made by exchanging the profession of a second-rate lawyer for the position of sole director of the biggest firm selling calculating machines in Belgium. I kept quiet, however, because he had no sense of humor, and I still hoped to be able to eat his dinners. He finished his lecture by telling me to go back from where I had come.

How could I answer his arguments? I could not disclose to him that I had decided to study medicine for no practical commercial reasons but for the kind of reason for which one goes on polar expeditions or becomes a monk. Had I told him this, he would have thought me mad or infantile. I also knew perfectly well that by going back to Wilno I should not really help myself, because the hopelessness of my life there would make me bitter and disgruntled. I tried to explain to him the position of the Jewish youth in Poland, the feeling of impending tragedy we all shared there. I could not convince him. He was enjoying life and the advantages provided by his money too much to want to see the gathering shadows. He finished by telling me that it was my kind of young Jews, with our intellectual restlessness, who were responsible for the Russian Revolution and the rise of Hitler.

When I did not give in to his arguments and sarcasm, he came to hate me in a way that left no doubt as to his sentiments. He ignored me when he met me in his house and taught his two-year-old daughter to call me names. I finished by feeling afraid not only of him, his wife, and his daughter but even of his cook, a Russian peasant woman.

My first reaction was to avoid him and his house. I tried for a few weeks to live on a kilo of bread a day and an occasional bowl of soup. Hunger broke my determination, and I started going to his house again on weekdays when he was away. On Saturdays and Sundays he ate at home, so those two days, which in Belgium are so gay and plentiful in food and drink, were my blackest. I used to spend them studying, lying on my bed, thinking of food, or debating with myself whether I should borrow some money from my landlady and buy myself a good meal. Then, no longer able to concentrate on my books or to stand the loneliness of my room, I would take a stroll along the Chaussee d'Ixelles, resounding with music and the voices of people crowding its restaurants, or along Avenue Louise, with its opulent houses and stream of limousines, before returning to my room to try to study or sleep. And all the time I would be unable to prevent myself from asking why it should be so.

Having swallowed my pride, I had to realize that life was going to pile up in my way more obstacles, which would make pointless my readiness for self-abasement. The university was half an hour's fast walk from my room; it was a forty-minute tram ride from my cousin's house. When laboratory work commenced, I had only two hours between the end of lectures and attendance at the lab. In those two hours I could just manage to have dinner at my cousin's, if I took the tram both ways and she had the meal waiting for me. But the facts were that most of the time I had no money to pay the fares and that the dinner was usually finished by the time I arrived so, not daring to ask the formidable Russian cook if there was anything left, I had to take the tram back to the university hungrier than before. Thus my dinnerless and dry-bread days increased, after I had been in Brussels for some three or four months, to three or four a week.

When summer arrived and my placid cousin left for the seaside, my position became even worse. Very often I did not even have the odd franc with which to purchase a loaf of bread. There were many days when I lived entirely on the stale bread that the lodger on the floor below me would put out on the landing to be collected by the landlady for her chickens, which I stealthily appropriated. On several occasions I was reduced to the degrading necessity of borrowing sums of money not exceeding twenty francs from people I hardly knew, and to whom I would explain my financial embarrassments as due to the bank having refused to pay me my remittance either because the money order had been wrongly addressed or because my name had been incorrectly spelled by the sender.

I had not taken my examinations in July, because I was too far behind with my studies as a result of linguistic difficulties, ignorance of mathematics, and inability to concentrate due to a permanent state of semistarvation. It was therefore during the summer months that I had to make ready for October, when the second examination board would sit. But with hunger as my constant companion and utter loneliness sapping all my optimism, my memory and powers of concentration became worse than ever. I could work only in snatches and spent the little money I received from home on food, thus ending by owing my landlady three months' rent. When she threatened me with the police and deportation, I swallowed my remaining pride and wrote to a very dear friend in Wilno, received from her the equivalent of some five pounds, and thus managed to survive until the examinations, which I passed by some miracle.

Thus ended my first year in Belgium. I was sent from home enough money to pay the university fees for my second year's studies and began another year of continuous, soul-destroying struggle against hunger, loneliness, and adolescent pride. I made my visits to my cousin's home as rare as possible. I lived mostly on bread and soup and dreamed of the day when I should no longer have to see her and her husband at all. Having come to

Belgium as a student, I was not allowed to accept any kind of work; the penalty for breaking that law was deportation to Poland. But I had been working on my English since my departure from Wilno, and before 1938 was out I felt confident enough in my knowledge of that language to start looking for pupils who were beginners. Halfway through my second year at the university, I earned enough by giving English lessons to half a dozen Belgians and German Jewish refugees to be able to cease going to my cousin's home altogether.

By now I had become sufficiently fluent in English to begin writing naïve tales of adventure set in the forests and jungles of Africa. An American agent sold two of them and paid me the fantastic sum of $150. With this windfall I could enter my third year in Belgium still poor and very lonely but no longer condemned to outright starvation.

I had spent almost three months in Brussels when I visited for the first time the man whose mother's story had influenced my choice of career. I found him living in the top flat of his own house, an ultramodern building consisting of a shop and three apartments. He was a simple, clearheaded, unromantic, and slightly eccentric bachelor of thirty-five. He was meticulously clean and methodical in his habits, and he had one hobby: music—he played both the violin and guitar. Although he had completed his medical studies in a Belgian university and had spent several years in the Belgian Congo, he was not allowed to practice medicine in Belgium because he was a foreigner. Still, he did not seem to be much affected by this restriction. He had saved enough money while in the Congo to build the house in which he lived, and by practicing great economy, and avoiding the expense that matrimony would involve, he managed to live as a *rentier*. I had expected to find a man who would have something in him of the heroes of Conrad's *Heart of Darkness* and reflect some of Albert Schweitzer's idealism, but all I met was a man who at the prime of his life had lost all sense of adventure and could speak of his years in the Congo only in terms of money. As for his profession, even if once he had looked upon it as a vocation, he now saw it as a hopeless cul-de-sac. He advised me to profit by his experience and give up medicine.

It was even worse at the university. To my fellow Belgian students, the Congo was a place one went if one could not find a practice in Belgium.

Although I heard many of my liberal-minded colleagues criticize British rule in India, I never overheard them express the slightest doubt about the right of a small country like theirs to rule over an immense empire and alien races thousands of miles away.

I also began to notice the chinks in the democratic structure that had at first seemed so impressively solid and sure of itself. I saw them first when I asked my fellow students what they thought of the world around them. They replied without any feeling of embarrassment that they had not given it much thought. When I asked them what they lived for, they answered, without any shame, *"Pour s'amuser."* I tried to find out how they were going to defend the democratic way of life that had been bequeathed to them. They told me they did not care. They were glad to be Belgian because nowhere else could one get chips and steak and beer as cheaply as in *la petite Belgique*. A good enough reason to be proud of one's country, no doubt, but in the struggle that I knew was forthcoming, would their ideals be strong enough to make them die for a way of life that meant only the satisfaction of their senses and their stomachs?

I had arrived in Belgium armed with a very simple and uncomplicated Marxist outlook: capitalism in the West was doomed and still survived only because of the cowardice, treachery, or muddleheadedness of social democratic leaders. But I had common sense enough to realize after a few months' stay the fallacy of my oversimplified view. I realized soon that an economic system capable of providing its unemployed with more to eat and more fun than a socialist system could not be written off as one that needed only a coup de grâce. I could also perceive the much deeper failings of the decadent capitalist system.

It was prostitution that made me recognize the system's utter immorality and absurdity. The part of Brussels in which I lived, called Ixelles, is the Montmartre and Montparnasse combined of the capital of Belgium. I met *les poules* everywhere, in the house where I lived, in cafés, in restaurants, in the streets. Having been deeply impressed by Tolstoy's *Resurrection* as a boy of fifteen, I pitied them. I remember a little *poule* with the most doll-like and angelic face in the world. I used to see her sitting on the terrace of a café at the Porte de Namur. Lonely and imaginative as I was at that time, I almost fell in love with her. I imagined myself rescuing her from the clutches of vice, making her my wife, and educating her to be my equal.

One night, however, she accosted me. Despite her resemblance to a Dresden china shepherdess, her voice was very ordinary and her speech very vulgar. The spell was broken when I asked her why she had chosen her particular way of making a living. She told me that, as she had not been well educated, the only kind of work she could find was as a maidservant or a salesgirl in a department store with a salary not exceeding five hundred francs a month. In her present occupation, she could earn as much in a single night.

That confession shook me considerably but did not change my ideas about the causes of prostitution. Then I found out that the majority of her colleagues adduced the same reasons for their occupation. I saw that not only were they satisfied with their way of earning a living but they even managed to remain quite respectable. There was one who used to be accompanied to her place of business by her own mother. Once arrived, they used to kiss and part, the mother going off to do her shopping at the nearby department stores and her daughter starting on her beat.

In Poland, with her capitalist system hardly developed and already decaying, prostitutes were forced to choose their profession by their own stupidity, by the cruelty of men, or by hunger. Their profession was disagreeable at the best and debasing, exhausting, dangerous, and badly paid in most cases. There was no doubt in my mind that, given an opportunity, the majority of prostitutes in Poland would have returned to an honest way of earning a living. There vice did not pay, unlike in the West, where it paid better than virtue. And here was the crux of the whole problem of decaying capitalism.

Thus a moment came when it seemed to me as if I had left behind me, in the East, a world of robust barbarians, only to find in the West a world of degenerate egotists. Which world was I to choose? Both repulsed me.

Such was my state of mind at that distant time, when Spain was being cynically sacrificed and the rape of Czechoslovakia prepared. Then Munich came. I could not understand without forgiving the ignoble motives behind the actions of British politicians, because what was Czechoslovakia to them if not another pawn on the bewildering chessboard of world politics? But I could not even begin to understand the attitude of the rulers and a large number of the people who inhabited the country of my birth. Poland's part in the rape of Czechoslovakia made me decide to get rid of my Polish nationality and never fight in a Polish army.

At the same time the much deeper bond of language with my native country slowly dissolved. I say dissolved because there was no sudden severance. I had wanted to become a member of the English-speaking world since I was sixteen, and the example of Joseph Conrad gave me hope that such a thing was possible. But I never formulated that hope in words, because I doubted my linguistic abilities. However, toward the end of 1938 my knowledge of English, added to my interest in all things English, made my position—that of a Polish Jew studying in French in Belgium but interested only in England, her language and literature—unbearably absurd at times. I was like a scholar who had fallen in love with ancient Greece. Instead of learning to know my Englishmen as living persons, I learned to know them as if they were Homeric or Sophoclean heroes: arrested in time, finite, unchangeable, and immortal. The dangers of such a method are obvious, its contradictions all too numerous. I tried to build a transcendental figure of an Englishman by amalgamating the traits of all the Englishmen, or rather Britons, I had met within novels or read about in history. I had before my eyes Robinson Crusoe, Mr. Pickwick, General Gordon, Livingstone and Stanley, the unexpected heroes of Aldous Huxley, D. H. Lawrence, and J. B. Priestley, and I tried to telescope them in time and space, create a synthesis of all of them, and obtain God's own Englishman. Naturally I failed. If my obsession with her was not to become a kind of madness, the only way out was to see England. But how was I to achieve it? To cross the Channel as an emigrant was impossible; to cross it otherwise one had to prove to the cautious British immigration authorities that one was financially independent—a demonstration beyond my capabilities.

With this idea master of my thoughts and dreams, my medical studies receded into the background and I became ready to sacrifice them for even a short stay in England. But nobody was interested in my willingness to sacrifice anything. At last I could see only two ways leading to my goal. One was Conradesque: to master the English tongue, write a book in it, and be invited to come over to England. The other way seemed easier: England needed soldiers; notwithstanding all kinds of recruiting campaigns, she appeared unable to find them. Why not enlist as a private, show thus that I loved England well enough to be ready to die for her and, at the same time, satisfy my urge to live the life of a man of action?

I wrote to the British Embassy in Brussels for the first time in 1937. Then Munich came and I wrote again. This time I was not even favored with a reply. Yet the problem had by then become serious. I was already convinced that war was inevitable, and when it broke out I wanted to fight against Germany; even if Poland were to fight against Germany, I had no wish to join her army and serve under anti-Semitic, sword-rattling officers and arrogant, semiliterate NCOs.

Finally came the spring of 1939. A disgusting cowardice and refusal to face facts still held Western Europe in chains. It was not until after Jozef Beck's speech, in which that sinister Polish foreign minister dared tell Hitler the Poles would fight for the integrity of their land, that the West appeared to begin facing realities and gathering courage at last. I felt better than I had felt since the days when Franco's forces had been stopped at the gates of Madrid. My shock, therefore, on reading of the Stalin-Ribbentrop pact was very great. My heart went cold and my brain numb when the news broke on that beautiful, sunny day.

It took me some days to collect my thoughts. My heart was full of dreadful forebodings. I knew that I was going to witness, and become part of, a great tragedy. I saw this as having a double aspect: one, personal and Jewish, the other, universal and human. I foresaw the Jewish tragedy in Poland. I felt sure that Poland would be attacked, and although I never expected her to be vanquished in a fortnight, I knew that she would be invaded. Nazi troops in Poland, apart from giving vent to their own hatred of Jews, would release the scarcely controlled native anti-Semitic furies, and a massacre would follow—a massacre worse than Chmielnicki's pogroms in the Ukraine, during which more than two hundred thousand Jewish children, women, and men had been slaughtered. (Of course, I could never imagine the full magnitude of the disaster that was to overtake European Jewry.) As for the universal aspect of the tragedy, my belief that all the forces of progress always rallied and united when it came to the real test was shattered. For to me, in spite of all the differences between capitalist Britain and France on one side and the Soviet Union on the other, the three shared fundamentally the same beliefs derived from the ideas that had spread over Europe after the Religious Wars and had found their classic expression in the French trinity of liberty, equality, and fraternity.

Faced with this onslaught of unsettling events, I took refuge in an increased attachment to England. Her calm, unruffled common sense—so snaillike at times but so human and near to my heart just because of its limitations—became like a beacon in an ocean of uncertainty and heart searching.

As it turned out, in that summer of 1939 little time was left for intellectual debate. Hitler acted, the Second World War broke out, and the acid test of blood, force, and determination took the place of mental arguments in which one played an eternal, inconclusive game of chess against oneself.

The outbreak of war meant that I was left without any source of income. No more money could come from home, and all my pupils gave up taking English lessons for a while as well. Yet I do not remember that period as a time of physical privations, for at last I met people who gave me their friendship, company, and even love. I was befriended by a Walloon couple, who had moved into the house in which I lived in the terrible days of September. Monsieur and Madame Caprasse, who came from the Ardennes, preserved the friendliness and freshness of the large families and forest in the midst of which they had been born and brought up, and professed a form of Catholicism that was sincere, tolerant, and mitigated by their Gallic mentality. Although deeply fond of children, they had none and gave me much of the affection they would have bestowed on a son of their own.

In the same memorable September I made friends with a middle-aged Flemish couple. The Minnes owned a grocery that I began to visit regularly after the outbreak of the war. As I always purchased the same article—potatoes—Madame Minne conceived the idea that they formed my only food and one day, while the shop was full of chattering housewives, told me in her brusque, tactless Flemish fashion to take some ham with my potatoes and not to worry about the payment. Nobody's embarrassment can compare with that of a proud pauper; mine was so great that I could feel myself go crimson. I left the shop without the ham, but returning again I discovered the simplicity of heart, uncalculating kindness, and deep humanity of the brave little woman and her guileless husband. They gave me their friendship and confidence without stint or reserve and bestowed on me the supreme gift of their race: outspoken loyalty.

The urge to fight Germany became stronger every day, and I decided to try to join the RAF. One late February day in 1940, I bought a copy of *John O'London's Weekly*, read on its front page an article on Stendhal by Sir Samuel Hoare, then secretary for air, and became convinced that Sir Samuel was the type of man to understand my motives. I found his private address in *Who's Who* and wrote to him. Some ten days later came an impersonal acknowledgment of my letter written by his secretary. And a week or so after that, as I came down from my attic one morning, I found the letter described at the beginning of this book awaiting me on the table in the lobby. The impossible had happened: I was granted permission to join the Royal Air Force Volunteer Reserve as an aircrew.

BELGIUM IN MAY

I DID NOT RUSH OFF to the British Consulate for a visa; I did not celebrate; I did not even tell my newly acquired Belgian friends what that
letter meant to me. How could I? It would have meant opening my heart
and disclosing all my dreams to strangers.

I decided first to see the British air attaché and was received by his secretary, an elderly gentleman who, to my inexperienced eyes, looked like a
British cabinet minister. He took my letter to the air attaché, left me waiting
a short while, and then ushered me into the presence of the attaché, Wing
Commander Davies, who got up and shook hands. He was over six feet
tall, lanky, and did not look at all like the colonels I had learned to know in
Poland. He had a face that was a cross between that of a playboy and that of
an intellectual; I can think of only one face that resembled his: Noël Coward's. His exquisite courtesy and boyish grin set me at ease the moment I
came into his office. His deprecating manner made me feel as if we had
known each other for a long time. We chatted for about a quarter of an
hour, he listening to me as if it were his duty as air attaché to spend his time
meeting rather odd young men of my kind. He then told me to go to the
Passport Control Office, obtain a visa there, and cross the Channel. When
I left him, I was the happiest man in Brussels.

I went directly to the Passport Control Office, had my passport taken away, and was finally brought into the presence of the passport control officer himself, a certain Major B. The major was a highly unmilitary figure: handsome, groomed to the point of slickness, he had about him an air of cool arrogance. He fixed on me with a cold stare and said, "Sorry, I cannot give you a visa."

That was all. The shock was so great that I did not even have the presence of mind to ask why he refused to issue me one. I left the office and walked back to the house where I had my room, at first too dazed even to speculate as to why my request had been refused. I have since asked myself many times, without ever being able to find an adequate answer. I did not go back to the air attaché then and there and ask him to intervene on my behalf. The anticlimax was so great that in my then state of mind I felt like saying, "Damn you all, you British."

The invasion of Denmark and Norway came; so April ended and May began. A few bombs had fallen on Brussels, but there had been no intentional bombing of the city. The streets were crowded, the trams crammed as full as matchboxes. There was an air of animation that, somehow, did not convey to me the meaning of war. On the first day of the inevitable invasion there was no panic, none of the despondency, animal terror, and near hysterics of the days that preceded Munich. The only disconcerting feature of those first days of war was the constant passing of German planes over Brussels. The defenses of the capital fired all the time but were obviously insufficient and absolutely ineffective. The sirens went continuously, but on the second day of war nobody paid any more attention to their wail, because obeying their warning would have meant spending at least half of every hour in shelters, and also because the German planes were obviously not interested in bombing Brussels. The most ominous feature was, however, the absolute absence of Allied aircraft.

An experienced observer, however, would have seen signs of panic on the very first day, which I failed to notice. Some people who owned cars were leaving for France. They were, of course, people who had decided on such a step a long time before. There were Jews among them, mostly wealthy ones. On my way home I saw a mob in front of a Jewish furrier's shop, encircling in a menacing manner the furrier's car and calling him a *Boche* and a fifth columnist because he was leaving for France. Looking obviously foreign, I was stopped twice by eager Belgian Boy Scouts and asked to produce my identity card. To them, of course, as an *étranger*, I was a potential Nazi agent.

We were all waiting for the French and British armies to appear. There were vague rumors to the effect that *les Tommies* were approaching Brussels from Charleroi. It must have been early in the afternoon when I heard the people, massed on Avenue Louise, cheer wildly and rather hysterically. I was having lunch at the Caprasses'; I dropped my knife and fork and raced down Rue de la Concorde to Avenue Louise.

A stream of British lorries, Bren carriers, and motorcycles was flowing from Chaussee de Charleroi into Avenue Louise. The vehicles were freshly painted, the soldiers wore their helmets at rakish angles, and the fresh green of their uniforms seemed to bring the breath of spring and green fields into the anxious city. The soldiers were young, smiling, and sunburned. There was nothing of the heaviness and clumsiness of Belgian soldiers about them, nor anything of the grim, ruthless, and cocksure air Polish soldiers display. They looked strikingly boyish and friendly, and, somehow, there was something Boy Scoutish about them. The Belgians lining both sides of the avenue threw chocolate, cigarettes, and even bottles of beer at them, and the soldiers caught them with great agility and raised their thumbs in a salute that looked half serious, half comic. It was the first time in my life that I saw so many Britons together, and I felt as proud of them as if I were already one of their company. Sadly, the flow of men and vehicles dried up all too soon.

I managed to see the air attaché again on the second day of the invasion. He told me to wait until things got more settled, then he would see about getting me over to the United Kingdom. When I asked him how long it might take for things to get settled, he replied with a grin that it depended entirely on Hitler. Seeing that I was far from reassured by his reply, he soon presented me with a document in English and French that ran as follows:

To Whom It May Concern

This is to certify that the bearer of this letter is Mr. R. AINSZTEIN
He is endeavoring to go to England, via France, to join the RAF. Will
you please do everything in your power to help him on his way?

Wing Commander E. P. M. Davies,
Air Attaché, Brussels

I read it and felt as honored as if I had been knighted. With that document
in my pocket I felt as certain of reaching England as if a special airplane had
been assigned to fly me over there. However, although it was already May 12,
I did not feel in a special hurry to set out and called on the Caprasses to tell
them of my letter of recommendation and to offer my assistance.

I found Madame Caprasse alone watching the street through the large
bay window of their sitting room. Her husband had gone to the Belgian
War Ministry in order to find out whether he was expected to stay in Belgium or leave for France. I cheered her up as well as I could and dismissed
any possibility of immediate danger, although the German tide had already
swept through all the frontier defenses of Belgium. This fact had, however,
become known to the inhabitants of Rue de la Concorde, who were suddenly displaying the most astounding degree of familiarity with one
another. The street became like any alley in Naples, with people talking to
one another through opened windows, cars being driven out of garages
and stopped in front of the house entrances; bags, trunks, cots being
stowed inside them or strapped outside; mattresses fastened to the roofs of
the Fords, Chevrolets, Citroëns, Buicks, and Packards as precautions
against machine-gun attacks from low-flying German aircraft.

I was glad when Monsieur Caprasse came back, because his wife had
become almost hysterical with fear at the sight of all this activity. He
arrived with his mind made up to leave for France. We decided to catch a
train that evening, and I declared my willingness to help them with their
luggage and to accompany them as far as Paris, from where I intended to
make for the nearest harbor and sail for England.

It was almost midnight when we were finally packed and ready to leave
for the station. I went out to look for a taxi and found none but saw an
armored car spraying the Porte Louise with its automatic weapons. I was

relieved to get back without being shot or arrested. I found the Caprasses listening patiently to the discourse of our landlady, who was inventing enemies where there were none, exaggerating dangers, and generally being of more use to Hitler's armies than a fully armed German paratrooper dropped in the center of Brussels.

When she finally left us, we tried to snatch a few hours' sleep. At five o'clock in the morning we were again in the street looking in vain for a taxi. We had to wait for the first trams; in spite of the early hour they were closely packed, and it was only after some struggle that we managed to board one. Had I been alone with my small suitcase, which was just big enough to hold a few articles of underwear and a very large Anglo-Polish dictionary, I would not have found it difficult to reach the Gare du Midi on foot or by tram. However, it was a much more difficult proposition to do so laden as we were with two large suitcases and a fair-sized hamper containing provisions for at least a fortnight.

When we finally arrived at the station, I almost gave up hope of ever being able to board a train. The immense square in front of the railway station was tightly packed with people, and when we somehow or other managed to get inside the station, we were informed that it was no use boarding trains for France without a French visa, because the French turned back everybody who was not in possession of one. Of course, with the wing commander's letter in my pocket, I felt absolutely convinced that no Frenchman would dare to turn me back, but Monsieur Caprasse and his wife hurried off to the French Consulate.

I sat on a bench in the Boulevard du Midi and observed the wide thoroughfare. As midday approached the wide boulevard became ever more congested with traffic. I could not but marvel at the number of motorcars that kept driving past me in an unending stream. Then came bicycles. Thousands and thousands of Belgians, dressed in black and wearing caps, with red blankets on their backs or strapped behind the saddles of their steel steeds, filed past my astonished eyes. Then came immense numbers of slow, two-wheeled carts, drawn by deliberate and powerful Brabant horses, with whole farmer families—grandmothers, canaries, cats, and all piled on top of their belongings—and the ever-present red blankets spread or neatly rolled. I never imagined that there were so many red blankets in the whole of Europe, let alone in Belgium.

Although it was past noon, the Caprasses had not returned yet from the consulate. At two o'clock in the afternoon, I went to the café at which we had arranged to meet to find a slip of paper covered in Madame Caprasse's handwriting telling me that they had just returned from the consulate but had not obtained any visas and that they were sorry but they had been told that there was a train on the point of leaving for the South of France and could not wait for me.

To see the effect of panic reflected in the behavior of people whom I loved and respected made me painfully sad. I felt as disappointed and hurt as I had been only on those occasions when, as a child or adolescent, I had learned about the gaps between idealism and reality. Luckily I had no time for recriminations as I struggled inside the Gare du Midi and fought my way through a terrorized and stupid mob in order to reach the platforms. When I finally did get near the trains, I found that all of them were going toward the Belgian coast. I did not want to board any of them, because I thought that the Belgian ports would be completely choked with refugees trying to cross to England; determined to reach France, I finally found one bound for Paris.

It was five o'clock when the train steamed from underneath the great shadow of the Gare du Midi into a late May afternoon. The light, sun, and the green fields that surrounded us as soon as we left Brussels cheered me up a little but could not entirely dispel my mood of sadness. The fact that I was on a train and on my way to England came as an anticlimax after the excitement of the last three days. For the first time since the early morning of May 10, I ceased living in the immediate present and began to think of what was to come.

At Baisieux, the French frontier station, a very tall Frenchman told us to leave the train with our passports ready for inspection. The gendarmes accompanying him asked us whether we had been bombed; the train preceding ours had been hit and carried some twenty dead.

I was one of the first to take my place in the queue, confident that with my letter of recommendation the whole business would be a mere formality. The same tall Frenchman was now seated behind a small table and applying a big rubber stamp to the proffered documents. I handed over my passport; he glanced at it, put it away, and told me that being a Pole I could not cross at Baisieux but had to enter France through another border post. I endeavored to make him read the air attaché's letter and explain to him that I was not on my way to join the Polish Army in France but he refused to listen. He looked up at the sky, jumped at the slightest noise resembling the drone of aircraft engines, and was impervious to reasoning. He wanted the train to be out of his station as soon as possible and had no time for me. *"Foutez-moi la paix!"* was his only comment. *"J'enmerde votre attaché . . ."*

I left him in peace, got my suitcase out of the train, and decided to adopt a fatalistic attitude. My bad luck presently became obvious to me, for hardly had I taken my suitcase out of the train when a plane, which had been hovering above us in the darkness, dropped a flare. The flare was enough for the Frenchman to give up checking the passengers and to have the train pull out of his station as fast as the brakes and steam allowed. I remained at Baisieux, because I did not want to lose my passport.

I went inside the station building and lay down upon a bench. Finally I sank into an uneasy sleep, through which I could still hear the droning of a plane turning overhead like a moth around a lamp, but I was suddenly awakened by a deafening explosion that almost threw me off the bench and by a Frenchman's cry of terror: *"Nom de Dieu!"* I remained lying on the bench for some time to prove to myself that I was not scared, then got up and went into the small square outside the station. The bomb had fallen practically in the middle of it and destroyed the memorial erected to the dead of the First World War. It was almost five o'clock in the morning by now, and the workers' café was open in the square. I had a cup of bitter black coffee and then started chasing after my passport. It took the Frenchman some time to find it, and when he did I boarded the local workers' train.

The railway station at Mons was burning as we pulled in, for it had been hit a short time before our arrival. I made for the buffet; there was nobody inside, and beer was pouring freely from the taps and out of shattered barrels. The whole place looked like a Wild West saloon after a gun battle.

We pulled out of Mons very promptly but, instead of turning west, we turned north back into Belgium. Still, I did not worry too much. We were no more than thirty miles from the French border.

Altogether I spent two full days and two full nights aboard that train, and when we reached Courtrai, only forty miles west of Mons, I decided to continue my journey on foot.

In a café I asked the way to the nearest frontier point, which turned out to be in Menin, some ten miles away. As I was on the point of leaving, a Belgian who had been sitting in a corner came up to me and asked me if he might come along. "Of course," I said.

He was a slim man of about thirty, dressed meticulously but quite inappropriately for tramping—a typical clerk. Married, a father, the proud owner of a house, he was afraid of wet grass and too much walking, and absolutely out of his depth whenever there were no houses and trams to be seen. His wife had packed a suitcase that was more like a trunk, and he had managed to get it all the way from Brussels to Courtrai. He was making for the South of France, where, he had been told, the Belgian Army would be reorganized.

I helped him carry his suitcase. After so many days and nights spent in a cramped position, it was a real pleasure to use my muscles again. It was hot, and we felt very thirsty but, as we had taken the shortest cut across fields, there was nowhere we could slake our thirst. Thousands of people were trudging along the same road; I began to sing Polish and Russian marching songs, and their rhythmic cadence helped my companion to keep in step and use his lungs. Freed from the petty worries of how I was going to pay my next month's rent or where my next meal would be coming from, I felt carefree and young again, and almost indestructible.

We reached Menin only to find that the French frontier was closed, so we tramped on to Comines. Unlike Menin, it had not been invaded by refugees and therefore appeared orderly, quiet, and enchantingly peaceful. We stopped at a café that stood opposite a bridge spanning the banks of the canal that formed the frontier between France and Belgium. French customs officials were drinking in the café, while French and British soldiers were strolling over the bridge into Belgium, buying cigarettes and drinking Belgian beer, then returning without formalities to the French side.

It seemed absurd to me that I should not be able to cross that bridge. I approached two British soldiers and explained to them my problem. While they debated my case, a French soldier approached our group and inquired in broken English if he could be of any use. Explaining my predicament to him, I won his sympathy. He had been taken prisoner by the Germans in the First World War and had been interned in a part of Poland which I knew very well. He also had a son of my age fighting somewhere in Belgium, so by helping me he felt that he might be helping his boy. At last the appropriate French official was found. The French veteran and the two British soldiers slapped my shoulders and repeated: *"Bon homme,* very *bon homme";* the French official declared that he could not permit me to cross the bridge because the border was closed. The French soldier called him a bureaucrat, a *couillon,* and, last but not least, a saboteur preventing a brave lad from joining the Allied forces. The bureaucrat surrendered and, having shaken hands with my Belgian companion, I crossed the bridge and found myself in France.

The Roads of Flanders

I T WAS THE HOUR OF CURFEW and I had nowhere to sleep. I decided
that the only thing to do was get stopped by a patrol and spend the night
in a guardroom. I advanced along the deserted streets cherishing that hope
until, at last, I heard the heavy step of a soldier. I turned a corner and found
myself in front of a French *poilu*. He called on me to halt, which I did
promptly. He then asked me who I was. *"Ami,"* I replied. *"Ne bouge pas ou
je te creve,"* he said, placed the point of his bayonet between my shoulder
blades, and pushed me forward. His unsteady gait and idiotic repetition of
"Ne bouge pas ou je te creve" made me realize that he was drunk. So I kept
quiet, hoping fervently that he would not pull the trigger on his rifle by
mistake with his shaking fingers. At last we reached the guardroom—a former shop of some kind—and he allowed me to lie down on the floor. I fell
asleep and was awakened in the early hours of the morning by the insistent
drone of a hovering plane. Ack-ack guns were barking in concerted outburst against it, but without any obvious results. At last the plane dropped
its bombs and quiet returned. I tried again to sleep, but the day was breaking and soldiers started coming in. They all went to the corner where I was
lying to have a look at me as if I were some kind of a prize catch. I pretended I was still asleep, and I could hear them telling one another that I
was a German paratrooper or spy arrested in the dead of night.

At five o'clock in the morning their sergeant entered and made his arrival ominous to me by his loud *"Où est ce sale Boche?"* I got up and told him indignantly that I was no *Boche*. He told me to shut up. I answered that I had to talk in order to explain who I was. He pulled out his pistol, pointed it at my chest, and invited me to try. He was a head shorter than I, had the broken nose of a boxer, the eyes of a pig, and cauliflower ears; and his breath was laden with the sour vapors of wine. He searched me, looked contemptuously at my identity papers and credentials, flung the contents of my suitcase upon the floor, tore my Anglo-Polish dictionary out of its cover, and emptied my last tin of English pipe tobacco upon my shirts and socks. After that he told me that all my documents were forged and that if he could have his way he would shoot me on the spot, called me the filthiest names he could remember, flung my papers into my face, and left the guardroom.

It took me quite a while after he had gone to get over my feelings of indignation. The other soldiers in the guardroom, visibly ashamed of their sergeant's behavior, brought me a mug of black coffee, a packet of their own issue tobacco—black and strong as powder—and consoled me with remarks such as "You know, *mon petit*, there are so many spies about."

At about seven in the morning their officer arrived and I was taken into his presence. He was an elderly captain who gazed in silence at my passport and letter of recommendation and, having satisfied himself as to their genuineness, returned them to me, then advised me to make my way through Armentières, Hazebrouck, and Saint-Omer. He came out with me into the street to show me the way, and I said good-bye to him and his soldiers.

I arrived at Armentières tired, thirsty, and hungry. This clean, modern town was empty of its inhabitants and invaded by refugees. I tried to buy some bread, but none was to be obtained, for the bakers, many of whom owned motorcars, had been the first to flee. I went into a café full of middle-aged Frenchmen in uniforms that went back to the First World War. Although I instinctively refused to reflect, I could not help feeling anguish at this sight of unpreparedness and disorganization. They were on their way to mobilization depots that were already inside invaded territory, and most of them were drunk and full of the spirit of *m'en foutisme*. I left the café in a hurry.

By now the heel of my right foot, which I had hurt on the way from Menin to Comines, was causing me acute pain. I stopped by the first stream I came to and bathed it. On my heel there was a red patch of raw flesh looking very much like one of those sores I used to see on the backs of poor hacks in Polish towns. I had to set my teeth when I put on a fresh sock and the down-at-heel shoe. I had decided to reach Hazebrouck in the evening, and I was determined to do so, sore or no sore, and in spite of the agony that shot through my body with the monotony of a toothache at every step I took.

My natural curiosity helped me along, for the spectacle offered by the highway was of an elemental nature that transcended simple misery, wretchedness, suffering, and terror. A stream of carts, motorcars, taxis, bicycles, and humans advanced slowly along the road, both sides of which were strewn with abandoned vehicles. Impressive American limousines, mostly from Belgium and even Holland, symbols of their owners' importance, wealth, and often their very raison d'être, lay stranded by the roadside for lack of petrol, because they had broken down, or because they had been thrown off the highway by an impatient military column. War, that great but very unfair leveler, had been abroad on this road and had hit out indiscriminately at rich and poor, strong and helpless, women, men, and children.

The end of the day found me a few miles from Hazebrouck. There came a moment—a moment I never experienced before or since—when my legs simply refused to obey my will. I stopped full of disbelief that such a thing could happen: that the pain caused by my heel could achieve such a total divorce between my brains and my muscles. I tried again to advance ever so slowly—without much avail. I gave up trying, sat down against a bunker, and hid my head in my hands in a wave of weariness and pain. When I looked up again at the road, there was a pause in the stream of refugees.

The road in front of me remained empty and silent. All of a sudden a little girl of four or five appeared, hopping along on each of her tiny feet alternately. The spectacle was unbelievable. Her quiet enjoyment of herself and the world, her being alone on this straight highway, seemed incredible and unaccountable to me who, at that moment, almost began to doubt my own reality. Then, after a very long while, her mother and a number of other women, pushing barrows loaded with household goods, appeared, and the world became real again.

A derelict hut stood not far from the bunker, and from it a French boy emerged and came over to me. "You don't look too cheerful," he said. "Where are you making for?"

"Saint-Omer and Calais," I replied.

"Well, that's a long way. Why not spend the night with us in the hut?" he suggested, and I accepted.

The hut was filled with hay. I lay down and was given some bread and cheese by the boy's father and then offered a good *coup de rouge*. After that I felt better. My hosts were workers from Lille whose factory had been closed without any warning the day before. Before leaving for the South of France the management forgot to pay them their full wages but did remember to tell them to make their way to some city beyond the Garonne. They were on their way.

The following morning I entered Hazebrouck. I begged the first Frenchman I met standing outside his little house for an old pair of sandals or slippers and was given a pair of the latter. With the worst of my pain now gone, I set out on my way to Saint-Omer. I was now in a frantic hurry to reach the coast. The innumerable motorcars, taxis, and even buses from Brussels that rested in the ditches by the road gave the impression of a human wave that had passed in a terrible hurry. Coming in its wake, I could not help feeling very late, perhaps too late, yet I could not accelerate my pace because of my heel. I was also getting weaker by the hour and suffering constantly from thirst. I had not had a hot meal for days, and I could now notice my thinness. The weather was still glorious and hot.

A few miles on I noticed a British three-ton lorry and a strange looking contraption, whose name I learned later to be a dumper, parked outside a café. The driver of the dumper, a young, fair-haired Englishman without any headgear, his shirt open and his sleeves rolled up, had left the wheel of his strange vehicle and was drinking beer out of a bottle. I showed him the air attaché's letter and asked if he could give me a lift. He told me to wait for the sergeant, who was having a drink in the café, and show my documents to him.

The sergeant, a dark-haired, wiry-looking English soldier, his steel helmet aslant, agreed and pushed a bottle of black beer into my hands.

The bottom of our dumper was filled with kit bags, petrol tins, and blankets. On top of them there was an Englishman fast asleep. His face was covered by his helmet, but as our vehicle drove forward its movements made the helmet slide and uncover his face. I could see that he was young and fair, and that he had a small and well-groomed mustache the color of ripe oats. Even asleep his face bore a careless and daredevil expression. After some time he awoke, took no visible notice of my presence, emptied a bottle of beer, and went off to sleep again. The dark soldier spoke to me, but I could hardly understand his Cockney English. The driver had limpid blue eyes and a kind of grin. I learned from him that they had set out from Le Havre almost twenty hours earlier, and that he had never left the wheel all that time because the dumper could not cover more than fourteen miles an hour. The idiocy of the order that had sent the dumper from the relative safety of Le Havre to Boulogne in order to be evacuated from there to England struck us fully only a day later, when we learned about the true position of the front line.

I enjoyed every minute of the ride. For one thing, I could rest my heel; for another, I was among British soldiers. Not everything about them was as I had expected. For instance, they swore continually and I, who had derived most of my knowledge about the English from Victorian books, imagined that Britons never used anything worse than the word *damn*. Coming from a country where swearwords are numerous, picturesque, and judiciously employed, I found their obscenities dull and unnecessary. As for their constant use of the word *bloody,* I felt absolutely incapable of appreciating its universal utility. I changed my opinion later, of course.

I liked their friendliness, their obvious ability to enjoy every situation, and their soldierly spirit. Our driver, despite the twenty-odd hours he spent at the wheel, wore a constant grin and never swore. The dark-haired Cockney gave me his address in London and, in intervals between the most horrible obscenities and blasphemies, he asked me to visit his missus and tell her that he was having a good time. Another soldier, sporting a mustache, had one laconic explanation for everything: *"C'est la guerre."* I found it very restful to drink beer and not have to take part in an argument about the necessity of the war, its causes, and its prospects.

We stopped with Saint-Omer in view on the horizon. A unique spectacle of war surrounded us. On our left an immense field was literally covered with glittering petrol cans. Jerry cans were still unknown then, and the silvery tin reflecting the sun must have been visible from many miles away by airmen. On our right British batteries of antiaircraft guns were dug in all over an immense and level Flemish plain. A column of three-ton lorries filled with Territorials was moving in the direction from which we had just come, and my companions exchanged banter with their comrades who were moving up to meet the Germans. Thumbs were jerked on both sides; we threw a few bottles of beer to those who asked for them and had cigarettes flung at us in return.

Suddenly a nervous shock seemed to move along the tremendous column of lorries. Helmeted heads looked up to the skies. The field on our right, covered with antiaircraft batteries, came to life. We looked up to the sky as well but at first saw nothing. Then we heard a noise of aircraft, and irregular formations of bombers approaching from the direction of Haze-brouck began flying over our batteries of antiaircraft guns. We immediately abandoned our vehicle to take cover in the roadside ditch. Several formations of German bombers passed over our heads; then we heard muffled explosions and saw columns of smoke arise over Saint-Omer. The raid was soon over, and the squadrons wheeled in the sky and flew back without passing over our antiaircraft batteries.

When we reached the outskirts of Saint-Omer, people were standing outside their houses, their faces still white and contracted. My companions grinned and showed them their thumbs. The soldier with the mustache sat with his legs dangling outside the bucket of our dumping wagon, holding a bottle of beer in his right hand and shouting now and then, *"C'est la guerre."* There was little response from the Frenchmen, whose town had just been blitzed, but when it came it consisted mostly of raised arms crowned with clenched fists. I could read in their eyes that they looked on my companions as men fighting their own battle on somebody else's soil, and abandoning their ally in her hour of need. Without knowing it at the time, I was witnessing the birth of the Vichy spirit.

BOULOGNE IN MAY

WE MOVED ON AND STOPPED for the night in an abandoned cottage just outside Boulogne. I had a huge meal of corned beef and bread and could not help envying the soldiers' vast quantities of food. We slept on blankets spread upon the floor, but before falling asleep we had a chat about the way the war was going. I was still optimistic, because I ignored the facts of the situation and because I wanted to be. So were my British companions. But there was a Scotsman in our midst who fearlessly declared that we were beaten, because Hitler had the best generals and officers in the world. Nobody tried to deny it, and we fell asleep.

We were up at five o'clock the next morning. I could hardly move for the crowds of refugees and soldiers wandering aimlessly. In the square in front of the citadel a throng of French soldiers, looking tired and hungry, were surrounding old-fashioned horse-drawn field kitchens. I made my way slowly to the harbor, where I found many thousands of Belgian refugees, mostly women and children, waiting outside the Gare Maritime. A line of steel-helmeted English soldiers with fixed bayonets was preventing them from storming the gangway to the few available boats.

Having obtained a British visa without any difficulty from the British vice consul's office, I walked briskly past the guard and down to the dock.

There was only one boat left—a tug. A company of soldiers was clambering down the dock wall into her, and I followed.

We were well over two hundred aboard, crammed like sardines, apprehensive and at the same time breathlessly happy to be there. The tug cast off almost as soon as the last man managed to scramble aboard, but we did not steam out far. We were still within the harbor when the antiaircraft batteries defending the port opened up. German bombers were flying over our heads. We were now outside the zone protected by barrage balloons against dive-bomb attacks. We watched one of the German bombers detach itself from the formation, dive to the sea, then make for us, and we were much too terror-struck to do anything but lie on our faces. Luckily for us our French skipper had not lost his head and was steering a zigzag course. The German dropped a stick of bombs, the nearest of which fell close enough to our tug to drench us with brine. His gunner then sprayed us with bullets. When we came back to our senses, we found our tug's starboard staved in, several of our comrades dead, more dying, and over thirty wounded. There was nothing to do but steam back into the dock we had just left.

I helped to unload the wounded. Once that work was finished, I found myself again a civilian, without anybody's protection and very hungry. There were no more boats in the harbor and, according to rumors, a German armored column was already approaching the southern outskirts of Boulogne. I left the harbor area in search of food but with the intention to return later, as I had not lost all hope of finding a ship that would take me to England. I was convinced the Germans would not easily take Boulogne. I reasoned that since during the First World War they could never reach the Channel, surely they would not now be allowed by the British to master its shores in a matter of days. It was a different thing, I told myself, to race across France, because the Frenchmen were not ready to die for their country. But Boulogne in the hand of the Germans would be a pistol pointed at England, and therefore a town for the British to defend.

I was strengthened in my belief by the sight of a battalion of Welsh Guards marching into Boulogne instead of leaving it. They had just landed and were the finest body of soldiers I had ever seen in my life. They marched in single file on both sides of the street, led by amazing sergeant majors—giants with defiant mustaches armed with arrogant swagger sticks. As for the soldiers, they were no less amazing. Their boots shone like the patent shoes of a Spanish *caballero,* every piece of brass on them glittered like pure gold; their webbing was so perfectly fitted that it must have made them very uncomfortable; their step was full of nonchalant swagger; they whistled "Roll Out the Barrel" and had ever-ready grins.

I pilfered an abandoned Belgian Army lorry full of loaves of bread. I carried one away but found it was stale and moldy. Trying to find my way back to the Gare Maritime, I emerged out of a maze of mean streets into an open, sandy square bordered by warehouses on three sides and by hills on the fourth. Behind those hills was the Channel. In the middle of the square was an air-raid shelter consisting of a trench whose roof was protected by sandbags. I had hardly had the time to take in my surroundings when everybody in the square made for the air-raid shelter. I did not hesitate a moment, for a formation of German bombers had appeared in the sky. But the Germans kept their bombs for somebody else, so we left our insecure shelter and eagerly followed their flight.

Once beyond the line of hills, they began to circle in the sky not unlike vultures soaring over crags on the lookout for prey. Then puffs of smoke began to appear all around them, and I realized that I was witnessing an antiaircraft barrage put up by ships. And a very effective one it seemed to be. Yet the Germans continued their merry-go-round, the shells kept bursting around them, and nothing seemed to happen. Then, when we had almost given up believing that the antiaircraft artillery could ever do them any damage, we saw a shell looking like a small ball of fire speed upward, a bomber dive as if to encounter it, and a gigantic ball of fire slowly leave the sky to disappear behind the hills.

The German aircraft had scarcely accomplished their mission when shells began to tear the air over our own heads. We raced back to the shelter. There was no sort of lighting in it; struggling over limbs and bodies, I found at last a place for myself. Squatting in the absolute darkness of the trench, I could hear the shells overhead with almost clockwork regularity, terrifying in their passage.

Constant anticipation of the whistling, eerie sound and the roar that followed it made me taut with fear. Entombed in the dark and smelly shelter, I was haunted by the idea of being buried alive. Then I remembered that sound did not travel very fast and, therefore, as long as I could hear explosions I could be certain that the shells were dropping at a reasonable distance away. I also began wondering who was lobbing the shells and, by listening to the talk of people who had entered our warren later than myself, I learned that they came from a British cruiser, and that they were aimed at a German armored column approaching Boulogne from the south.

The following morning I left the shelter and found my way back to the harbor. There were no ships in the docks, and most of the barrage balloons were gone, punctured by machine-gun fire from the German aircraft. People were emerging everywhere from the solid cellars that are to be found underneath practically every old house in Boulogne; they were hungry and thirsty, but there was no water and little bread in the town. The shortage of food was in danger of causing a riot.

There and then I decided to leave Boulogne and make for Calais. But not far from the citadel my progress was stopped by a roadblock manned by French marines. From them I learned that the best place for me to be was in an air-raid shelter, as the German onslaught was expected any moment.

In fact, the first German shells fell on the town only a few minutes after I had left the marines and was crossing the square in front of the citadel. I took cover in one of the slit trenches, although it was not easy for a civilian to find room in any of them because they were filled with Belgian soldiers who had taken the precaution of ridding themselves of their rifles some time earlier. As a consequence of their voluntary disarmament, the cellars, gutters, and sewers of Boulogne were full of Belgian rifles, bayonets, grenades, and cartridges.

The shelling lasted for some time, but it was neither as imposing nor as frightening as the deep booming of the cruiser's guns. When the lull came I made for the harbor but found no ships there. As I was wandering aimlessly and listlessly away from the Gare Maritime, thinking of the days lost in Brussels and on the trains, the shelling recommenced and I took shelter in the first cellar I came across.

There was only one foreigner down there, a Belgian from Liège. He had a big basket full of bottles: cognac, vermouth, wine, and Schiedam stood side by side in his hamper. He drank steadily and leisurely. As soon as he saw me come down into the cellar he offered me a drink, and I did not refuse. He seemed friendly, and I was young, lonely, and bewildered. I told him about my plans for joining the RAF, about the damaged tug and my hope of finding a means of reaching England come what might.

In the late afternoon a young French soldier with flashing dark eyes and dazzling white teeth came into our cellar and demanded our identity papers. Most of us in the cellar were able to satisfy his demand, but there were several Frenchmen who had left their papers at home. The young soldier, with that most disarming accent of Toulouse that did not leave a single vowel unpronounced, earnestly insisted on seeing their identity cards and launched into a long explanation of the reasons that made his demand necessary. His good humor was like a ray of sun and a breath of fresh air in this dark and smelly den. But when he left the cellar there was no mention of his youthfulness and cheerfulness. Instead, the occupants of the cellar imitated his accent, made fun of his way of expressing himself, and told one another stories about the Midi, the strange people who live there, and the reception a Frenchman from the North—a *Boche du Nord* to the natives of the Midi—could expect from them. Everybody became so heated, arguing the differences between the North and the South, that I could not help asking them whether they were at war with Germany or about to declare war on Toulouse, Bordeaux, and Marseilles. That brought them back to reality but did not endear me to them.

Shortly afterward we were visited by another soldier. As he came into our cellar, one of the women shrieked and threw herself upon him. Kisses followed, although I could hardly see why anybody should want to kiss her. Apparently, they were husband and wife, and they had not seen each other for some days. He had come to see her and say good-bye before going with his detachment into action. After they had hugged and kissed each other, the woman whispered something into his ear and began to stare at me. The soldier had practically no forehead, an extremely large nose, immense ears, a cavernous mouth, and a chin that was conspicuous by its absence. He called to me to come over to him from the corner where I was sitting. I did so, and he demanded my identity card. I showed him my passport, and when he saw that I was a Pole his rage burst out. He accused me in one breath of being responsible for the war and of being a fifth columnist. He then told me that he felt like shooting me on the spot but that, out of the goodness of his heart, he would take me to the gendarmerie instead. However, if he happened to find me again in the cellar, he would not hesitate to carry out his threat. Having kissed his wife again, he left the cellar, taking me with him.

It was night now, and there was sniping throughout the town, although the Germans had not pierced the perimeter yet. Lorries and cars were burning in the streets; here and there a shell-struck house showed its entrails. We reached the gendarmerie, and my escort handed me over to a gendarme and left without waiting for the outcome of the interrogation. The gendarme saw my papers and let me go. I found myself back in the street, where darkness reigned and tracer bullets tore the night into fantastic ribbons. I had to leave the deserted street at all costs if I did not want to be shot by a German sniper or a trigger-happy Frenchman.

The following morning was dull and cold. I made for the harbor in order to see whether there were now any boats there but found it deserted. There were no ships in the docks, no antiaircraft guns, no barrage balloons, no British uniforms. I turned back, lost my way in a narrow street, and saw a fifteen-hundred-weight Bedford guarded by a British soldier. Although it was May he wore his greatcoat. He was the first soldierlike figure I had seen since I had been stopped by the French marines. He had a ruddy, honest face, a straight nose, a good chin, very fair hair, and a kindly smile. He was young—twenty-four as he later told me—and his name was Jim. He came from Durham, and he was a miner. I could hardly understand his dialect, yet he has remained in my memory because of his kindliness and quiet determination.

He befriended me immediately. I asked him if he knew of any boat still likely to sail for England, and he told me to wait until his sergeant's return, as the sergeant had gone to find out the very same thing. In the meantime he offered me a drink. I asked him what kind of a drink he had, and he told me to choose. He lifted the flap of the canvas covering the lorry; I looked in and found that the back of the lorry was full of blankets, boxes, hand grenades, petrol tins, antitank ammunition, and bottles. I hoped to discover a bottle of beer, but there were none. So I relented and accepted a drink of Dubonnet. The aperitif did not quench my thirst, but it gave me the courage to inquire of him if he had any food. "Only some biscuits and chocolate," he replied. I accepted both gladly and was munching them when his sergeant and two other soldiers arrived. The straight-backed sergeant appeared to be in his thirties but was actually in his early forties. The two others were the driver, a young and sturdy Scotsman, and a diminutive Cockney who must have lost his dentures because he looked a perfect Punch.

Jim introduced me to his companions. The sergeant had a look at my credentials and accepted me. I asked him if there were any boats likely to arrive in Boulogne, and he replied that not the slightest hope remained that we would see one, and that our only chance was to make for Calais or Dunkirk.

We got rid of the ammunition in the back of the lorry and started on our way. The sergeant sat in front with the Scottish driver, while the three of us settled upon petrol tins in the back. The next thing we saw was petrol gushing from the tin on which Jim was sitting. The driver stopped to inquire if we were all right, and the Cockney took advantage of our stationary position to jump out of the lorry. He left us to continue our venture without him, saying he preferred to be a live prisoner than a dead hero. A Polish sergeant would have heaped him with abuse and threats; our sergeant merely told him to take care of himself, and we started off again.

We drove through narrow streets until we emerged in a square. The Bedford stopped, and I could hear the Scottish driver arguing with the sergeant about the route to follow. As I had a map in the back of the lorry, they left their seats in order to come and consult it. Just then Jim and I heard a sudden outburst of machine-gun fire and the sergeant's exclamation of pain. We both fell flat on our faces. After what appeared to me a very long while, the firing stopped. I looked up and saw the canvas above my head neatly holed. The sergeant and the driver had taken cover under the lorry and were lying flat on their faces against the wheels. As soon as the firing stopped, we let the backboard down and helped them in. The sergeant was wounded in his right shoulder—almost in the same spot in which he had been hit by a piece of shrapnel in the 1914–1918 War.

Looking out of the back of our fifteen-hundred-weight, we could see a square bordered by a canal. It was obvious that we could not continue in our lorry, because the German sniper would open up at us with his tommy gun as soon as we tried to drive on. If he had stopped firing, it was probably because he thought we were all dead. The problem facing us was, therefore, how and when to abandon our vehicle. The Scotsman was for waiting inside the Bedford until it became dark; the sergeant and Jim were for leaving it immediately. The way to achieve a getaway was to leap out of the lorry, sprint some thirty yards to a Belgian lorry standing nearby, take cover behind it, and then run again to the shelter offered by another lorry blocking the canal bridge. There we should have been safe. The sergeant, of course, being wounded and thus unable to sprint, would have to remain inside the Bedford until we came back to take part in the expedition against the German sniper. The cheek of that man, sitting on the roof—or somewhere near it—of a building in the center of an enemy town and killing off Belgian, French, and British soldiers as if they were some kind of game.

The question of deciding when to leave our lorry was settled for us by German artillery fire. Shells began to explode in our neighborhood and set some of the warehouses on fire. Without much hesitation Jim jumped out and sprinted to the Belgian vehicle. I saw him fall behind one of the rear wheels of the lorry and then became too frightened to watch. I fell again on my face and heard bullets whistle over my head. This time, when the German sniper decided that he had finished with us and took his finger off the trigger, I could see a neat row of holes in the woodwork of the lorry on the side close to which I was lying.

We did not talk for a long time after that. The Scotsman broke the silence quite unnecessarily by saying in a most lugubrious voice, "Sarge, we're doomed."

The sergeant answered cheerfully that we could come through all right. There was now nothing else to do but wait until darkness fell. We were not uncomfortable lying on the blankets, and we had enough cigarettes and chocolate to keep us busy. I, for one, resigned myself quite easily to the idea of waiting until night came.

After some time I remembered Jim. I looked out and saw him lying behind the wheel in the very same position in which I had seen him immediately after his fall. Apparently he had been fired at by the German and was pretending that he was dead. Like ourselves he was probably waiting for darkness in order to make a dash for safety.

The disconcerting and fantastic aspect of our situation lay in the fact that, as I looked out of the lorry to my right, French civilians and soldiers were strolling or hurrying in the street that led into the square while we, only a few hundred yards away from them, were reduced to the fate of pheasants cowering under a bush in the hope that the sportsman might not notice them.

When I had a look again at Jim, he was still lying in the very same position, but some change seemed to have taken place around him. What that change was I did not realize at first. I called out to him: "Jim, are you all right?" but there was no answer. I called out again and again, at almost regular intervals, but still there was no reply. However, I could now see that he was lying in a rapidly spreading pool of blood.

Soon after that I became conscious of an eerie sound that was partly a groan, partly a complaint, and partly an animal expression of intense physical agony. It took me some time to connect this weird, inhuman noise with Jim. However, there could soon be no doubt about its origin and, as I listened attentively, I could construe the sounds into words: "Water! Help! Water! Help!"

What were we to do? The sergeant thought that we had to clench our teeth and wait until darkness. The dour Scotsman said nothing. Neither of them looked out of the lorry. But I did, and could see the red around Jim's body becoming darker and darker. Nor did he stop groaning and calling pitifully for help and water, so I decided that I must do all I could.

"Be careful, lad," said the sergeant.

I jumped out of the lorry, stuck my hands into my trouser pockets, and walked up to Jim without looking back over my shoulder. My heart thumped wildly, but nothing happened: the German did not shoot me in the back.

I tried to lift Jim and realized how weak I had become. He groaned and cried as I managed to throw him over my right shoulder, where he hung not unlike a half-clasped knife. The inside of his right leg, from the knee to the ankle, was gone. The bullet must have ricocheted from the cobbles before tearing the flesh and muscles off his limb. And now the slightest movement was agony to him. The awful wound almost made me vomit, but his pallor was even more frightening. At last I managed to stagger to the lorry with him over my shoulder, and the Scotsman helped me get him inside. I then said peremptorily that we had to take him to a hospital immediately.

The Scotsman left the safety of the lorry's back without a word and started the engine. Almost at the same moment the German opened up again, and the windscreen went to pieces, but by some miracle the driver was not hit by a single piece of flying glass. He put his foot on the accelerator and roared past the corner house, where the sniper was perched, into the safety of the narrow street, only to find that it was barricaded by burnt-out motorcars. However, Jim's groans brought pale, unwashed, and disheveled Frenchmen out of the cellars in which they were hiding, and with their help we cleared a way for our truck.

We pulled up in front of the Hopital de Saint Pierre et Saint Paul. A Frenchwoman received us and told me curtly to take the wounded Englishman to another hospital, because this one was overcrowded. All the excitement, fear, and frustration that had been bottled up within me exploded. I told her what I thought of her selfishness and callousness. She replied by calling me a dirty foreigner and a saboteur. Again I had to show my passport, Belgian identity card, the air attaché's letter, and every other scrap of evidence I had on my person to avoid being arrested on the spot. The shouting and commotion had, however, the result of bringing a French major out of the hospital. Having had a look at Jim, he called for stretcher bearers and told them to take him and the sergeant into the hospital. When I asked him what was going to happen to Jim, he told me that his leg would have to be amputated.

I was not allowed to stay with my three companions because I was a civilian, so I shook hands with the sergeant and the driver, took a blanket from the pile inside the lorry, and moved aimlessly on.

Again I felt my loneliness. But despite everything I was not unhappy. I thought of all the jeers, accusations of cowardice, and cheap sarcasm I had had to suffer at the hand of Poles as a child and boy. In my heart of hearts I had always known that I was a better man than my tormentors, and when the sergeant had called me "good lad" I had felt as if this praise, coming from an Englishman, had chased away forever all those doubts. To have achieved self-respect, obtained a better knowledge of myself, rid myself of a complex, and fulfilled an ambition in one day—what more could I wish for? And so, although I realized that I had failed in my main purpose, that of reaching England, and although I now knew that I could not avoid being under the Germans, I did not feel quite as despondent as I ought to have been as I left my comrades and walked off into the maze of Boulogne's narrow streets.

Without actually intending it, I found myself again in front of the very same cellar in which I had spent my previous night in Boulogne. I had one desire, to sleep, but as I descended into the cellar, I met with a reception that was quite unexpected. A Belgian who had shared his hamper of bottles with me the night before and had been quite friendly in the morning declared that every time I left the cellar the German shelling followed, and every time I returned to it it ceased: ergo, I was a spy. I was too over-whelmed to protest. Besides, I had no time to protest, because a young Belgian officer, in splendid riding breeches and tightly fitting brown boots, appeared from nowhere with a miniature Browning in his fist. He stuck it in my back and told me to march. He was the first Belgian officer I had seen in Boulogne, and he frightened me badly because his hand shook so uncon-trollably that I was afraid he might unwittingly pull the trigger of his pistol. Luckily for me, we had only to cross the street to reach a French guard-room. The brave Belgian lieutenant, having done his duty, left me in the hands of a tall, comfortably drunk French soldier, who searched me for arms, had a look at my papers, and let me go. I told him I could not return to that cellar and I badly wanted to sleep. Did he know of a place where I could spread my blanket? He pointed to a house opposite the guardroom, which had been badly damaged by German shells but whose cellar remained intact and empty.

I wrapped myself in my blanket there and fell asleep. When I woke up it was some time after four o'clock in the morning, and the shining sun promised a glorious day. I was still very sleepy, and it took me quite a while to realize what it was that had roused me from my sleep: my ears were ring-ing, and there was an eerie, almost unearthly quiet abroad. My conscious and subconscious selves had become so used to the continuous din of machine-gun fire and shelling that their sudden cessation had chased my sleep away.

I was overcome by a tide of anxiety and self-reproach. Why had I not left Brussels earlier? Why had I not continued on the train for Paris even if it had meant leaving my passport behind? Why had I not made for Calais instead of Boulogne? But I had no time for self-torment and recrimina-tions. The door of the cellar flew open, and a German soldier appeared in the entrance.

He was over six feet tall, dressed in black with his sleeves rolled up, jackbooted and helmeted, a submachine gun at the ready. I raised my hands, and he said in German, "We, Germans, make no war on civilians." I let my arms fall.

He disappeared and I remained for a lengthy while in a state of indecision as to what I should do now. A tall Catholic priest with a submachine gun, accompanied by three black-uniformed panzer troopers, appeared on the other side of the street. The priest kicked the doors of a cellar and shouted in perfect French: "The fighting is over! You, civilians, need fear nothing." He then addressed his men in German, and they made for another cellar.

I hid the air attaché's letter in one of my shoes and left. All I was thinking of at that moment was how to find a place where I could get enough water to drink and wash. I walked through the streets of Boulogne expecting to be stopped at any moment by the Germans. But they were too busy fighting a war to worry about civilians. I decided to head south, in the direction of the Somme, because I imagined that the front line ran along that river and I still hoped to be able to reach the Allied lines. I ran into a young Catholic priest and asked him the way out of Boulogne. We walked together almost as far as the outskirts of the town, and during our walk he talked about the fall of the harbor and blamed the British for its loss. We met a column of French prisoners, beaten, dejected, and despairing. Their backs were hunched, their tread was heavy, their soldierly pride was gone. There was not a spark of defiance or resentment left in them.

I parted company with the young priest. I was now out of Boulogne and found the road strewn with untold items of equipment of a beaten army. It was the first time I saw the waste that is war, and I felt overwhelmed by it. I looked at all the abandoned guns, vehicles, ammunition, piles of uniforms, rifles, ambulances, and it seemed to me that their value was so tremendous that no army should have given them up without a fight to the last round. For, as I walked through this immense depot of war matériel, mostly of British origin, I could not help calculating how many of his soldiers Hitler would be able to clothe and equip with it. I was not wrong: I soon met Germans driving British fifteen-hundred-weights and three-ton lorries on which they had already put their Wehrmacht number plates.

That was the first example of the formidable German organization about which I had heard so much. But before I met any more of it, I saw the British spirit embodied in a column of prisoners of war. They were escorted by a much more numerous and businesslike number of Germans than the French prisoners had been, yet they managed to make their escort look like Jerries and not like Germans. Despite their ominous helmets, heavy boots, and sub-machine guns, the Germans appeared too self-conscious and tense to be real victors. Their prisoners might be beaten, but they did not look defeated. In their battle dress they appeared almost elegant in a vaguely bohemian way. Many had their hands in their pockets; others smoked cigarettes; some grinned at me; a few winked. I waited until their column had passed before I moved on. The realization that I had almost become one of them came with a pang. My personal bad luck had made me almost forget the larger issues of the war.

AFTER BOULOGNE

I VENTURED OFF THE MAIN ROAD onto a lane that led into a farmyard. Only when I emerged in front of the farmhouse did I realize to
my dismay that a German tank detachment was billeted in the place. My
first reaction was to turn back but, as my emergence had already been
noticed by several Germans, I decided to go on.

The farmer was away with the army, leaving his wife—a nervous and
sickly-looking woman—to run the place on her own. Her farmhouse
already served as a refuge for a dozen or more Dutch and Belgian refugees,
so my arrival was at first a cause of alarm. However, when I explained to
her that I only wanted to wash and shave and then move on, the farmer's
wife became more sympathetic and showed me the way to the washhouse,
where a young Dutch priest helped me by swinging the recalcitrant handle
of the pump.

While I was washing and shaving, I noticed that the Germans were frequent visitors to the place. They came in either to wash or to polish their
heavy boots until they shone. There was one among them in particular,
young, fairish, slender, and not very tall compared with his comrades. He
swaggered as he walked, and his voice was loud and guttural. He proceeded to explain to me that England was responsible for this war, respon-

sible for *all* European wars; that she had always been the cause of Europe's divisions; that the Fuehrer did not want to fight the Frenchmen, Belgians, and Dutch but was forced to invade their countries in order to get at the British. After that I learned that he was a Saxon; that his division had taken part in the Sedan breakthrough; that he was a regular soldier with some five years' service behind him despite the fact that he was only twenty-two; and that the Frenchmen were good fighters but they tried to fight this war with the weapons of 1914. As he had also taken part in the Polish campaign, I asked him what he thought of the Poles as soldiers. He replied with visible disgust that he did not think much of them. They had fought from behind hedges and did not know when they were beaten. Of course, they were brave, but who was not brave when defending his own homeland? And what about the British? Oh yes, they could fight, they were Nordic enough for that, but they lacked the discipline and toughness to withstand the onslaught of the rejuvenated German nation.

I must have looked very tired because, as I was going to start on my trek to the Somme, the farmer's wife proposed that I spend the night at the farm. I was only too glad to accept her invitation. Opposite the farmhouse was a big barn full of hay, in which I buried myself, though I was fated that night to sleep badly.

The French family consisted of a mother and two daughters. One daughter was a cripple from birth and paralyzed; she was carted about in a wheelchair. The other was a relatively good-looking female, whom the Saxon courted in the most guttural and barking German I had ever heard. The girl did not understand him but kept repeating *oui* in all the right and wrong places. Throughout the night I could hear him extolling the Fuehrer, deprecating Western immorality, praising German womanhood, and then keeping relatively quiet while making love. I was still young enough to be outraged by the gruesomeness of the occasion: the French girl submitting to her enemy only a few yards from her unsleeping mother and paralyzed sister. Yet the whole occasion was so different from what I might have imagined such a situation would be like: the girl did not resist, the German did not behave like a brute and did not look like one. His worst crime was a horrible, confident, barking voice.

I woke up late the next morning and met the Saxon in the washhouse, polishing his boots. He interrupted his polishing and left the place in a hurry at the noise of aircraft flying overhead. I followed him and looked up. An irregular formation of some thirty German bombers was passing high in the blue sky—a very impressive sight in the spring of 1940, when the thousands of RAF and U.S. bombers were not yet dreamed of. The Saxon's face expressed the most childlike admiration. *"Unsere Flieger!"* he exclaimed. *"Wunderbar! Wunderbar!"*

He certainly had good reason to admire his Luftwaffe. He had hardly finished straining his neck in his effort to follow the flight of the bombers when a dispatch rider arrived on a motorcycle with mail for the detachment. The mail was only three days old and had been brought by air. I admired the organization of his army and hated him and his Wehrmacht all the more. I could not help thinking of French soldiers who had to queue for bread in their own country.

It was time to go. For the Belgian and Dutch refugees, the war was over. They had already forgotten their apprehensions about German barbarism and were talking of German orderliness and kindness. Their only interest at present was how to return to their homes. But for me the war was only beginning.

I said good-bye to the farmer's wife and the refugees. But as I was on the point of leaving the farmyard, a German playing with the farmer's baby daughter, thinking that I was on my way home, told me to wait and disappeared for a short while into the barn. He came back with a packet of English biscuits for me, and a bar of French chocolate for the little girl, and expressed his belief in a very early peace. "We did not want this war," he said. "It was forced upon us. Our Adolf has known war himself, and he is the last man in the world to desire it. It is the Jews and the British who have provoked this war. All we Germans want is justice—justice denied to us by the Treaty of Versailles."

I asked him cautiously whether he thought that Germany, having become the victor, would be just to those she had vanquished. Would not Germany demand territories from the French—for instance, Alsace and Lorraine—and thus make the French claim that they too had suffered a Versailles and plan for a war or revenge? To put it in a nutshell, did he think that wars solved anything?

He expressed his belief that *der Adolf* would avoid the pitfalls of a peace of revenge. The people of Alsace and Lorraine would probably be given the choice between Germany and France. However, I could tell that he was struck by my way of seeing war as a vicious circle.

He hoped that the war would be over before the end of the summer. Twenty-eight years old, he had spent nine years of his life in the army; he hoped to spend the remaining three years of his military engagement in the recovered African colonies, then return with a pension and get married.

We parted, and he wished me all the best. I have often wondered whether he knew that I was a Jew. I suppose he did, because I look unmistakably Jewish, and he hardly used any anti-Semitic arguments in the course of our conversation.

I do not remember how many days it took me to cover the thirty miles that separated me from the Somme. I was too hungry and worn out to register places and people. I reached the Somme only to find that the Germans had already crossed it and were now many miles to the south.

I knew that I could not hope to overtake their tanks and motorized troops, or even keep up with their infantry. So I decided to try my luck along the Channel coast. Animated by the hope that I might find a fisherman ready to take me to England in his boat, I walked back along the Channel as far as Hardelot-Plage, a seaside resort some eight miles south of Boulogne, where I gave up my quest.

I found a room with a real bed and blankets on the top floor of an abandoned villa and slept off the worst of my fatigue. The first floor of the villa was occupied by a Belgian family from Ghent, who had left Belgium in two cars and a van. Half of their luggage consisted of food, and I soon discovered that walking downstairs and crossing the lobby, which adjoined the kitchen, could be a most atrocious form of torture. The smell of food and freshly ground coffee was enough to give me stomach cramps and make me hate all those whose stomachs were full.

The resort had no provision shops of any kind, not even a baker's. Bread was brought from Boulogne every morning and shared out by a committee set up by Belgian refugees. That bread and German army soup kept me alive. I discovered that practically all the Belgian refugees, notwithstanding their supplies of food, were begging from the Germans. I did the same and managed to obtain once a day a big bowl of fat, nutritious soup containing all kinds of vegetables and meat.

One day I found a kayak in a shed behind our villa and decided to try to get to England in it. I had paddled a kayak as a boy on the river Wilya, and I felt confident of being able to cross the Channel, which in that sunny June of 1940 looked as smooth as a pond. Of course, I knew nothing about the tides and currents of that narrow stretch of sea, and the only thing that made me hesitate in my venture was the lack of a compass. When, a day or two after finding the kayak, I managed to secure a compass from a Belgian Boy Scout and made up my mind to set off in the early hours of the following morning, my plans were dashed by the German high command. Only a few hours after I had secured the compass, the Channel coast was declared a forbidden zone, and all civilians were ordered to leave Hardelot-Plage by six o'clock the next morning. My Belgian neighbors offered me a perch in one of their cars, and I thought it advisable to take advantage of their kind offer and to return to Belgium. And so, at five o'clock in the morning, we left the resort, drove through the ruins of Saint-Omer and Armentières, and reached Ghent in the evening. As their three motorcars were crammed with people and luggage, I sat all the way on the right front mudguard of the van and almost scalded my hand clinging to the overheated bonnet.

I had been all alone during that period. Left to myself, I had avoided too much brooding in daytime by driving myself about in search of food or a boat in which to cross the Channel. But at night there was nothing else to do but to think. My faculties for feeling were numbed to a great extent, but my brain was more lucid during that period than it had been for a long time. And there were two never-ending themes to provide material for thought: myself and the war.

As far as the former was concerned, I could not help thinking of myself as a failure. If I had not lost time in Brussels waiting for my Belgian friends to make up their minds whether to stay or to leave; if I had not remained on that Belgian train; if I had walked a little faster—the ifs never seemed to end. I called myself a fool, and yet in my heart of hearts I knew that, if it were to be done all over again, I should act in exactly the same way.

I also knew, however, that I was no longer the same as when I had set out from Brussels. I had regained that simple physical confidence in myself which I had lost in Brussels, where money in one's pocket seemed to go a much longer way than one's intelligence, determination, and physical fit-ness. But much more than that: I had learned during that month of May to know myself as I had never known myself before, and I had also had the opportunity to shed another of the ghetto complexes foisted on my conscious and subconscious minds by a hostile Christian environment. I now knew for certain that I was not a coward. I felt grown up and, somehow, free: a man capable of both thought and action. Even if I had failed in the eyes of the world, this adventure was not a failure as far as the evolution of my own self was concerned.

When I returned to Nazi-occupied Brussels, I was more than ever resolved to take an active part in the struggle against Nazism. And my attachment to England, far from having abated, was greater than ever.

THE TIME OF
HELPLESSNESS

HAVING BEEN BORN in a country with the history and traditions of a century and a half of foreign oppression, I had very definite ideas on how a conquered people should behave toward their oppressors. I also had preconceived ideas on what the invaders' behavior would be like to those whom they had conquered but, on returning to Brussels, I found that my ideas had hardly any counterpart in reality.

I came across an émigré Russian paper published in Berlin that contained an article entitled "Warsaw and Paris." Its text has remained in my memory because to me it described in a striking manner the difference between the way the West at first accepted Nazi domination and the way the Slavonic peoples reacted to defeat.

The author of the article had found that although Warsaw had been occupied by the German armies for more than ten months when he visited it, it gave the impression of having just been conquered, while Paris impressed him as a city occupied for years. He visited Paris while the French armies were still fighting. Yet the Parisians behaved as if they had accepted their conquerors for good and were waiting for the fall of London to have peace at last. The people of Warsaw talked and behaved as if the Polish Army were still fighting in Poland, and likely to liberate their city any day. Their refusal to face reality was amazing. One heard people in cafés telling one another stories about "murderous RAF raids" on Hamburg, or the Royal Navy having forced its way into the Baltic.

Both the Belgians and the French tried to regain their self-esteem by blaming their allies for their respective defeats. The Belgians blamed the British and the French; the French blamed the British and the Belgian king.

At the end of a miserable summer of waiting and waiting the Caprasses returned from the South of France, so I no longer felt lonely. There were also the modest and simple Minnes, whose kindness and goodness made one think of two Dickensian good souls. Befriended and helped by these two families, I lost a little of my single-minded obsession with the war and my failure to join the RAF.

I tried to earn a living by giving English lessons, but the only people to take lessons in English in the summer of 1940 were the Germans. Moreover, the profession of a language teacher, desperate in the most normal times, was absolutely hopeless as a means of earning a living at a time when a kilogram of potatoes was worth two hours' teaching, and when the monthly bread ration lasted twenty days at the most.

I owed my introduction into black market activities to one of my pupils. The man was a civil servant employed at the Food Office of one of the boroughs of Brussels. It took me some time to realize that he was engaged in illicit traffic, although he kept proposing to me the sale of chocolate, peas, sugar, honey, rice, and potatoes in the intervals between learning German conjugations and declensions. To begin, I agreed reluctantly to try to sell some of his goods to my acquaintances. I acted as intermediary without taking any commission for my trouble but, having realized that nobody believed in my disinterestedness, I decided to merit my reputation. I never managed to make much out of these transactions, although I risked being sent to a concentration camp if caught with a few pounds of sugar or peas, but at least I earned enough money to eat bread every day of the month, have a hot meal at least once a day, and buy myself a pair of shoes when I needed them. To be quite honest, I was better off than I had been as a student before the outbreak of the war. I need hardly add, however, that I was neither blinded nor corrupted by the relative ease with which I earned a living under the Nazi occupation.

This was not the general rule. Many Belgians, who had at first felt that being at war would disallow business as usual, soon became corrupted by the facility with which money could be made by trading with the Germans and forgot that their wealth would be of little avail to them if the Germans won the war. The clever Nazi policy of encouraging "normalcy" in Belgium was far from a failure. Had the German occupation authorities managed to honor the monthly food rations, they could have counted on the passive tolerance and even cooperation of a large part of the population throughout the war.

But it was not only the Belgians who were lulled by the orderliness and seeming humanity of the German invaders in 1940. Even the Jews were taken in. Panic-stricken, they had fled at first to the South of France. But now, having learned of the comparative quiet on the Jewish front, many of them decided to return to Belgium. Some, of course, had to return because they had exhausted their financial reserves and could find no means of subsistence in France. But many returned simply because they had left behind flourishing businesses or because they hoped to make money thanks to the easy spending habits of the occupants.

They founded their optimism on Hitler's imaginary respect for the moral standards of the West. They wanted to believe at all costs that Hitler would not treat them in the same way he treated the Jews in Poland, because they imagined that the civilized Dutch, Belgians, and French would not stand for similar barbarism and atrocities. They trusted in the protection of the Queen of the Belgians and the Cardinal of Malines. They refused to see the terrible truth out of stupidity, unjustified optimism, cowardice, or selfishness.

My own trust in Hitler's single-mindedness and German thoroughness was not misplaced. It was soon justified when an ordinance appeared ordering all Jews to register at their respective town halls. Now I could be certain that the day the Gestapo was ready to commence the deportation of Western European Jews to the ghettos and camps of Poland, they would know where to find me.

I believed that the only sensible thing for a Jew to do was to escape, to leave Hitler's Europe. To stay and fight Nazism in Belgium struck me as a mad undertaking. As a Jew, I would have to fear not only the Nazis but their anti-Jewish allies among the Belgians themselves. But how was I to get out of Hitler's European prison?

Before I had the time to make any serious plans to escape, unexpected offers of help from all kinds of people began to appear. The "underground" had arrived, and every Belgian worth his salt started to imagine himself to be a member of it. People came to me offering to arrange my departure to England by air, boat, or submarine after I had told them that I wanted to enlist in the RAF.

I met all sorts of Belgians in all kinds of places—cafés, parks, pedicure parlors—and was promised that I should be in London within a fortnight at the latest. But the weeks lengthened into months, Christmas 1940 came, my Belgian "underground" contacts disappeared, and I was left where I had started. Then a different "organization" approached me, the same game was played all over again, and the spring of 1941 came.

The first concentration camps in Belgium were established by now. The Jews of Antwerp were forbidden to appear in the streets before and after certain hours. Access to cinemas and cafés was prohibited to them. The process by which the Belgians were to be made accustomed to the idea that Jews were not entitled to the same rights as other human beings was initiated.

The most important event I experienced during those fifteen months spent in Brussels under Nazi occupation was on June 22, 1941.

I had left my room at midday and walked through the sunny streets to my Flemish friends, the Minnes, who had invited me to share their Sunday dinner. There were no newspapers, no blaring loudspeakers to announce the news. And when my Belgian friends told me of the Nazi attack against the Soviet Union, I would not believe them at first. The news appeared to me too good to be true. I could hardly believe that Hitler would commit such a mistake as to open up a second front without having first disposed of Britain.

During the first week of the war in the East, all hopes were permitted. There was no news about the progress of the campaign in the newspapers, nor did any come over the radio. The Germans in Brussels walked about with long faces and neither clicked their heels nor stamped their boots as loudly as was their wont. There were rumors abroad of gigantic tank battles and serious engagements along a front more than a thousand miles long. At last German blood was flowing; at last a soldier as determined as the Nazi superman, and animated by a weltanschauung even more comprehensive than the one based on blood and soil, was the enemy.

A week of hopes and dreams of retribution. Another Sunday came. I was at the Porte de Namur when a special edition of the *Bruesseler Zeitung* appeared. It was literally torn out of the vendors' hands by Germans, who read their sheets on the spot. Before they even finished reading them, their faces beamed, their salutes became smarter than ever, and their heels clicked with gusto.

I bought a sheet myself and read the headlines about thousands of Soviet tanks, guns, and aircraft destroyed and captured; prisoners running into hundreds and thousands; Lvov, Minsk, and Riga occupied.

Wilno fell two days after the German armies had struck in the East. I realized with despair that there could have been no time for my family to escape into the protective depths of Russia.

ACROSS THE
TWO FRANCES

I DETERMINED TO SET OUT across France, Spain, and Portugal, with Lisbon as my ultimate goal. From there I expected to be able to reach Britain. Having made up my mind on how I was going to get out of Hitler's European prison, I bought Otto Sauer's *Spanish Conversation Grammar* and took to studying Castilian. I also became money conscious and began to hunt for all the peas, sugar, and beans the big black market operators were willing to sell to such a small fry as myself. In this way, in addition to accumulating some four thousand Belgian francs, I found a companion for the adventure.

Leon was a Jew from Warsaw without the slightest look of Jewishness about him but with many Jewish characteristics, the most important of which were restlessness, ingenuity, tenacity, and ready generosity. He held a Brussels University degree in chemistry but, being a foreigner, he could never find work in his profession because of the Belgian labor laws. Thanks to his Nordic appearance, our acquaintance was made in rather amusing circumstances.

With another Pole I used to frequent a café at the Porte de Namur, into which Leon used to come, greet everybody present, sit down beside us, take out a Penguin book, fill his pipe, order a coffee, and spend the evening reading and listening to other people's conversations. Although he read

English books, I knew that he was not British. Although he spoke French like a Belgian, there was something in his wit that declared him un-Belgian. I decided to make certain whether my suspicion was justified, and one night, when he was sitting next to us and had just paid for his coffee, I said in Polish to my companion: "He's dropped twenty francs."

The old trick worked: he glanced at the floor. After that there was nothing else for him to do but join in our hearty laugh.

Leon was an extraordinary person for making "contacts." He knew literally hundreds of people from all walks of life, ranging from ministers' wives to suspect owners of nightclubs. He had agreed to leave Belgium with me and make for Portugal, from where he hoped to sail for New York, where part of his family lived. However, he was not in a hurry to leave Brussels because, for the first time in his life, thanks to the Nazi occupation, he was earning enough money to have two good meals a day and a bottle of wine with each. He was selling zip fasteners to the majority of establishments that specialized in providing the ladies of Brussels with corsets and represented a firm that was still in possession of large supplies. The passing of the first Nazi anti-Jewish laws coupled with my insistence made him decide to sell his business and fix a day for our departure. And, thanks to his "contacts," he learned about a beautifully simple and easy way of reaching Marseilles, which put an end to his hesitations.

Belgium and the North of France, with the Somme as the southern border, formed a forbidden zone; without a special permit from the German military authorities, one could neither leave it nor enter it. We had no hope, of course, of ever obtaining such a permit. From the Somme to the Pyrenees, all along the coast, stretched another special zone, which was neither easy to enter nor easy to leave. It had been my original plan to pass through Paris, enter the coastal zone, and then carry on as far as Bayonne. I trusted my own pluck and luck—a plan that did not especially appeal to Leon.

Thanks to one of his friends, however, we learned that the forbidden zone inside which we dwelt stretched not only along the Channel as far as the Somme but also eastward along the borders of Alsace and the Swiss frontier, ending only in the Jura mountains. Being inside the forbidden territory, we could board a train in Brussels, cross the French frontier without having to show our passports, traverse Lorraine, enter Franche-Comté, and leave the train at Besançon, twenty miles from the demarcation line separating German-occupied France. Thus, instead of having to cross two demarcation lines before reaching the Spanish frontier, we would have only one to negotiate.

Before leaving Brussels, Leon obtained two Belgian identity cards, and on the last night of September we boarded a train for Besançon at the Gare du Nord. It was the first time in my life that I assumed a false identity, and I felt anxious throughout the journey. Late on the following day we stepped off the train at Besançon, where we spent the night. I forgot a little about the road ahead of us and went around admiring the city. There is something about the ancient capital of Franche-Comté that no other French city possesses. Its stone houses have a dignity that is Spanish in its forbidding severity. The people display a dignified politeness that has something of the aloofness of the mountains that surround the city. The massive citadels built by Vauban give the place the air of an outpost. Roman columns and a Roman arch bear witness to its antiquity.

In the afternoon of the following day we boarded a charcoal-driven bus. We were a mixed company, consisting of local farmers and German soldiers. Our bus crawled slowly through valleys and penetrated deeper into the mountains, which were the kind that inspire one with wonder at, and love of, nature. There were deep forests of mysterious firs and picturesque hardwood, soft slopes covered with grass or furrows, spacious farmsteads, and solid villages in stone. We drove along the bottom of a valley, and on either side of it the mountain peaks were crowned with massive citadels or medieval castles. I had never seen a country like this in my life, yet I felt as if I had always known and loved it.

We spent the night at a village inn whose landlord was going to put us in touch with a guide who would lead us into Vichy France. Built in stone, the inn stood on the banks of a small, swift river that was harnessed by means of a lock to form a placid millpond. The old mill with its moss-covered wheels formed part of the inn's buildings. One reached the inn itself by walking through an old timber house—the café—and crossing a wooden bridge that had been roofed and glazed and looked like some picturesque gallery.

However, reality in the shape of German soldiers was present even at the inn. In the evening we shared the same table with them. They were mostly middle-aged, thickset, and dull-faced peasants, smelling of horses and manure, for they belonged to a horse-drawn transport column. One of them switched on the radio, and we heard Hitler's voice. Having waded through the usual vituperations against the Jews, Western plutocrats, Bolsheviks, and the Treaty of Versailles, he announced that the final offensive of the German armies in Russia had resulted in the encirclement and annihilation of some sixty Red divisions and the disappearance of the Red Army as an organized fighting force, and that Moscow's fall was a matter of days.

I found some consolation in observing the faces of the Germans. They went on chewing their food, their expressions as dull and unenthusiastic as they had been before their Fuehrer's voice filled the inn. My consolation, however, was of a very strained quality. The Fuehrer was a liar, but the fact was that his armies kept advancing and tearing the very entrails out of Russia's body. I could not help asking myself whether the war might not end even before I managed to reach Britain's shores.

In the afternoon we met our guide, a Frenchman who was in his early twenties. He took us for a couple of escaped French prisoners of war and demanded only two hundred francs per person for guiding us across the demarcation line. We agreed readily, had a drink together, shook hands on the deal, and, after his departure, waited impatiently for the night to come.

In the evening the rain stopped. The night was dark but not black enough to make all progress guesswork. We left the inn and the people in it with regret and set out along a lane that soon changed into a narrow country road. As we advanced, single persons and later whole groups left the shadows on either side of the road and joined us. At length we found ourselves in the midst of a singing fir forest and could stop to take stock of our companions.

We numbered more than twenty. There were two German Jewesses, a mother in her early sixties and her daughter, of some thirty-five years of age. Both were healthy, buxom women, cheerful, great cigarette smokers, and both spoke fluent French. Both had visas for the United States and hoped to be able to sail for New York from Marseilles. There was also a couple of Polish Jews, husband and wife, pale and frightened. All the others were Frenchmen, mostly from Alsace and Lorraine, who had escaped from German prisoner-of-war camps or had to flee in order to avoid serving with Hitler's armies.

We left the forest road and cut across soft meadows until a mass of farm buildings loomed in front of us. We had to spend a couple of hours at this farm waiting for a group similar to ours to arrive from Vichy France before we could proceed. It was the first time in my life that I had visited one of those mountain farms, and I was amazed at the spaciousness of the barns and the number of cows. We were received by the farmer's daughter, and her appearance was as much out of the ordinary as everything else that occurred during that night.

She was a girl of sixteen, and our arrival had brought her out of bed. Her cheap and old frock clung tightly to her body and displayed a figure that was beautiful in its youthful vigor and clarity of outline but forecast a Junoesque maturity. There was still sleep in her eyes; her skin was sun-tanned and golden. She had the kind of physical beauty that usually goes with a blond, Nordic type, but she possessed black hair and dark, flashing eyes. She was shy and silent but prodigal with her dimpled smiles. She gave us milk and bread, but I do not remember having heard her utter a single word during the couple of hours we stayed at the farm.

At last the group from Vichy France arrived, and we set out on the most dangerous stretch of our trek. We cut across woods and forests, slithered down slopes, and clambered up mountains. The Polish Jewess fainted, and we learned from her husband that she was at an advanced stage of preg-nancy. We helped her climb breathtaking slopes and get across swift and cold mountain streams. An icy, penetrating rain, which made everything slippery, began to fall. As the moon disappeared, the night became Egypt-ian in its blackness. I began to wonder whether our guide might not lose his way.

But he knew this country too well for mere darkness to make him lose his bearings. At last we were lying in bushes bordering a road that was the demarcation line between the two Frances. We heard a noise and waited with bated breath. A German patrol on bicycles approached the place where we were lying, passed it, and disappeared. We crossed the road, dived into a young beech wood, and advanced in silence for another twenty minutes or so, after which we were free to smoke and talk. The rain had stopped falling, and the sun had risen to give us a glorious autumn day. Walking on through the gold and red hues of the beech wood, we finally reached a road.

A bus, which would take us to the nearest town, was waiting. Two *gardes mobiles* scrutinized all of us but said nothing. The young guide joined them in a long conversation. We boarded the bus and, driving along winding, serpentine roads, we commenced our descent into the valley where Lons-le-Saunier lies. The blue mist that shrouded it looked like a lake.

The bus stopped outside a large building housing the local food office and the gendarmerie headquarters. We were told to report to the food office for temporary ration cards. I noticed that the two German Jewesses and the *gardes mobiles* did not leave the bus.

We received temporary ration cards, and on leaving the food office we met our guide. We stopped to thank him, and I asked him why the two German women stayed with the gendarmes. He replied that he had had them arrested by the gendarmerie because they were *Boches*. To bring people across the frontier into Vichy France was a responsible job, and he was not going to help Germans cross it. I asked him what would happen to the women. "Oh, they will be delivered to the *Feldgendarmerie*. Thus the Germans will not be able to say that our police do not guard the demarcation line."

"But these women are Jewesses," I said.

"*Qu'est-ce que ca fait?* They're German, aren't they?" he replied.

I was going to explain to him the difference and would have probably finished by having a violent argument when Leon intervened and changed the subject. We left the guide, and Leon and I had a violent quarrel, he accusing me of stupidity in trying to intervene on behalf of other people when my own fate was in the balance, and I calling him an egoist and a coward.

Of course my accusations against my companion were unjustified. Neither a coward nor an egoist, Leon was more of a realist than myself and accepted the injustices that are entailed in being born a Jew much better that I did. It was these women's fate to suffer in Germany because they were Jewish; it was their destiny to be treated as enemies by the young Frenchman because they were German. The young Frenchman could not even be accused of being anti-Semitic. To him they were nothing but Germans—the twentieth-century aberrations of race were probably unknown

to him. He was still a *liberal* to whom the place of one's birth and one's language determined one's nationality. It was the supreme irony of the two
Jewesses' fates that they should be delivered into the hands of the Gestapo
by a Frenchman who refused to accept the Nazi ideas on nationality.

We managed to get a train to Lyons on the same day. I did not enjoy the
landscape, dominated by the swift, rebellious Rhône, as much as I should
have done under different circumstances, because my thoughts were still
with those women. To be so near safety and yet to be sent back to certain
death because of the whim of a thoughtless boy! I could not help reflecting
on it, since my fate might be the same.

We arrived at Lyons and went to a hotel that had been recommended to
us by Leon's friend in Brussels. Its owner did not ask us to register or to
show our identity papers. We spent two days at the hotel and then boarded
a train for Marseilles.

I know of no gloomier and more forbidding French city than Lyons. Of
course, my impression is absolutely subjective. It is not just the outcome of
my two days' stay in that city, with its tall, massive tenement houses and the
turmoil of its two stone-bordered rivers. It is rather the result of ideas and
moods fed on boyhood readings about the Gironde episode of the French
Revolution. During my two days in Lyons I felt as if I were living among
people and surroundings that came straight out of a Zola novel.

It took me almost half of the journey to snap out of my depression, but
outside Marseilles I discovered that I was in a world I had never seen
before. The old earth, the familiar skies, the very air—all acquired a clear-
ness and transparency that were like a revelation. I knew nothing of van
Gogh at that time, and the discovery of the South came like a shock.

To look out and observe the fleeting landscape was the only thing one
could do, as there was nothing inside the train to distract our attention. We
were as reserved and shy about starting a conversation with our companions as any proverbial English travelers. The reasons for our reserve were
not, of course, the same. Although Leon and I had been in so-called Free
France for only a few days and our elation on not seeing German uniforms
had not yet died down, we could not avoid noticing many ugly facts that
made us wonder whether we were really any freer and safer here than we
had been on the other side of the demarcation line. We saw and felt dangers
that we had never feared while we had been in German-occupied France:

we were afraid of our neighbors. Made to realize only too soon after crossing into Vichy France that there were Frenchmen who hated other Frenchmen more than they hated the Germans, we kept as silent as the rest of our
fellow travelers.

When the train steamed into the Gare de St. Charles at Marseilles, we
were among the last passengers to leave it. The exit was guarded by gendarmes and members of the new Vichy police, who asked the passengers
for their tickets and identity papers. We had already been warned that, once
we fell into the hands of the Vichy police, our documents would not save us
from the usual journey through prison, concentration camp, and finally, if
one was very unlucky, a period of forced labor. Naturally enough, we had
no desire to test the truth of this warning, so we decided to avoid the main
exit of the station. We went into the cloakroom to deposit our luggage and
there saw an unguarded exit into the main street through which we
escaped.

In Brussels we had been given the address of a boardinghouse in Marseilles whose Belgian proprietor would not ask us any awkward questions
or demand a residential permit. We found it without much difficulty and
went to bed with the intention of calling on the U.S. Consulate the following morning. I hoped to find somebody there who, on the strength of the
air attaché's letter, would help me to reach England.

It was the first time in almost two years that we had seen a big city without a blackout and a curfew. We felt exhilarated and almost intoxicated by
the lights, advertisements for Hollywood films, and the warm, stuffy air of
the Mediterranean. But the following day had a sobering effect on us.

At the U.S. Consulate I was admitted, thanks to my letter of recommendation, into the presence of the consul general himself, only to learn that
he could do nothing for me. He sent me to one of his officials who dealt
with British nationals and escaped prisoners of war, and who was obviously British himself. That official told me to go to my own Polish authorities for aid.

We went to the Polish Red Cross and found it to be a typical Polish
office abroad. It was full of gentlemen giving themselves airs and graces,
and its atmosphere was heavy with signs of internecine strife, scarcely
camouflaged by a typically Polish politeness. It was badly controlled by

young and pale priests with little charity or fervor. We were told immediately on entering the office that, first, the Polish Red Cross in Marseilles was very poor in resources and therefore unable to help us; second, as we had not served with the Polish Army, we were not entitled to any help from them; and, third, they were very sorry indeed but could not give us any advice or information because they knew nothing at all.

From them we went to the Polish Consular Office. A similar, although less suave, reception awaited us. We were received by another dignified gentleman who told us in polite but firm tones that he knew nothing about the ways and means of crossing Spain. And yet, as I learned later, both the Polish Red Cross and the Consular Office in Marseilles knew enough to have saved me from at least a year's stay in a Spanish concentration camp had they only wanted to help.

They knew enough, however, to notice that our Polish passports needed renewal, and, before we knew what we were doing, we'd paid a couple hundred francs for absolutely valueless stamps and signatures.

There remained little else for us to do in Marseilles. I was not too downhearted by the lack of success we had had at the U.S. Consulate and the Polish offices, because I had set out on this adventure expecting little help from anybody and was prepared to have to struggle and triumph on my own. But Leon's ideas were different. There was little of the romantic in him, and odds, instead of being a challenge to him, had a sobering effect. He proposed that we try the Belgians.

We found the Belgian office, a modest little place, and felt strangely relaxed as soon as we entered it. We knew that we were no longer among enemies, as we had been while staying on the premises of "our country's" offices. The people in the Belgian office might not help us, but they would certainly not hurt us. The Belgian representative found it quite natural that we, Polish Jews who had enjoyed the hospitality of his country, should come to him for help, for he was quite familiar with the treatment Polish Jews received at the Polish Red Cross and Consular Office. *"Les Polonais d'ici sont des Nazis spirituels,"* he remarked in a final tone that dismissed the whole matter. He told us that he would help us because he looked upon us as being partly Belgian, since we had studied in a Belgian university, and also because, being Jews, we had few friends and needed help more than others.

He proposed to obtain for us visas to the Belgian Congo. He told us not to worry about passports and Spanish transit visas because he would take care of everything, even provide us with medical certificates stating our unfitness for military service, without which the Spaniards refused to grant transit facilities to citizens of Allied countries. He told us to go to ground for a month or so, away from Marseilles, while he was making the necessary arrangements. Marseilles was too dangerous a city to stay in, because it was out of bounds to all foreigners, even those with regular permits to live in France.

We decided to go to ground in Montpellier, because it was a convenient distance from Marseilles as well as not too far from the Spanish frontier, and because my companion had a half brother who had fled from Belgium in 1940 and settled in that old university city.

We stayed with a Polish Jewish family who were refugees from Paris. Leon found his brother, now a very sick man, and soon, with his usual facility, made friends with various people, in particular with the university students. I enjoyed my stay in the city as long as I could find something new to see and learn as, for instance, at the University of Montpellier, with Europe's oldest faculty of medicine. I made no friends and very few acquaintances among the local French population, but I became quite friendly with several Catalans, for the city was the center of Catalan immigration. One could find half of the Catalan government and parliament in the principal café of Montpellier. Having become acquainted with the personal secretary of the president of Catalonia, the unfortunate and luckless Companys, I was soon admitted into their company and even permitted to share some of their secrets.

Halfway through November, however, I had exhausted all the resources of Montpellier, and there had still been no news from our Belgian friend in Marseilles. I decided to take the bull by the horns and travel there by train. I located the Belgian office, but not our friend. The Vichy police had found out about his activities and banished him to some small village in the department of Côte-d'Or.

I avoided being caught in a street razzia and boarded a train back to Montpellier, determined to set out immediately for Spain while I still possessed a few thousand French francs and before the Pyrenees became snowbound. Luckily I was partly immunized against feeling the full weight of my own problems by the terrifying news from the Russian front, into which the German juggernaut kept advancing and devouring space and armies.

Our sojourn at Montpellier was not made any easier by the fact that we suffered from acute undernourishment due to the general scarcity of food in this department, which the French call *le desert du vin,* and also to our lack of normal ration cards. Consequently, I felt much more keenly the defeats and my own inactivity than I might otherwise have done.

Leon could afford to wait longer than I because he had set out on this adventure with almost three times as much money. He now tried to persuade me to stay until something turned up. He marshaled all the facts and rumors he knew or had heard that referred to the difficulties of crossing the Pyrenees, the dangers of traveling across Spain, the horrors of Spanish prisons, and the concentration camp of Miranda, in order to convince me that to undertake the crossing of Spain without a guide and help was sheer madness. He was convinced that, if we waited a little longer, he would manage to find some "contact" and obtain all the necessary information and aid. In the meantime, he was prepared to share his money with me.

Leon's pursuit of "contacts" had some amusing consequences. There was, for instance, the case of the cashier at the tearoom where we used to spend our evenings. The place used to sell a concoction that was very unjustly called *chocolat au lait* and contained a fine supply of Napoleon brandy—it was a very versatile tearoom indeed. The lady behind the desk had a most striking appearance: raven black hair and flashing, dark, intelligent eyes. She was in her late thirties, and in my eyes she appeared positively ancient. My taste in women was pretty unsophisticated in those days; charm had little effect on me, and I was therefore strictly reserved and indifferent in her presence. But to make up for my reserve and indifference, Leon flirted with her assiduously. The result was that we could buy sandwiches at this tearoom without having to surrender bread coupons—a very precious concession and privilege in those days.

Leon found out that she was married to a man some twenty years her senior, but he also learned that she had a lover who was a police inspector in the newly formed Vichy militia. Having learned about his influential position, Leon conceived the plan of obtaining all the necessary permits from the inspector thanks to the cashier's intervention. Leon believed that this would be possible if he could become her lover, which was, we both considered, a likely event.

The first intimation of a miscalculation on our part came to me one evening. We invited the cashier and her husband to come to the cinema with us. Whether by accident or design she happened to sit next to me. As soon as the lights went out and the film show began, she got hold of my hand and squeezed it with the nervous strength that only a woman in love would be capable of. I decided it was merely an expression of perversity on her part and did not tell Leon what had happened.

A few days later she invited us to have dinner with her. She took us to a secret black market restaurant, where we were served a dinner that would have been elaborate even in prewar times. We had sole meunière swimming in butter, steaks that melted in our mouths, golden fried potatoes, a salad full of imagination, white bread, as much butter as we could eat, and rich burgundy. The good food and wine made us feel carefree and voluptuous. And when Leon tried to pay for the meal, he found that it had already been paid for.

We were quite alone in the room, the three of us. We went on drinking wine, feeling elated and lazy, and as soon as Leon left the room for a few minutes the lady put her hands behind my head and pulled it toward hers until our lips met.

When Leon came back he did not need much explanation to know that our plans were in need of adjustment. He felt surprised but not upset. Later on he gave me all the advice he thought I needed. I listened to him without demur, but I doubted inwardly whether I would rise to the occasion.

On her first free evening following the dinner, I took the cashier to the pictures. Had the program consisted of any film save Disney's cartoons, I might have carried it off. But, after almost two years of German films, Disney's world of color and fantasy was like a draft of fresh air or a few hours of freedom. I answered her kisses halfheartedly; I scowled at the screen instead of losing myself in her eyes; I laughed so heartily that I destroyed all vestiges of erotic feeling.

When we left the cinema, I still had a chance to make up for my mistakes. I knew from Leon that she had a pied-à-terre where she received her inspector. Naturally, the thing for me to do was to ask her to show me her flat. Instead, I told her that it was late and offered to accompany her home. She declined.

I had failed signally on my mission and knew that I could expect nothing but Leon's wrath. It was high time for the two of us to part.

The first snows were falling in the Pyrenees, and practically every day the papers reported cases of Frenchmen, Poles, and Yugoslavs found in the mountains either frozen to death or in the last stages of exposure. But instead of being scared by the news, I took it as a challenge. Somehow or other I refused to believe that snow could stop me from crossing the mountains. After all, I reasoned, I come from a part of the world where we have snow every year.

I was now faced with the problem of finding enough money to pay for my train fare to the Spanish border, and enough pesetas to keep me alive until I reached Barcelona, where I hoped to contact the British consul and obtain the necessary documents and money for my further journey. But for a while my position looked quite hopeless: Leon had almost run out of money; my own resources were so low as to make my dinners dependent on the trust and benevolence of the Jewish restaurant owner whose establishment we patronized. I tried the Jewish Refugees' Committee, which was run by an Alsatian rabbi, a very patriotic Frenchman. He offered me the paltry sum of four hundred francs, which was the monthly allowance Jewish refugees received. Even that sum, he intimated to me, was a favor, as he had no right to help a person deprived of a police permit to stay at Montpellier.

I took the money he offered and went to the representative of the Belgian Red Cross at Montpellier. He agreed that my present impecunious state was partly due to the promises of his colleague at Marseilles, thanks to which I had lost almost two months waiting in Montpellier, and offered me a thousand francs with his apologies for not being able to give me more.

I purchased a hundred pesetas for this sum, packed into a French Army haversack those of my belongings that I considered necessary for my journey, and bought a railway ticket to Perpignan. At the last moment Leon decided to accompany me, and I bought a ticket for him as well. We arrived during the second week of January 1942, with a ghastly cold wind blowing from the Pyrenees.

A German armistice commission had its headquarters there, so the town was full of Vichy militia and plainclothes policemen. Consequently, we could not lodge at any hotel. A Catalan we knew allowed us to spend the night in the garage he owned and offered to introduce us to a guide. I knew that it was a sheer waste of time to try to obtain the services of a guide, poor as we were, but Leon insisted on seeing him.

He was a young Republican refugee who looked so unreliable that I should have expected him to lead me straight into the local Gestapo headquarters. Without any sign of embarrassment, he demanded forty thousand francs for piloting us across the Pyrenees. We promised to consider his offer.

Leon and I then spent one of the most miserable nights of our lives trying to fall asleep on tires in the garage. The wind kept blowing like a malignant intelligence bent upon seeking out the slightest layer of warmth around our bodies in order to destroy it. We greeted the day with gladness.

I put on all my shirts and underwear, so that I could hardly button up my jacket, and at noon took the bus to Le Boulou, a village lying some seven miles from the Spanish border. Leon did not accompany me—the night spent in the garage must have had something to do with his quitting. I traveled on the slow bus outwardly composed but feeling taut and jumpy.

Halfway to Le Boulou the bus stopped and a gendarme got on. I thought that my adventure was over there and then. I expected him to start checking the passengers' identity cards at any moment, and I even began to make plans for escape from the concentration camp where I expected to land within a few days. But the gendarme was not on duty.

The bus stopped in what appeared to be the high street of Le Boulou, which ended at a river, shallow but broad. Across the river the plain continued for a few miles, then ended abruptly as the Pyrenees rose suddenly like a wall.

The bridge that spanned the river was long, and as I started crossing it I could scarcely see the other end. A car overtook me when I was almost halfway across it. The car reached the opposite end, came to a sudden standstill, and two gendarmes, whose existence I did not even suspect, appeared and began to examine it. I stopped dead, leaned over the balustrade, and gazed at the swift stream. At last I managed to collect myself sufficiently to realize that it was neither the time nor the place to dither. I retraced my steps and at last reached the village without either of the gendarmes calling after me or running in pursuit.

I turned upstream and walked along the river until the falling darkness made me realize that I would have to give up the idea of crossing it that day and begin instead to look for a place where I could spend the night.

There were no farms along the riverbank and very few houses. At last I saw a small cottage and a man working in the garden outside it. I begged him for permission to spend the night under his roof. He refused in an apologetic tone, telling me he was only a *metaire,* that the cottage was not his own, and that, being a Swiss, he was afraid to take any risks. But he advised me to keep on walking for another mile or so until I arrived at a small village. There were two cafés in that village, and if I went to one of them and told its owner that I had been sent by him, he would not refuse to let me stay.

I left him, continued along the bank of the river, and found the village and the two cafés, which were almost next door to each other. I first entered the wrong café and had some difficulty in extricating myself from its owners' inquisitive questions as to the purpose of my visit. I then entered the second and found the proprietor's wife busy cleaning some vegetables in front of a smoking fireplace. When I told her what had brought me there, she asked me to wait for her husband, who arrived a few minutes later. A big and heavy man many years older than his wife, who was herself in her late forties, he looked me over suspiciously and asked me many searching questions. Hoping to appear even more deserving of help than I actually was, I told him that I was an escaped prisoner of war on my way to England across Spain. He demanded to see my documents, finished his examination as abruptly as he had commenced it, and told his wife to set another place at the table for me.

I was invited into the kitchen, where a big fire was blazing in a vast fireplace. After a while their son arrived, a young and handsome fellow to whom I was introduced. We had a drink together, and he told me about his war experiences.

That night I shared his room. A warm and comfortable bed was like paradise to bones that had been bruised by the tires on the previous night, but I could not fall asleep immediately, thinking as I was of the difficulties and risks I would have to face on the following day. I talked to my room-mate about the mountains that reared their peaks outside the windows of the bedroom and asked for his advice. I had a map, and he showed me which path to take, where to avoid the gendarmerie posts, and how to keep my bearings. He apologized for not being able to guide me himself, saying his mother would not let him. But for her, he declared, he would have left a long time before to join General de Gaulle's forces.

I remember that before falling asleep I asked him in whose bed I was sleeping, and he told me that his sailor cousin had used it when on leave. He would never again sleep in it, for he had been killed by British shells at Mers-al-Kabir. "All because of those men of Vichy," he said sadly.

Into Catalonia

I WOKE LATE on the following morning. My roommate was already up but had not had the heart to disturb me in my deep sleep. I looked out the window and saw that the whole landscape was covered by a white blanket of snow. Big, lazy, fluffy flakes kept coming down and cushioning the ground. I hurriedly shaved and washed and came downstairs. As usual I could not eat anything for breakfast but drank a cup of coffee made from corn. My kind hostess's eyes wandered anxiously from the weather outside to me sitting in front of her fireplace. I could read her thoughts, full of compassion. If it had depended upon her, I am sure that she would have tried to dissuade me from sallying forth in this blizzard. But I knew that my hosts were taking risks in keeping me under their roof, and I did not want to abuse their hospitality.

I left them at ten o'clock, crossed the bridge, and followed the road leading into the mountains. I felt warm with the snow falling evenly and gaily, but I could not see far ahead and my face was wet. My plan for crossing the frontier was very simple. I intended to keep to the right of the highway that leads to the Perthus Pass and, having reached the border, which generally runs along the peaks of the mountain ridges, cross into Spain. If everything went smoothly, I should reach the frontier in the evening and thus be able to cross it under the cover of darkness.

I realized very soon, however, that I had not set off on a lucky day; because the snow had narrowed my field of vision, I was unable to get a glimpse of any landmark. Then, early in the afternoon, remembering the instructions my host's son had given me, I began to wonder where I ought to leave the road I was following in order to avoid the gendarmerie post. My host's son had marked the position of the post on my map, and I now looked for the map in my haversack only to discover that it was not there. I had forgotten to put it back before going to bed. This meant that I would have to trust my luck even more than I had intended on this side of the border, and that once in Spain I would be practically blind.

Until then I had been in open country. As the ground was covered with snow, I could not tell whether it was tilled or pastureland. But after having washed my feet in the stream and walked on along the same faint path, I found myself in a hollow wood with beeches and ashes. It was much warmer among the trees, and there was a little snow on the ground. By now, anxious to find somebody of whom I might inquire as to my present whereabouts, I accelerated my steps and found that the path I was following led into a lane, at the end of which I saw a collection of buildings in red brick. Not a sound came from any of them. I ventured toward them, became bolder, and knocked at the windows of some, but nobody replied. I could not make out what all these fine houses were doing in this apparent wilderness and why they were not inhabited. But there was no time to stray aimlessly about, and I left the main body of buildings, walked past solitary pavilions, and again found myself in the surrounding wood, which, I decided, must have been a park.

Cutting across the wood, I climbed over an elaborate iron fence and found myself on some unknown road, face-to-face with an old woman wrapped up in a black shawl, who told me that the strange domain I had just crossed was a spa, open only in summer. When I asked her whether I was on the right road to Perthus, my question had an immediate effect. Instead of answering me she shook her head sadly and said, "I know why you want to go there. Have you not had enough of war? Better go back to your parents, who miss you. We have stopped fighting the Germans, and we ought to keep our obligations. It is because of boys like you, who love war, that my grandson is still a prisoner of war in Germany."

I was so much taken aback by her words that I was at first at a loss for a reply. "But, Grandmother, do you honestly believe that Hitler will free your grandson if I give up the fight? He will free the French prisoners only if France joins him in the war against England or Russia."

She shook her head again. She had not listened to my words at all. "You, *Francais du nord*," she said, "you can never make peace with the Germans. Why not end the quarrel once and for all? This is not our war. Why not let the English spill their own blood? Go home, my boy, go home."

I forgot that she was an old woman. My temper rose and I almost shouted, "You cannot buy happiness at the cost of other people's sufferings. There are millions of women in Europe with grandsons suffering your grandson's fate or worse. Hitler's Germany is responsible for their unhappiness, but you are ready to make peace with him so that you alone should be happy with your grandson. You are a bad Frenchwoman and a bad grandmother!"

She shook her head ruefully but did not answer. As she made ready to walk off, I repeated my original question. She nodded affirmatively. I then asked her whether I was far from the gendarmerie post. She answered that I was only some five minutes' walk from it, and that at the next turning of the road I would find myself in front of it.

We parted. I disappeared to the right of the road in brushwood of a kind I had never seen before, which covered the slope of the mountain. I hoped to hit the road again, but beyond the gendarmerie post. I found a path meandering among the bushes and followed it, treading through slush and mud until it brought me to the top of the mountain. But when I looked over its brow, I found that my climbing had only just begun.

I had reached what looked like the brow of a saddle. I had to descend and climb the full arch of the saddle before I reached the other brow, which was an even higher peak than the one I had just ascended. What lay beyond that I did not know.

The saddle between the two peaks was full of snow. There was no track, no path, no trace of human or animal feet to be seen. I commenced the descent at random, strayed into deep snowdrifts, got thoroughly wet, and at last reached the trough. I climbed, slipped, climbed again, fell, crawled on, with my heart beating wildly and my body all covered with perspiration, until I finally reached the opposite brow of the saddle. The view from the top was a splendid reward for the effort involved in reaching it. Looking out to the south, I saw on my left the Perthus Pass crowned by its immense Belegarde citadel, and on my right innumerable peaks, snow-capped and glistening in the sun.

The descent took me longer than I had expected. Now and then cars drove up and down the road; their occupants could have been gendarmes or *gardes mobiles*. My solitary figure coming down the mountain pass might have aroused their suspicions, so I had to keep to wooded parts of the mountain, force my way among snow-laden saplings, wade through drifts, slide down uncovered soil, and travel quickly. The sun was setting, and I was still nowhere near the border.

I soon learned that geography was not on my side. As the ranges were running from east to west and I was making south, I was doomed to climb and descend, and climb and descend again until I had reached the range along whose crests ran the frontier. Nor was nature kind to me. The hills were covered by a real jungle of stunted timber and brushwood, interlaced and interlocked by their own branches, wild vines, and lichens. Apart from supple and vigorous legs, one needed powerful arms and a machete to advance.

I had, of course, no machete with which to cut a trail for myself, and my legs were far from being supple or vigorous. I had not eaten anything since waking; I had simply forgotten the necessity of taking food. I now decided to drink some of the condensed milk I had brought and felt at once better: warmer, more cheerful, less dissatisfied with myself. I braced myself for climbing again. I was lucky that I wore a solid trench coat, which stood very well against the wrenching and tearing of unknown shrubs, tree branches, and thorns. I followed trails that had not been trodden for so long that vegetation had again claimed them as its own. I had to leap over torrents, crawl under low-hanging boughs, and still have enough breath left for climbing. I forced my pace but to no avail: it was almost night and I was alone, in the mountains, and still in France.

I struck a path that led me into a clearing filled with rectangular stacks of timber. I had seen very similar stacks in the old forests of the Wilno province and realized that they were charcoal kilns. The burning had not yet begun and, as it had become quite dark, I decided to spend the night in the clearing.

To sit and rest was enough to make me content for an hour or so. But January nights are long and cold, so that soon I was stiff and shivering. I had to get up from the log on which I was sitting and keep walking about swinging my arms until the increased circulation had warmed my body. Then I would sit down, become stiff and cold again, and, before drowsiness overcame me completely, get up and keep walking until I felt warmer. The disappointed but generous cashier had given me a bottle of brandy before I left Montpellier, and whenever I felt the cold getting the better of my determination I had a sip of it.

My spark of courage was glowing bravely but was not sufficient to shut out completely the assaults of the cold and long night. Toward the morning I was very stiff and craving for something hot to drink. If there had been the slightest trace of human dwelling around, I would have taken the risk of approaching and testing the hospitality of its inhabitants. But temptation was out of my sight and reach. I just had to go on slumbering, waking up, running around the charcoal kilns, having a sip of my Napoleon brandy, going off to sleep again, and repeating the whole process like a litany.

At last, reluctantly, came the morning. A glorious sun appeared. There was a breath of spring in the air, as if the snow of yesterday had never been.

I still had the same struggle in front of me: climbing and descending by clearing a trail through tangled shrubs, evergreens, and cork trees. The effort involved in this work put a constant strain on my willpower. I drank my second and last tin of condensed milk and struggled on doggedly.

An absolute silence reigned in the mountains, as if no human being was alive within miles. I found tracks leading to clearings with the characteristic charcoal kilns in the center of them. Swift, gurgling torrents forced their way through crag, rock, and vegetation, dashed forward in breathless haste, fell down in cascades, and, as if ashamed of their hurry, dwelt for a while in meditation in dark pools. My impulse was to sit down near one of these pools and fall asleep in the warm sun, but a furtive glance at my watch kept me moving forward.

At midday I saw a spiral of smoke rising above a wooded valley. I quickened my step and, as I turned around a bend in the road, beheld two

French customs officers leaning against the mountain rock through which the road had been cut. Their eyes were half closed and their faces raised to the sun. They were obviously basking in its rays and, perhaps, dozing off every now and then.

I quickly moved back behind the bend, but not fast enough to avoid detection. I dove down the bank of the road into bushes, tore through them, found myself in a clearing, raced forward in the direction of the valley above which I had seen the swirling smoke, met a torrent, raced splashing up its stream, and sprawled to find myself half in water and half lying on stones under a rock overgrown with evergreen bushes, making me invisible from the bank. I lay there with my nose washed by the torrent and my heart beating wildly.

I heard the customs officers forcing their way through the thick shrubs, but they were beating the bush in the wrong direction. My escaping forward instead of backward was to prove my salvation. They searched the little valley conscientiously but never reached the place where I was hidden. At last they passed my hiding place, walking parallel to the road and back to their point of vantage. I could hear one of them repeat heatedly, "But I tell you, I did see a man in a beret and trench coat!"

I stayed in my hiding place for half an hour after the last echoes of their voices had vanished. Then I crawled out of the hollow through which the torrent was speeding and emerged on the opposite side of the little valley. To my right I could see the smoking chimney of a house hidden in a thicket; to my left was a small cemetery. Miles beyond the cemetery was the towering mass of the Perthus Pass. I knew that I was on the border between France and Spain and not far from the customs officers' place of ambush—some four hundred yards in a straight line at the most. The reasonable thing to do was to disappear into the jungle of alders on the other side of the stream. But, having crept into the heart of a thicket, I took off my shoes and trench coat to let them dry in the sun, lay down, and, gazing into the sky with its scudding clouds, dozed off.

On January 15, 1942, at five o'clock in the afternoon, I crossed the stream, cut through a plantation of alders so thick that the path seemed like a tunnel, and, after more than half an hour's brisk walking, emerged into the open.

The valley of Figueras lay ahead of me, illuminated by the light of the setting sun. To my right it was bordered by the wooded ridges that flowed down from the mass of Andorran peaks. Its left flank disappeared in the gathering darkness; I could see it stretch as far as the highway lined with telegraph poles of a peculiarly Spanish nature: short and uneven, they leaned over wildly in all directions, as if they had been erected in a treeless desert.

I briskly followed the path and soon found myself in a street, among houses, and in front of a grocer's shop lit up and displaying fruit I had not seen for almost two years: oranges and bananas. I realized that I was in La Junquera, a village I had been warned to avoid at all costs, because it was the headquarters of the carabineros and *guardia civil*. Nevertheless the attraction of the fruit was too great for me to turn back on the spot. I took a chance, went into the grocer's shop, and asked for a kilo of bananas. I had never learned the Spanish name on the assumption that it was the same as in English or in French. The woman therefore, being obviously a Catalan and having been asked for *bananas* instead of *plátanos,* assumed me to be a fellow countryman of hers and spoke to me in Catalan. Unable to understand what she was saying and not realizing at first that she was speaking a language I had not studied, I answered curtly, *"Sí, sí,"* paid for the fruit, and left in a hurry.

Before leaving the village I passed a civil guard wrapped up in his cloak and looking very much like a raven, but he never stopped to ask me for my documents. The reason, I suppose, was the fact that he was alone, and civil guards seldom dare to carry out their duties unless there are two or more of them.

I found that the greatest difficulty on my journey was overcoming my desire to fall asleep; marching remained the only reasonable way to do so. The Spanish countryside struck me by its absolute silence; the familiar noises of the Polish countryside at night were entirely missing. The road took me right through villages and hamlets, brilliantly lit by electric lamps. In the glaring, cold light I saw white houses shuttered and inhospitable, painted with immense slogans proclaiming: "Nothing for myself, all for Spain, Spain for Franco, and Franco for God."

I had never been so far south in my life. The springlike warmth of the January night; the white windowless cottages; the towering churches; the

mountains, purple and violet before sunset—all combined to make me feel
that I was indeed in a strange land and under an unknown sky. But I felt no
foreigner; I experienced the same feeling as I have had on entering every
land in Europe: a feeling of curiosity at seeing another part of the stage on
which a chapter of my people's past had been performed.

By about five o'clock in the morning I was no longer alone on the highway. Peasant carts drawn by mules or donkeys emerged from side roads;
groups of silent men passed me without a word of greeting. A mile or so
from Figueras I had to proceed between two guardhouses, standing on
either side of the road. Civil guards were looking out of them at the stream
of people and animals. The carts had to stop and undergo some kind of
examination. I kept in the shadow and passed without being stopped.

At Figueras I found my way to the marketplace by following the stream of
traffic. At a small milk bar that was already open, I had one *café con leche*
and then another. I paid four pesetas for those two drinks. I knew from my
Catalan friends at Montpellier that the average wages of a Spanish worker
were eight pesetas a day. This legal black market economy frightened me,
for I had less than a hundred pesetas on me, and at least another four days'
marching to Barcelona.

A Catalan at Montpellier had given me the address of a small hotel in
Figueras, where, he assured me, I would find food and shelter if I men-
tioned his name. I sat on a bench, waited for the day to advance, and
shortly before nine o'clock in the morning I found the small hotel, whose
owner received me cautiously. He was glad to hear that his *sobrino* was in
good health; he was confident that Señor Churchill would win the war and
then help the Catalans to throw off Franco's yoke; but he had a wife and
children to think of, and all the hotels were watched by the *guardia civil*,
carbineros, and the Himmler-organized *policía armada*. Therefore he could
offer me a meal and let me sit in his restaurant, but as for letting a room—
no, it was quite impossible, not even for the day.

I washed and shaved and then sat down on one of the hard chairs in the
dark dining room and tried to sleep. My head kept slipping off the back of
the chair, and I would wake up with a start, afraid that I was falling down.
In this manner I spent the hours separating me from the midday meal,
which turned out to be a miserable affair. The hunk of bread he served with

the meal was of maize and not much bigger than my fist. Nevertheless, he told me that it was the equivalent of two days' rations and, as I later found out, he was telling the truth.

I had had enough of marching, and I thought of continuing to Barcelona by train or bus until I learned from my host that this was not feasible. In order to be able to buy a railway or coach ticket, a Spaniard had first to apply to the police for a travel permit. Every ticket collector on the train or bus was accompanied by a plainclothes policeman who inspected the permits. Consequently I decided not to take any of the risks involved and to continue on foot. At five o'clock, when darkness fell, I said goodbye to my cautious host and set off for Gerona, a distance of twenty-five miles. I had heard from the hotel keeper that there was a British vice consul at Gerona, and that piece of news was almost as good as a night's rest in a bed. I was confident of my ability to get there before the following morning.

A few miles out of the town I was overtaken by a tremendous pig, which, in spite of its bulk, kept up a good gallop and soon disappeared in the distance. Hardly had I overcome my surprise at seeing a pig race along a public highway on its own when a motorcyclist overtook me and stopped in front of me. The rider, obviously a representative of law and order, asked me politely whose pig it was.

I answered rather curtly: *"No sé. No es mío."*

"Gracias," he said and raced off after the animal.

After eight o'clock I met no living person on the road. The night was cold, and my brandy was almost all gone. I tried again to steal some sleep in the hayricks, but their dampness made any kind of rest impossible. To march on and to follow on my wristwatch the passage of time were the only two things I could do.

It was hard marching, too, because the road was rising continually as it penetrated the hills that separated the valley of Figueras from the larger valley in which Gerona lies. I was covering on average three and a half miles an hour—a pace fast enough to allow me to reach Gerona in the late hours of the following morning.

There were two recurrent themes in my mind. The first was a blind, stubborn desire to succeed, embodied in a kaleidoscope of images express-

ing the importance of achievement, of reaching England. The second
theme was more a symphony of feelings, *un etat d'Ame,* which I had known
for the first time on reading Joseph Conrad's *Youth.* That narrative had
always struck me as being the most perfect romantic ode to the divine self-
assurance of youth, to the godlike feeling of personal indestructibility, and
to the irrational, youthful conviction of being able to overcome any external odds and any opposition presented by one's physical body. But in that
indetermined hour that precedes sunrise, when the first cock crows, the
cold penetrated to the very marrow of my bones. A burning thirst for some
hot drink got hold of me. It possessed me with the same demonic intensity
as the urge for liquor possesses its addicts. To obtain it I was ready to knock
at the first door I saw, and before long a lonely cottage appeared by the
roadside. Smoke was coming out of its roof and voices could be heard
inside. There was a big wooden door, at which I knocked. Nobody replied,
so I pushed the door and found that behind it there was a stable, beyond
which I detected another door. I knocked and thought I heard a voice
telling me to come in.

It took me a good many seconds to take in the place and the people.
There was a fire burning on the stone floor right in the middle of the room,
the smoke escaping through a hole in the roof, but not a single piece of fur-
niture was visible in the place. An old peasant, bent and gnarled, was shap-
ing a piece of wood into the handle of a hoe. He cast a glance at me and
went on working. Another man was crouching by the fire and heaping
brushwood on it. He looked as powerful as an ox. His face was covered
with the growth of several days, and his eyes had a menacing look.

"Buenos días, señores, " I said apologetically. "You would not have some
hot milk to sell me by any chance? I have got all frozen in the cold." The
man interrupted me peremptorily in a well-modulated and distinct voice
that formed a strange contrast with his uncouth appearance. He said, "How
dare you, *señor,* enter my house without first knocking and waiting for my
permission to do so?"

His dignity was there; his indignation sincerely felt, but I hastened to
assure him in my faltering Spanish that I had knocked at both doors and
entered his home only after having heard sounds that I had taken to be an
invitation to do so.

During the whole scene, the old man, who must have been either the younger man's father or his father-in-law, went on with his job without paying the slightest attention to my presence. He did not pay any more attention even when the younger man accepted my explanation and told me in his warm, expressive voice, "We have no milk."

"Then would you permit me to warm myself at your fire?" I asked him.

He said something to the old man in Catalan and received a mumbled monosyllable in reply. "You may," he replied.

I crouched by the fire. After a few minutes he brought a stool from the stable and offered it to me. I thanked him and sat down upon it. Not a word was spoken after that for a good quarter of an hour. At the end of that time a door, which I had not noticed before, opened and a woman came in, walked through the room, and went into the stable. She was about the same age as the younger man, broad, dressed in black, and wearing a shawl over her head. I said, *"Buenos días,"* but she did not reply. She came back, disappeared again behind the door whence she had first made her appearance, turned up again, and hung up something over the fire.

I almost forgot my fatigue. I watched the place and people with a fascination I had rarely experienced. Never before had I seen such a primitive abode. The poorest peasants huts I had known in Polish Belorussia had some kind of window; the way into the *izba* was never through the stable; they always possessed stoves and ovens; they were often filthy, with lice in winter and fleas in summer, but always warm and cozy. This Catalan cottage looked so poor and primitive that it made one wonder whether its occupants did not try to keep it in such a state for some special reason.

And then fragments of stories I had read as a boy about travelers who had put up at Spanish inns or houses only to be murdered and robbed by their hosts came to my mind. My imagination got out of hand for a while. I even began to consider my chances of being able to get away from this place alive. My terror became quite real when I saw the woman whisper something to her husband. Then he opened his mouth and spoke to me. "Would you care to have some soup my wife has warmed up? It is poor soup, but warm."

I thanked him for his kindness, and his wife handed him a plate, which he brought over to where I sat. The soup smelled and tasted strange, but it was warm and I ate it voraciously.

When I had finished, I asked him how far I was from Gerona. Like most peasants anywhere in Europe, he had no definite idea of distance in miles. All he could tell me was that I had some two hours' walk ahead of me.

It was almost eight o'clock and time to go. I had nothing on me except money that I could offer the cottagers as a sign of gratitude for their hospitality, so I asked the husband how much I owed them.

He answered in his dignified voice, "We are poor but not without manners, *señor*. There is nothing to pay for a little warmth."

I thanked them all and went through the stable back into the open.

The highway was still practically deserted save for an occasional bus or motorcar. On hearing the sound of an engine, I invariably left the road to avoid being seen by any possible policeman, a practice that, of course, held me up considerably.

Toward noon the road lost its arrowlike straightness and became full of bends, which proved both dangerous and useful. Dangerous because I did not know whom I might meet around them. Useful because they hid me from whoever was watching around the bend. Twice I detected pairs of civil guards patrolling the roads. I avoided them by cutting across the fields and striking the highway a mile or even two beyond their beat.

By noon the temperature was more like that of a late English spring than January. The fact that I had all my shirts and underwear on did not help. I felt hot, thirsty, and sleepy. In search of a drink I wandered into two or three taverns and had glasses of red and white wine. Nobody had ever warned me that Spanish wine is heavy, that it affects one's legs before making an impression on one's brain, so it further sabotaged my progress toward Gerona.

At last I found myself on a long and winding street full of color and light. There was the white of the houses, the yellow and brown of the factory buildings; there was the bustle of workers going home; the restfulness of old people sitting outside their front doors and basking in the sun; there were the sudden splashes of color presented by the shops. And, above all, there was a sky of a delicate blue with clouds as exquisite as lace, a warm wind, and a mellow, happy sunset.

There was a sudden bend in the street. As I turned around it I found some twenty paces ahead of me a river, a wooden bridge, and a whole bunch of civil guards watching it. Instinctively I rushed back beyond the bend in the street, saw a doorway, and took cover in it. My heart was beating fast. What was I to do? Turn back or go on? I made up my mind to go on. My French Army haversack was swinging over my shoulder. Its military shape might attract the attention of the civil guards, so I decided to carry it in my hand, and by a movement of my right arm and shoulder I let its strap slip into my right hand.

My eyes had followed the movement of the falling strap. As I raised them, I found myself looking at a tall, young man in his shirtsleeves, who was pointing at me the biggest pistol I had ever seen outside the cinema and signaling me to follow him. We walked back across the street, entered a house, and went upstairs and into a big room whose window looked onto the street.

"Polaco?" he inquired curtly.

I was so much taken aback that although I had a Belgian identity card I replied affirmatively.

His ridiculous black tricorn hat was lying on the bed. His green tunic was hanging on the back of a chair. He had been shaving in front of a small mirror hung up on the window frame and had, quite unwittingly, observed what was happening in the street below. He had noticed my sudden rush into the doorway right opposite his window. He had arrested several Belgians and Poles before me and thus had an eye for my kind of traveler. He had wiped the lather off his face, grabbed his pistol, and raced into the street to arrest me.

He now searched me thoroughly and found both my Belgian identity card and the Polish passport but not the air attaché's letter. He expressed a liking for one of my two pipes, and I let him have it without arguing. Then he noticed my wristwatch and declared his readiness to buy it, but I answered that I was not ready to sell it.

"When you have been in prison for a few days, you will sell it for a loaf of bread or a few cigarettes," he replied.

He then began to ply me with questions about my knowledge of Spanish. Where had I learned it? Had I been in Spain before? Was I not a former member of the International Brigade? Had I not been sent to Spain by the Reds?

I replied that I had never been to Spain before and that the little Spanish I knew I had learned with the aid of the book I had in my haversack.

He changed the tone of his voice to one of understanding. "I could not do anything else but arrest you. It was my duty to do so. However, nobody has seen me. I could take you out of town the way you have come, show you the right road to take, and set you free. What do you say to that, *amigo mío?*"

"Muchas gracias, señor," I replied, all ready to believe but not entirely convinced.

He told me to sit down and have patience while he finished shaving. He shaved very thoroughly but held his pistol within easy reach and observed my slightest movements in the mirror. Having finished, he donned his well-fitting tunic, scented his well-made person, put on his long greatcoat, and declared himself ready. Then he asked me whether I had reconsidered my reply to his offer to buy my wristwatch.

"I do not want to sell it," I replied, "but I shall give it to you."

"Give it to me!" he called out sternly. "We, civil guards, have as our motto 'Honor and Glory.' You cannot bribe us!"

I felt as if I had really made a very false move, although he was staring at me with my own curved pipe between his healthy white teeth. I mumbled apologies and made myself look as dejected as possible. Then I offered to sell him the watch, which he generously accepted. He had it for a crown.

It was dark in the street when we emerged. We turned left, toward the bridge, which made me realize immediately that he had lied to me about his intentions to set me free. The civil guard post was close to the bridge. He led me inside it, handed me over to his superior, and disappeared.

I decided that it was better to keep my mouth shut. Having spent the first eighteen years of my life in a country run by colonels and policemen, I knew enough of the dangers attendant on the pursuit of justice when the malefactors and the judges are the very same people.

THE OTHER SPAIN

Two young civil guards took me into their custody after their superior at the post had finished interrogating me. One of them was a friendly and talkative fellow, who complimented me on my Spanish and told me that they were taking me to see the civil governor of Gerona.

He was a dapper young man in his early thirties, with a feminine face, a well-tended mustache, and shiny, carefully combed hair. He wore the insignia of the Falange—a knot of thunderbolts looking like a nest of vipers—in the lapel of his coat. A bevy of young girls in white blouses and blue skirts surrounded him. They all had animated faces, as if they had been having a jolly good time just before my appearance. Having saluted the civil governor, the talkative civil guard explained who I was and handed over an envelope containing all the documents and money found on my person. The governor looked through them and gave me back my Spanish pesetas. The envelope also contained some fifty French francs. When he came to them, he said to me, "These will be of no use to you, señor, will they?" and pocketed them.

Having finished with the formalities, he passed on to the more pleasant part of our *entretien*. He asked me where I had learned my Spanish, how I liked Spain, what I thought of Spanish women. I replied fully to his first question. As to the second, I explained that I could not answer it because his good civil guards had not given me much time and opportunity to make up my mind. As to the third, to judge by the young ladies around him, Spanish women looked as glamorous as the poets had described. The governor liked my reply, and so did the young ladies. The latter spoke all at once, so that the room was filled with a sound like the chirping of flocks of sparrows.

After that the civil governor told me not to worry and bade me good-bye. "You will spend a few days in prison here until there is a police escort ready to take you to Barcelona. There your consul will effect your release." I thanked him and his young ladies and left with my two protectors.

Once we were in the street, the young guard advised me to buy some food and tobacco before I went into prison. We went into a grocer's shop where I bought a few kilos of bananas and oranges. As tobacco was rationed, I could not buy it legally without being in possession of the necessary ration book. But the guard meant for me to have tobacco, so we wandered along the street until he saw a man standing in a doorway, went up to him, and asked for cigarettes. Apparently the black marketer had been in the habit of providing the guard with that scarce weed, for he handed me the stuff without any hesitation. I paid him a price 500 percent above the official one, and we set off for the prison along an ill-lit street.

The approaches were guarded by soldiers warming themselves around braziers. Old women in shawls and young, shivering and stockingless girls were waiting outside with baskets in which they had brought food for their incarcerated sons, husbands, and brothers. A small door in a very large gate opened up, and we entered the jail.

An unexpected sight greeted my eyes. We were in a patio brightly illuminated by electric bulbs swinging in the air. Galleries ran around the courtyard. Men of all ages, dressed in all kinds of civilian clothes, were rushing about carrying chairs, tables, benches, mattresses, and cases. The place did not look like a prison at all. I learned a day later the cause of this extraordinary activity. The two thousand–odd prisoners had been moved on the day of my arrival from their old prison, which was a former church, to the present one, which was a former convent. As I later discovered, there was nothing unusual about churches and convents being used as prisons in Catholic Franco's Spain.

We went into the prison office. Apart from one official, the office was run by prisoners. They took down my particulars, confiscated my shaving

tackle, and asked me what my military status was. When one of the clerks
hastened to explain to me that as an officer I would be permitted to keep my
hair, whereas as a noncommissioned warrior I would have it cropped, I
promoted myself without hesitation.

During the same interrogation I was asked what was my religion and I
hesitated a moment before replying. I thought of Spain's anti-Jewish traditions; I thought of the Gestapo's tentacles. But before I had time to answer,
one of the prisoners said, "He is a Pole; all Poles are Catholics," and I did
not contradict him. It was the first time in my life that I had denied my Jewishness, and I felt illogically uneasy about it to such a degree that as soon as
we left the prison office I wanted to turn back and tell the clerk to rectify
the error in his books.

The civil guards shook hands with me and wished me all the best. Then
a jailer took me to what I hoped would be a cell with a bed, where, at last, I
should be able to sleep off the three nights spent in the mountains and on
the road. Instead of a cell I found myself in a cellar, where not the slightest
ray of light and very few sounds penetrated from outside. Cold flagstones
were the only resting place. I thought of the damp and cold hayricks standing in open fields at which I had railed only the night before and realized at
last the depths of my misfortune.

I felt lonely and forsaken, with all my courage gone. I was afraid of
falling asleep on the cold stones on account of rats, whose scurrying I
could hear. I shivered but was too downcast to get up and try to warm
myself by swinging my arms and stamping my feet. The enshrouding
darkness and silence weighed heavily upon me.

I had lost all count of time, and when the bolts were pushed back and the
heavy door opened, and I emerged again in the courtyard, I was amazed to
learn that it was early afternoon and I had spent only one night and one
morning in darkness.

A big caldron stood in a corner of the patio. A yellow mess reeking to
high heaven covered its bottom. I was given a tin plate and allowed to take
as much as I wanted of the unknown pulpy substance. It was still warm,
and that made me eat it. The mess consisted of rice and beans, and would
have been quite appetizing were it not for its terrible smell. That smell
never left the food I was to eat during fourteen months of captivity, and I

never grew used to it. It was the odor of badly refined olive oil. I was surprised to find rice forming part of the prison menu, considering that this tropical food had become as rare as coffee and tea in Hitler's Europe.

There was a water tap near the caldron. I asked for permission to wash and was told to go ahead. I suppose I was expected to wash only my face and hands, because when I bared myself to the waist and washed the upper part of my body as well, I became an object of curiosity and wonder. I was asked whether I was not cold, and when I assured my questioners that I actually felt warmer after having washed, I heard them express amazement at the hardiness of the people of the North. As a matter of fact, the temperature on the patio on that January afternoon was extremely mild.

I was then taken for quarantine to a room on the third floor of the prison. There were no windows, and its door, opening into the main corridor, had no lock. One was supposed to leave the room only in order to visit the lavatory, and the *cabo* of the floor saw to it that this regulation was obeyed.

The room was some twelve feet square and contained ten people. The two most striking were an old shepherd and a gypsy. I never found out why the gypsy was in prison. He pretended that he was a political prisoner, while the other prisoners said that he was only a petty thief and ignored him accordingly. The old shepherd—he must have been almost seventy and was as gnarled and small as a gnome—was accused of having murdered a priest and of having set his village church on fire. I could hardly understand his Asturian dialect, but I managed to grasp enough of his replies to realize that he did not deny any of the charges against him, and that he had no regrets for what he had done. He was the first Spaniard to open my eyes to the extent of odium the Catholic Church provokes in some part of the Spanish people.

My other companions were young Catalans, whose occupations ranged from baker to shipping clerk and whose only crime was to have served with the Republican Army. Their terms of imprisonment ran from seven years, or seven years and a day, to fifteen years, or fifteen years and a day. They had already spent years in camps and prisons, had been freed under the terms of all kinds of amnesties, and had been taken back to prison because of some informer's report, their local priest's dislike, or a blue shirt's personal vengeance.

During my first day in quarantine I learned the most important features of prison life in Franco's Spain. First of all, I learned that no prisoner was given a bed, mattress, or blanket. Beds were actually banned. A prisoner had to bring his blankets and mattress with him. In daytime he rolled his sleeping kit into the smallest possible bundle and pushed it against the wall.

The prison I was in enjoyed a reputation for being humane. There were no premeditated beatings or solitary cells; as a matter of fact, apart from the cellars underneath the old convent building, there were no cells at all. The few rooms were used as sick quarters and offices, and the prisoners slept in the passageways and corridors, occupying exactly as much room as their respective mattresses, and lying so close to one another that an expedition to the lavatory at night entailed as much effort and concentration on one's part as tightrope walking.

Half an hour after my arrival I was reminded that, despite its casual and unorthodox appearance, it *was* a prison. I had hardly settled in my corner upon a blanket offered me by a young Catalan baker when we heard a shot. A short silence followed and was then broken by hasty steps and abrupt voices. One of our company looked out and reported that a prisoner was lying in the corridor, in front of a window.

I learned that no inmate of a Spanish prison was allowed to stand in front of a window. The soldiers who guarded the prisons were under strict orders to fire at every silhouette they saw appear behind a window's pane. Considering that the soldiers were conscripts, without party allegiance, without any special reasons for hating the people they were guarding, I found it puzzling that they should be so eager to execute orders they could easily neglect. However, the other prisoners explained to me that for shooting a prisoner a soldier was given a month's leave and a certain sum of money. For the average ignorant peasant lad, treated like a beast of burden by his officers and NCOs, shivering in his drill uniform and canvas sandals, constantly hungry, and often unable to buy his weekly allowance of cigarettes, the temptation was too great to be resisted.

The prisoner who had just been killed was only twenty-five. He had been originally sentenced to death and kept for months with that sentence hanging over his head like the sword of Damocles. The sentence was then commuted to a term of thirty years' imprisonment. His mother did not give up the struggle for her son's life and freedom and, at about the same time as my arrival in the quarantine room, was announcing to her son that she had obtained his conditional release from prison. Her son had rushed from the office in the patio, where he had received the happy tidings from his mother, back to the passage on the third floor to collect his few belongings. They were lying under his mattress; the mattress, neatly rolled up, lay below the sill of a window. The man forgot about the prison's regulations regarding windows. He did not duck low enough: his head was visible from the wall that surrounded the prison. Lead shattered his brain and reduced him to a corpse, his mother to a broken human being, and the poor ignoramus who pulled the trigger to a murderer.

On my second day in the prison I was taken to the sick quarters. Like everything else it was manned by prisoners; two doctors ran it. About one of them, the surgeon, I had already heard at Montpellier, for he was one of the most famous doctors in Catalonia. After he had inoculated me against typhus, we got down to the important business of talking politics and exchanging news. I told them all I knew about the world outside, and they gave me the latest news from the Russian front. I told them about the defeat of Hitler's armies at the gates of Moscow. They told me about the latest advances of the Red Army. Their enthusiasm and optimism were winged: according to their informants the siege of Leningrad had been lifted and Smolensk liberated. They forestalled events by years. As for the Japanese war, we consoled ourselves by agreeing that its course would be turned by the guns of Singapore.

I visited the two doctors several times during my stay in the prison, and our conversations always revolved around the same topics: politics and the latest news, which they seemed to receive daily from outside. Another topic was sex. They had a book with reproductions of Rubens's paintings. The doctors and their patients would spend hours poring over the pictures representing masses of female flesh.

The first few days of imprisonment passed away rather quickly, for I spent them sleeping and learning about the place and its occupants. I learned that the third floor, on which the quarantine room was situated, housed prisoners with sentences of thirty years and over, the second floor was occupied by those with sentences exceeding seven years and a day, and the first floor by political prisoners with terms of imprisonment under seven years, as well as by a certain number of petty criminals. I also discovered that the quality of the human beings who filled this cold convent generally increased with the level of the floor.

In the cellars underneath the convent were kept prisoners sentenced to death. According to my informants, there had been several hundred of them a few months before my arrival who had been either shot or reprieved, and at present only a score were left.

The prisoners under death sentence never knew the exact date of their execution, so that they could always go on hoping for a reprieve. They used to be taken away to be shot in the early hours of the morning; consequently every night brought the recurrent torture of expectation. They spent their nights smoking, talking, and waiting. So every time the other prisoners were given their tobacco and cigarette rations, one of them would go around with a small canvas bag, and they would all give part of their small rations for those whose nights were so much worse than their own.

I saw those tormented souls after leaving quarantine, when I was moved to the first floor. Every afternoon they were allowed an hour's walk in the yard of the prison. I could see them through the window of the prison classroom where I helped those prisoners who studied English. By standing on a table in the middle of the room and looking through the window from a safe distance, I could see them walking energetically to and fro, talking in an animated fashion.

On my fifth day in jail I was permitted to write to the British vice consul in Gerona but was still in the dark as to my fate. Nobody in a position to know had told me what was going to happen to me. The civil guards who had escorted me, and the amazing young governor, had led me to believe that I would be allowed to leave Spain if any other country proved willing to have me. Using all my knowledge of similar cases and applying all the common sense I was capable of, I reached the conclusion that the Spanish authorities could punish me for crossing their border illegally with a month's imprisonment and, having done this, would offer me the choice of a frontier across which I would prefer to leave their country. I was fortified in this belief by the other prisoners and thus swayed between the brightest of hopes and depths of despair. My hopes need not be described. As for my despair, it ranged from the possibility of having to spend years in this prison to being handed over to the Gestapo at Hendaye.

After I was moved to the first floor, my personal comfort suffered an immediate deterioration. First, I had to sleep in a passage instead of a room. Second, being a latecomer, I was assigned a space to sleep in that was next to the few criminals and the lavatory. Third, I had to lose the friends I had made on the third floor.

I particularly missed the *cabo*, a shy lad of twenty-two who had been in prison since 1938. He was an anarchist and a lover of Dickens with dreamy gray eyes and tuberculosis. He had fought during the Civil War alongside the Polish International Brigades and had since conceived the most profound admiration for Polish bravery. As he was also very deeply interested in everything concerning Poland, he had made it his job to befriend every Polish prisoner who happened to pass through the prison of Gerona.

Being a regular prisoner, I was now allowed out in the yard for the morning walk. The business was run on military lines. We marched out by floors and then drew up in the courtyard. The flag was hoisted, and we had to salute it by raising our right arms. Then we had to sing three anthems: the Falange anthem, the Carlist one, and the old Royalist one. In this simple way Franco satisfied the aspirations of all his supporters.

To give the Fascist salute cost me more internal struggles than I could have imagined, considering that I am a person to whom symbols remain only symbols. However, in that winter of 1942, saluting with a raised arm Franco's *bandera* was like saluting the swastika. Nevertheless, I did not try to refuse raising my arm. I lacked the physical courage to do it after having heard from the Spanish prisoners that foreigners like myself who had refused to give the Fascist salute had been beaten up and kept for months in solitary confinement.

After the *bandera* ceremony was over, we broke our ranks and were free to talk, walk, or loiter on the same spot. Consequently, the yard looked not unlike the speakers' corner in Hyde Park. There was even a prisoner apparently trying to convert these dangerous *Rojos* to Roman Catholicism. He used to stand on an empty orange box and read the Gospel. There was always a cluster of prisoners around him. Of course, I was interested in the phenomenon of repentance. I learned, however, that the reason for such remarkable religious behavior was the desire for freedom at all costs. Without the prison chaplain's favorable report, no prisoner could be free.

I did not meet the chaplain, although I was assured that sooner or later he would want to see me, as he took a very kind interest in all *Polacos católicos*. I had, however, the opportunity of listening to a sermon delivered by a young Dominican friar, a man with deep-set, blazing eyes and an ascetic appearance. He spoke a beautifully clear Castilian and, although animated by fervor and impatience, he did not hurry his sentences, so I could understand practically every word he said. He called us Reds, murderers, Antichrists, bandits, torturers, and devils. He told us that we deserved only the gallows in this life and eternal damnation in the life to come. He deplored the kindness and generosity of Franco's heart, which had kept us alive. Whether he was there to try to bring us back to the mother church or to make us even more stubborn in our ideas, I was never able to decide.

I went only twice into the courtyard, for I left the prison on the morning of my third day's sojourn on the first floor. But during the two mornings spent in the prison courtyard, I managed to meet some unforgettable characters. There is one whom I must mention.

He was a little chap, some five feet tall, about thirty years old, lithe in his movements, with a quizzical expression on his face. He had been in the Spanish Foreign Legion and, having escaped from it, had spent several years serving with the French Foreign Legion. He had fought in the Republican Army during the Civil War and was in prison for thirty years and a day. He was the complete soldier-of-fortune type who possessed the most amazing talent for observing his fellow humans. He kept me spellbound when describing the national characteristics of his fellow legionnaires: Germans, Russians, Poles, Italians, and Frenchmen.

From the other prisoners I learned that originally he had been sentenced to be shot. On the night of his expected execution he was sitting up and waiting for the baleful noise of approaching steps. During the day he had received a food parcel from his family, and he still had some milk left. When he heard the steps approach his cell, he drank the milk, not wishing to waste it. The door of his cell was opened, and he was informed that he had been reprieved. Having been left to live, he thought first about breakfast. He had nothing left for it. So he stuck two fingers into his mouth and regurgitated the milk.

Most of the prisoners were human beings as honest, decent, average, or superior in their intelligence as any two thousand human males could be. I met no Communists among them, although quite a few anti-Communists. They all had a touching faith in the inevitability of an Allied victory and believed that it would come very soon. Many of them even looked on Mr. Churchill as their friend, and all were convinced that the day of Hitler's and Mussolini's defeat would be the end of Franco and the beginning of their freedom.

Franco did not overfeed us in his prisons. No breakfast of any kind in the morning, a pulpous, reeking mass served twice daily, and a single roll made of maize flour was all the food we received. Those prisoners who had no families or friends to send them food from outside or money with which to buy the fruit and tinned food sold at the canteen were starving. Absence of any occupation made the lack of food even worse, since one had so much time to think about it. My neighbors were so hungry that they collected the orange and banana skins from the floor and ate them.

I still had enough money left to eke out an almost satisfactory diet, but I felt sorely the lack of bread and the complete absence of meat. I also suffered from insomnia after I was moved down to the first floor. The stench from the lavatory, the constant coming and going of sleepy prisoners making for it, the hardness of the floor, and the glaring electric light burning all night long did not help. It was a fantastic sight to see a few hundred people sleeping shoulder to shoulder, some breathing deeply and so imperceptibly that they looked as if they were dead, while others snored with an amazing regularity or in outbursts of grunting, obscene noises, or dreamed aloud, groaning or crying.

I was very happy when, after only twelve days in the prison of Gerona, I was told to get ready for immediate departure. Escorted by two civil guards but not handcuffed, I was marched to the railway station where I boarded a train for Figueras. I was traveling back to the place whence I had come and wondered anxiously whether I was not going to be delivered into the hands of the French gendarmerie.

Neither of my guards was young. One of them dozed most of the time. The other was a kindly old fool who tried to persuade me that the Germans meant well when they occupied Poland, and that I should not believe anything I was told about their cruelties and atrocities. He had known many Germans of the Condor Legion during the Civil War, and he had found them to be brave, clean, honest, and kind. He advised me strongly to return to my country and make peace with the occupying force.

At Figueras I was taken to a derelict, half-ruined building. The gate was guarded by soldiers. The patio was overgrown with grass, the gallery running around the patio threatened to collapse at any moment, the upper stories of the house were entirely uninhabitable, but its basement, into which I was ordered, was still solid. From the dozen or more people already there, I learned that the building had been occupied by the International Brigades during the Civil War and hit by Nationalist bombs.

My new companions were Spaniards whose families had been settled in France for many years and who had come to Spain in order to fulfill their military obligations, so as not to lose their Spanish citizenship. Some of them knew hardly any Spanish, and most of them knew nothing about the country of their birth. They were therefore very surprised when, having crossed the Spanish frontier, they were arrested by the civil guards, handcuffed, treated like common criminals, and then sent under escort to this old ruin. I felt a kind of sadistic pleasure in telling them the little more I knew about their country than they did, and in making fun of their patriotic feelings, which had sent them to serve with an army in which private soldiers were cropped like French poodles, dressed like beggars, treated like criminals, and forced to become either thieves or murderers in order to be able to purchase their tobacco rations or obtain a furlough.

I spent two nights in that basement, unable to get much sleep on its stone floor and as hungry as a wolf. During those two days our number increased to thirty—all future soldiers in Franco's army—before we were marched, shortly before midnight and under heavy escort, to the railway station, where we boarded a train for Barcelona. In the months that followed I often regretted not having made a break for freedom in the darkness, while our column was marching through the empty and ill-lit streets of Figueras.

We arrived at daybreak. Franco's future warriors were to catch another train, so I was separated from them and handcuffed to an indescribably filthy Spanish lad of sixteen. I protested vehemently at being manacled, but the civil guard officer who awaited us at the station roared at me to shut up. *He* had not invited me to come to Spain, and *in Spain* I would be treated *like other Spaniards.*

We were marched through the dark streets of the city. People were already hurrying to their places of work. Their womenfolk, in shawls and without stockings, stood shivering in long queues outside bakeries and grocers' shops. We reached the Ramblas and took an underground train. Silent, sleepy men and women were filling the carriages and gazing at us with eyes full of sorrow and compassion. Several obviously working-class women gave my young companion bread and oranges, which they had only recently bought after long hours of queuing.

At last we reached our destination: the Cárcel Modelo. The Model Prison of Barcelona is built on American lines and looks like any cage prison one has become familiar with thanks to Hollywood gangster films. The prisoner in charge of cell allocation must have liked me, for he gave me a cell all to myself that had no bed, mattress, or blankets but possessed a tap with running water and looked clean. The window was barred and covered by an iron hood, but some daylight came in through a slit. Not to be handcuffed and to have as much water as I wanted, as well as a clean floor to lie down upon, was enough to make me happy for the time being.

I had hardly settled down and started washing some of my underwear and shirts when a screwed-up paper ball was thrown into my cell through the judas. I unrolled it and read the following:

Hallo! I am a Canadian arrested by the Spanish police. I am in train to wait to be sent to Miranda de Ebro. If you desire something say so to me, and I shall send you what I can. Your camarade, Paul Vincent.

I read the note many times, found its English rather peculiar, and in the end decided that my Canadian was a French speaker. I also began to wonder how I could answer him. But before I had spent much time trying to solve this problem, the door of my cell was unlocked and a prisoner came in with a brush and pail. Uttering very few words but using his eyes and face quite a lot, he asked me whether I had read the note and where was my reply to it. I wrote on the back of the note:

Dear Paul, Thanks for the note. I am a Pole trying to reach England in order to join the RAF. I was caught at Gerona. I could do with some bedding and food. Any idea what is going to happen to me? Yours etc.

P.S. If you find it easier to write in French, do so. My French is quite good.

The prisoner took my note and knocked at the door. The door was unlocked, and he left. Paul's answer, as well as a blanket and a tin of sardines, was brought to me several hours later by another prisoner. This time he wrote in French:

Dear R, I am sorry I can send you only one blanket and so little food, but this is the end of the week. Tomorrow we shall get our food parcel from the British consul's representative. He will also provide you with a mattress and cigarettes.

I am really a Belgian, and the reason for my parading as a Canadian is the fact that only British subjects are released from Miranda de Ebro and permitted to leave Spain for Gibraltar or Portugal. I am surprised you have not been told of this state of affairs by the Polish authorities in France. With your knowledge of English you could easily pretend that you are an Englishman. You will be sent to Miranda de Ebro from here. Try to change your nationality on the way. Paul.

So that was that. The curse of having been born a Polish Jew was still pursuing me. Those well-dressed, arrogant Poles in Marseilles could have changed my present plight by a few words. I had left my parents, home, and the city I loved in order to get away from them and their active spite and hatred but, having kept away from them for so many years, I was to be overtaken by their malignant anti-Semitism at the opposite end of Europe.

The whole affair bore too much the imprint of fate to make revolt of any value. I accepted my destiny and settled down to sleep. On the following day I was visited by the British consul's representative, who was a political prisoner himself.

What with my mattress, which the consul's representative brought me, blanket, food, and running water, I felt quite happy. As I slept most of the time, I did not even begin to feel bored. But I spent only two nights in the Cárcel Modelo; after that I was handcuffed again to the indescribably filthy lad, and we boarded a train for Reus.

There the prison accepted the boy but refused to take me. So I was handed over to one of the local police stations, where, as there was no available cell, I was locked up in one of the two lavatory cabinets for a day and a night.

We picked up the Spanish lad at the local prison, then boarded a train for Saragossa. I was again handcuffed to the boy, and during our long journey across Catalonia and Aragon I had the time and opportunity to notice that his hands bore the visible marks of scabies. It was not a very pleasant sensation to be manacled to somebody both filthy and eaten by vermin, yet I could not bring myself to protest aloud. After our guards had told some peasants to get up and vacate their seats, we sat down opposite three other prisoners. One of them was a Catalan soldier; the other two were political prisoners, a boy and a soldier in handcuffs, who carried their mattresses, blankets, tin plates, and spoons with them.

The boy was the son of an Asturian miner. During the Civil War he had been evacuated to France to stay with some relatives. Whether his relatives could no longer keep him or he had felt a sudden urge to go back to his parents I did not discover, but the fact was that, on having reported to some Spanish frontier post in order to be permitted to travel to his village, he was promptly arrested and was now being sent home.

The soldier was a deserter. Some six months earlier he had been ordered to join the Blue Division fighting on the Leningrad front. He had deserted from San Sebastián, where he was stationed, and fled to his father's farm in Catalonia, where he worked quietly until denounced by some neighbor. He was now anticipating a few years of service with a penal battalion and then another four or six years in Morocco, building roads and hewing rocks. He looked at his prospects with the same kind of humility and fatalism as a Russian muzhik.

The train was a *correo*, which meant that it stopped at practically every station, and its wooden carriages were crowded with peasants. Used to the gay national costumes of Polish peasants, I found it strange to see their sober black garb, which made them appear as if they were wearing eternal mourning for their own fate and that of their grand and beautiful country. There was an air of dignity and grace about them. I saw no morose faces but many sad ones. The women—and they were in the majority—had immense baskets full of struggling poultry. A few walked up and down the train, with wicker baskets swinging from their arms, selling rolls filled with ham or omelets. In doing this they were, of course, contravening the rationing laws of the land, since each of the rolls was as big as a Spaniard's daily ration of bread. But the civil guards permitted them to carry on with their business after each of the women had contributed in kind toward satisfying their hunger.

One of our guards, a young, handsome fellow, made friends rather quickly with a lively country lass traveling on her own. He obtained a guitar from some passenger and was soon strumming it and singing *flamencas*. The sun was shining, and I felt warm inside the train, as if it were a July day and not the beginning of February.

We were out of Catalonia and traveling through a country of red soil, black boulders, and solitary olive trees; we saw small, thick peasants dressed all in black. Our train sped along a river, its steep banks turned into innumerable terraces. Immense stones, boulders, and pieces of rock had been used to build them. And on those terraces not an inch of soil was wasted; they were covered with vineyards, olive trees, vegetables, and fruit trees. This made me realize that it was not the Spanish peasants' laziness that had left the wide horizon uncultivated. It also showed me that nature was not ungenerous. There must have been reasons of human making to prevent the remainder of the country from looking equally fertile and rich.

It was night when we reached Saragossa and, after a short walk through badly lit and deserted streets, arrived at the prison. We were admitted by young wardens in civilian clothes. There was no nonsense about them. The soldiers and the political prisoners, the first to enter, were slapped on their faces before they had time to say "Jack Robinson" because they had not raised their arms in the Falange salute. I later learned that the wardens were Falangists, former officers in Franco's army and at present students in the local university. They did jail keeping as a part-time occupation.

I was separated from the other prisoners and taken to a transit cell. A terrible stench assailed my nostrils and, like all prison cells in Spain, this one was glaringly illuminated all the night long. I remained at the door for a good while fighting the desire to vomit and wondering whether I would have to spend the night on my feet, for it looked as if I would not be able to move without stepping on people's faces and bodies.

The cell was no more than twelve feet square, and with my arrival the number of its inmates was brought to sixteen. There was a bucket in one corner of the cell, emptied once every twenty-four hours, into which the prisoners relieved themselves. The acid smell of urine and the revolting stench of human excreta pervaded everything, even the tobacco one happened to smoke.

The cell, of course, was designed to accommodate only a few prisoners at a time. But as some, although officially in transit, had already spent three months there, it was easy to explain its overcrowding. Among the prisoners were a few "Canadians." By their accent I knew immediately that they were Belgians. They looked as if they had come from clean, bourgeois surroundings, but in the absence of the comforts and amenities to which they had been accustomed, they had lost their characteristic trait of cleanliness and were as repugnantly filthy as the poor Spanish lad to whom I had been handcuffed.

My arrival awakened almost all the prisoners. The usual questions were asked and answered. When it came to my telling them that I was on my way to Miranda de Ebro, and that I expected to spend only one night in the transit cell, my words were received with sarcastic and cynical remarks. The filthiest of the Belgian-Canadians remarked, "I was told *mañana* three months ago."

And so with a heavy heart I went to sleep between two Spanish prisoners, almost next to the bucket. But at the crack of dawn I was ordered to get up and catch the train for Miranda de Ebro. I carried away a souvenir of my single night spent at the prison of Saragossa that would not leave me for months: the most bloodthirsty and tenacious lice one could come across.

Our train advanced slowly through a landscape of rocks and mountains, quite treeless, badly cultivated, and often covered in snow. It was getting colder as the day advanced, and I was back in February and winter. At last our train reached the station at Miranda, and we took the road to the camp. In the distance I could see whitewashed houses, their roofs covered with red tiles, standing in regular rows. They looked gay, bright, and clean. I could not see any walls or barbed-wire barricades around them. My spirits rose. After all, the place did not look worse than any collection of barracks. All I had heard about the terrible conditions inside the camp must have been exaggerated talk and gossip. I walked through a gate guarded by a Spanish soldier in a better mood than I had known since the day of my capture at Gerona.

MIRANDA DE EBRO:
JUST TO EAT AND REST

A FTER WALKING through three gates, I immediately realized that the impression I had gained of the camp from outside was completely false. I had to walk about a hundred yards from the last gate to the first barracks, which housed the office, wading through mud reaching my ankles. There was nothing clean or bright about the camp.

Groups of prisoners in all kinds of civilian clothes, muddy and neglected, either walked about briskly or loitered in one place. Among them one national type stood out immediately. Broad, burly, with slightly bent necks like those of threatening bulls, fairish with high cheekbones and defiant, scowling looks, the Poles saw me pass in silence. One or two asked me shortly, "Canadian?" and answered my denial with contemptuous glances. The civil guards handed me over to the camp authorities.

A soldier was sent to fetch the *cabo* of what was going to be my barracks, who turned out to be a young Pole. He owed his post to the fact that despite his youth he had already spent two years at the camp, having crossed into Spain directly after the fall of France. He was a typical product of pre-1939 Poland: his hatred of Jews was so great that he was unable to look one straight in the eye.

I followed him across the square, wading through mud and snow. He stopped at one of the barracks and kicked its door open.

It was dark inside, and I could not see a thing for a good while. My nose was invaded by the smell of frying onions, while my ears had some difficulty in absorbing the noise of human voices and the abundance of swear-words. But when I had become used to the semidarkness, I saw that I was treading on the skins of onions, empty tins, and orange peels. I was in a corridor the walls of which were formed by blankets. There was no floor; the ground inside the barracks was almost as muddy as the compound outside. It looked as if all the rags of Spain were hanging from the rafters. Actually, the rags were clothes, and the clothes were far from being in tatters but, unwashed and unironed, soiled and wet, they looked as if they had been refused by a scarecrow. I was to learn very soon that for lack of space inside the cabins the rafters in the corridor served as a common cloakroom.

We marched almost to the end of the barracks and then stopped. The *cabo* shouted, "Hey, there, I've got a new lodger for your cabin!"

There was a short silence, and then a querulous voice replied, "Why the hell should we get a Jew? Send him to the Jewish barracks."

For a good while I didn't know what to do. I was not even quite sure which cabin was mine. All I could see were blankets stretching from the ground to the rafters. While I was thus standing in the corridor, the same voice belonging to one of my future cabin mates went on swearing at the idea of having a third man in the cabin, and a Jew at that. But unexpectedly the other occupant spoke up in an unmistakable Silesian accent and told his mate to stop wailing. He then moved the blanket serving as a wall to his cabin and told me to climb up. I realized then that the cabin was on the first floor, and that the way to reach it was to climb a primitive ladder formed by rungs nailed to the posts that supported both the rafters and the first floor.

The Silesian was the same age as myself: the owner of the querulous and capricious voice, a native of the Poznan province, was a few years older. He had the typical Polish anti-Semite's facility for ignoring other people's feelings: he received me without the slightest embarrassment and as politely as only a Pole can. I replied with the same false politeness.

It was the cubicle, however, that drew most of my attention. It was, as I realized later, far from being a superior cabin; the Silesian and Poznan were too lazy and untidy to make it into the cozy den many other Poles inhabited. But it appeared as a striking example of ingenuity and patience to my fresh eyes.

As far as I could ascertain, the Poles had devised the pattern for the cabins. They used the wooden posts that supported the roof and the first floor as natural cabin limits. They nailed blankets to the posts and built dens not exceeding seven feet in width and the same in length. The blanket walls were reinforced with paper and then painted over, so as to look clean and cheerful. Wooden frames were then made, the canvas palliasses nailed to them and, presto, cots were created. As there was enough room in each cabin for exactly two cots and a narrow passage between them where a small table could be squeezed in, the other two cots were hung above. Thus a shipshape cabin was created, the result of much work and ingenuity, and often enough almost a work of art.

There were only two cots in my cubicle, so I would have to sleep on the floor for some time until I had managed to make or buy the necessary frame for a suspended cot. But I was not worried by such considerations as the lack of a bed on my first day and night at Miranda de Ebro, nor during the many days that followed. The situation was terrible enough to make me set in motion the usual mechanism of self-defense, which consisted of refusing to take in the present, closing as many doors as possible to the past, and accepting the future only when it became inevitable.

The first day at Miranda ended with my being recognized by the Poles as a member of their group. I had to go to the so-called officers' barracks, where a good hundred Polish officers lived, see a certain captain, the paymaster to the Polish group, and answer numerous questions as to my origin, life, and military service. My pure and fluent Polish was of great help in convincing the captain that I was born and educated in his country, but my Jewish features prevented him from welcoming me as a fellow Pole. Moreover, the fact that I had lived in Belgium since 1936 made him suspicious as to my right to call myself a Polish citizen at all. He wanted to know why I had left Poland to study abroad at a time when Poland could scarcely afford to spend foreign currency.

I asked him whether he remembered that there had been a numerus clausus for Jewish students in Polish universities, and that since 1931 every academic year in Poland had begun with riots organized by Polish students with the aim of chasing Jews from all Polish universities. I then proceeded to show him the document delivered only a few months earlier by the Polish Passport Office in Marseilles, which certified to the fact that I was a Polish citizen, and then produced my letter of recommendation from the British air attaché in Brussels. I casually pointed out that if the Polish camp authorities were not willing to recognize me as one of their group, the British would certainly not refuse to help me.

The last remark clinched all argument. The captain did not want to see me go to the British and inform them that their Polish allies did not differ greatly from the Germans as far as the treatment of their Jewish fellow citizens was concerned. So he recognized me as a Pole, which meant that I would get seven pesetas a day and food parcels every month. How valuable this was I learned very quickly.

It was dark in the passage when I returned to my barracks. A solitary electric bulb illuminated the passage. I climbed into my cabin, where my cabin mates were busy frying onions and sardines. I now had a chance to admire two other achievements of their ingenuity and workmanship: our lamp and stove.

The Spaniards provided electric power only by the single bulb hanging dismally in the middle of each barracks's passage; the lighting inside each cabin was supplied by little lamps made from tuna-fish tins or others; the fuel was oil saved from sardines; the wicks came from the blankets. The result was a light that flickered and spluttered and stank. One needed to have very good eyes and be impervious to headaches to be able to read by this smelly and blinking flame. Some had managed to obtain the necessary electric wire and bulbs and tapped the main cable. As a result, the bulb in the passage hardly shone at all. The Spaniards would now and then organize raids and find the electricity thieves, whose bulbs and wire were confiscated, and the offenders were punished with solitary confinement in the *calabozo*.

Prometheus's gift to the human race was further applied for heating purposes, stoves usually being made of two large biscuit or jam tins placed one inside the other, with a layer of clay between the two for thermal purposes. Luckily, the Spanish camp authorities allowed the prisoners to use some of the wood destined for the camp kitchen in these stoves.

Whatever the faults of the Poles may be, lack of hospitality is rarely one of them. I was invited by both of my cabin mates to share their meal, and in the course of the same evening I could make up my mind as to the relative merits of my two companions. The Silesian was direct, honest, and kindly. The Poznan was moody, querulous, and cunning. The former's family were miners, who had lived for many years in France working in the mines. The latter had also spent some time working in France before the war. The Silesian spoke German and French quite fluently, and his Polish was far from being pure. The Poznan spoke very good Polish and passable French. After a few days at Miranda I realized that I was very lucky to have them as my cabin mates because their stay in France had taught them a certain measure of tolerance and had slightly mellowed their nationalistic fervor.

It must have been about eleven when I lay down on my bag, as yet empty of straw, and covered myself with the two blankets I had received, one from the Spanish camp authorities and the other from the Polish Red Cross. But my companions were not yet ready for sleep. They wanted to hear what I knew about the war and to hear about my adventures. Inevitably the conversation turned to the memorable September of 1939 and the invasion of France. Not only my cabin mates took part in the conversation. Voices of people in cubicles to our right and left, on the same floor as our cabin or beneath it, and from across the passage joined in. Very soon I knew that I was among my countrymen again; that they had not changed in the slightest since I had left them in 1936; that I was among enemies and barbarians, whose viciousness and stupidity were not mitigated even by a selfish understanding of their own interests.

The real shock came when they spoke of the war. Intellectually, of course, I had realized before that clerical, anti-Semitic, and semifascist Poles could never see Hitler's war in the same light as a Western liberal or a communist would see it. But on my first night at Miranda de Ebro I was made to realize that even my worst expectations had been exceeded.

That aspect of Nazism that ought to have outraged them most—the racial theory of German superiority, which condemned them as Slavs to either slavery or disappearance as a nation from the face of the earth—failed to evoke any real indignation in them. They hated the Germans for their brutalities, of course, but they hated them like people who, having been used to practicing brutalities against others, never dreamed that they might become the victims of similar treatment themselves.

They admired Hitler. He would lose the war, of course, because he did not have the Poles on his side, but he was an elemental force destined to clear Poland of the Jews and Europe of the rotten democracies and the Communists, both under Jewish influence. How did they expect the war to go? Because Hitler did not have the Poles as his allies, he would lose the campaign in Russia. But in the course of the war in the East, both the Germans and the Muscovites would lose most of their manhood. When that had happened, the British and the Americans would land on the Continent and invade Germany, the Polish underground army would emerge from hiding, the Polish frontiers would be pushed west to the Oder and east to the Dnieper, accounts would be settled with the Ukrainian traitors once and for all, and not even a Jewish baby in its cradle would be left alive in Poland.

It was two o'clock in the morning when the general exchange of views ended. But I could not sleep. I realized that I was being eaten by lice, which made me toss about, scratch myself until I bled, and feel repulsively unclean. But even more depressing were my thoughts. The idea that I had left my family and home as a boy to escape living in the midst of such barbarians and that I had now landed among a collection of the worst representatives of them at the other end of Europe struck me as a supreme irony of fate. To think that the war might really turn out according to their wishes, that all the blood and suffering of innocent people would result in their return to power when victory over Nazism had been won, was maddening. The very fact that there could be people alive who, having been dealt so many blows by history, could still refuse to admit their mistakes and learn to feel sympathy for other people's sufferings destroyed some fundamental belief in human nature that I still cherished. The realization that I would have to live among them, imprisoned and in unavoidable proximity, made me dread the coming day.

The reveille was sounded by a band of buglers accompanied by drummers. Nobody was allowed to miss the *bandera,* the ceremonial hoisting of the flag and, at the same time, the occasion for counting the prisoners. Anybody found in the barracks during the *bandera* by Spanish patrols was likely to be hit with rifle butts and would certainly have his head shaved.

We formed up in companies outside our barracks and marched off to the parade ground. There we lined up in three columns, some four thousand people strong. The band, dressed in military uniforms but composed of prisoners and led by a German Jew, a former conductor of a provincial opera orchestra, struck up the three anthems of Franco's Spain: the Royalist, Carlist, and Falangist. We took off our headgear while the column of shivering Spaniards in front of us raised their arms in the Fascist salute. Sleet was falling, and the mud under our feet became deeper and clammier.

The semiliterate Spanish NCOs took almost an hour to count us; at the end of this review the Spanish prisoners, who formed labor battalions and were dressed in khaki drill uniforms and sandals without overcoats, looked blue and shivered in unison. At last, wet and swearing, we marched back to our barracks.

There were still three hours left until dinnertime; I spent them looking over the camp. It formed an almost perfect oblong. The whole camp was surrounded by a brick wall some six feet high, which at first sight did not appear a very formidable obstacle to a prisoner determined to escape. But the approaches to the wall were guarded by barbed wire, and on the wall itself there stood every fifteen yards a Spanish soldier who would shoot at anybody touching the barbed wire in daytime or approaching it at night. Only a few weeks prior to my arrival a Polish lieutenant had rushed the northern wall, which he had approached by crawling along the cookhouse. While he was crossing the river, which flows along the northern side of the camp, a Spanish guard shot and wounded him. Nevertheless he managed to reach the opposite bank, where he remained lying on the ground, bathed in his blood and unable to move. The orderly officer of the day found him lying there and killed him with a bullet from his pistol. Thanks to such men, and the fact that a battalion of three reinforced companies—over six hundred soldiers—was guarding the camp, there had been practically no escapes between 1940 and February 1942, when I arrived.

At noon the prisoners began to gather in a double queue outside their respective barracks in expectation of dinner. Our caldron had not yet been fetched from the cookhouse, so our *cabo* gave the word to two burly Poles to bring it. They raced to the shed without demurring. Fetching the caldron was a privilege, because the men who hauled it were the first to be served and thus certain to obtain the few pieces of meat and potatoes float-ing in the mess. At last the bugler sounded the signal for *rancho*, and the *comida* was dealt out. The soup was hot water with a few leaves of an unknown plant floating in it. As I was not at the head of the queue, I did not find even a part of a potato in my portion of the liquid. The only compo-nent of nutritive value the liquid contained was a few drops of brown, unrefined oil, which reeked mercilessly. I tried to eat the unknown leaves and had to spit them out. I learned that they were called Spanish cabbage.

During the major part of my stay at Miranda, this was the kind of soup we received. We also received a little over half a pound of bread every day, of excellent quality compared with the same article in occupied Belgium and France. Our guards received the same food as ourselves, but twice as much bread. However, a few months after my arrival we were granted the status of war prisoners, and our ration of bread was raised to that of the soldiers. But without the food parcels sent to us by the Polish Legation and Red Cross, and without the money allowance of seven pesetas a day, we would have been condemned to a state of protracted starvation. The for-eign prisoners who had arrived in 1940 had actually known not only a regime of terror but also gnawing hunger for a good year until the sending of food parcels from outside was permitted by Franco's government. I had it impressed on me that very day by old prisoners that I had arrived at a time when things were getting easy, and when Miranda de Ebro was begin-ning to look like a rest center compared with its former self. We, the Allied prisoners, were now so opulent that we could obtain the services of the Spanish prisoners—the members of Franco's labor battalions. For soup that we saved for them and an occasional cigarette, they would clean our plates and fetch our water, which involved a long and shivering wait in impatient and morose queues.

As was to be expected, I spent my first few days at Miranda trying to find out how long I was likely to stay behind its walls. Unless some radical change in the war and the Allies' attitude toward Franco occurred, it seemed I would have to spend the rest of the war there. The position was a very simple one thanks to Franco's genius. In order to be belligerent toward the USSR, friendly toward Germany, and neutral with regard to Britain and the United States, Franco granted his Allied prisoners the privilege of returning to their own countries or staying within the hospitable walls of Miranda de Ebro. Those of us from countries now occupied by the Nazis would be delivered into German hands at Hendaye.

I felt deeply the fact that I had failed in my endeavor to reach Portugal and was condemned to spend perhaps years in this place while the fate of the world and the very existence of my people were being settled, but I did not feel it so sharply during the first three or four months of my imprisonment at Miranda as I was to do later on. With my body recovering its strength and my stomach pacified, I could not feel utterly despondent.

Just to eat and rest were the moving forces of my existence during my first months in the camp. To rest meant to sleep, but many factors prevented me from doing the latter. The most important factor was the lice I had brought from the prison of Saragossa. Another was my compatriots' inclination to Spanish wine and storytelling. They had, of course, never drunk wine in Poland. As for vodka, its price and potency had made it impossible for most of them to drink it back home in large quantities except on very special occasions. But here they had both the money and the liquor. Consequently, there would be at least one party nightly in our barracks, and the guests emptied literally pails of wine, for the stuff used to be fetched from the canteen in containers made from empty biscuit tins, each holding easily a gallon. The parties were noisy and boisterous, and at times they would end in fights.

One thing, however, that made my life considerably easier was my knowledge of English. My Silesian cabin mate was the first to suggest to me that I should teach him English, since there was still a hope that we might leave the camp before the end of the war and find ourselves in Britain. I agreed willingly, for I liked teaching in those days, and also because the prospect of doing nothing but brooding for months, perhaps years, frightened me. The question of payment was a delicate one. Both of us felt that I was entitled to some fee but, because I was a Jew among Poles in a concentration camp, the problem was far from simple. I might be accused by some Poles of lacking in the spirit of comradeship because I did not teach my compatriots without any remuneration, while even those who thought that I was entitled to some pay might suspect me of waxing rich on "Polish money." However, my predicament was solved by my first pupil. He suggested that my fee should be the Spanish pay to which we were all entitled as "military internees," which amounted to five pesetas every ten days. I agreed. After that I experienced no trouble in finding pupils from the Polish soldiers', NCOs', and officers' companies. Later I became so popular as to have pupils of other nationalities, and I even had to refuse some. A Belgian, a highly placed official in the Congo Customs, found it necessary to bribe me with the promise of a gold sovereign before I managed to find some time for him. I spent all my earnings on food, fruit, and keeping clean, so that when the day of freedom came I was no richer than the other Polish prisoners.

MIRANDA DE EBRO:
THE YEAR OF STALINGRAD

URING THE WINTER OF 1941–42, I had almost permitted myself to hope that the victorious Red Army might reach Wilno before spring came and save some of my family and the friends of my boyhood. I had avoided thinking about the fate of my parents and three sisters as much as I could. I imagined that death from hunger and cold would be only one of the scourges brought by the Nazis upon the Jews of Wilno. I also expected that massacres carried out by the Germans themselves, or by a Polish and Lithuanian rabble organized by them, would decimate the Jewish community. I therefore entertained only the flimsiest of hopes as to the chances of my family having survived.

In March 1942, I sent a letter from Miranda de Ebro to my parents' address in Wilno inquiring how they were getting on and telling them not to worry about me. I received the letter back some six weeks later, stamped in German: "Addressee unknown." Four years later I learned that at the time I wrote the letter my father's and mother's bodies had already been rotting away with those of two-thirds of Wilno's ninety thousand Jews for almost six months. My three sisters were still alive at that time, but they were behind the walls of the ghetto. Only a few hundred yards separated them from the address to which my letter was sent, but they were farther from it than I was in Spain. For many years I kept the letter as a memento of

German orderliness and culture, which made the systematic extermination of millions possible but did not permit the German postmaster in Wilno to throw a letter—even a Jewish letter—into the wastepaper basket.

Spring came to Miranda de Ebro in April, and the world around the camp covered itself with loveliness and opened up our hearts and souls to anguish and all kinds of longing. Timoshenko's offensive in the direction of Kharkov opened victoriously and then failed. The German tiger struck in the Crimea. Kerch fell, then Sebastopol, and the brown tide began its inexorable advance toward the Volga. In Africa, Rommel's cohorts struck like lightning and took Tobruk.

Our canteen began to sell cherries and strawberries from Aranjuez even before April was over. Parcels from Polish organizations in the United States were distributed to us before Easter. We had food, fruit, wine, and safety behind the walls of the camp. Outside the fate of the world was being decided and my own people were being systematically wiped off the face of the earth. Hopelessness returned, and the sensation of failure again began to haunt me.

To take stock of myself I needed occasional solitude and silence, but I could find neither. After two or three months in a better barracks, I had to return to a Polish hut. That meant an additional strain on my willpower and nerves. With the return of warm weather it also became impossible to sleep at night, even after all the drunken brawls and discussions had stopped, because of the thousands of bugs that sucked our blood. We called them paratroopers, because they used to come down in regular drops from the roof or ceiling. One night I killed more than three hundred of them and then gave up the battle. In the daytime it became so hot inside the barracks that it was impossible to snatch a few hours' sleep in expectation of the forthcoming night's trials, while outside there was no protection from the sun, and when the wind blew there was no escape from the winter's mud, converted by the sun's rays into dust. As the sun rose in the sky and the end of May came, water began to grow scarce. Only a small trickle would come from the pump, and at times it would take an hour to fill a single pail. There were days when there was no water at all, because the trickle was just enough for the needs of the cookhouse.

The late morning was for me the best part of the day. A mountain mist would cover the landscape until nine o'clock, but when it had disappeared I could see the plain to the east of our camp stretching as far as the horizon. Before the spring was over, it was already covered with tender variations of green. The horizon was bordered by a row of slender poplars, along which ran the railway line. A train as small as a toy would puff along it at times, and the smoke from its engine looked no blacker than that from a good cigar. The freshness and delicacy of the tints and hues of the pushing vegetation acted as an absolute contrast to the barren yellow of the soil within the camp, the dazzling white of the barracks, and the red of their tiled roofs.

To the north of the camp, the rising mist unveiled the hills across the river. Brown and grayish in winter and summer, they were now green and unrolled softly toward the horizon. Near the camp young corn covered their contours; beyond, sheep grazed in idyllic peacefulness. A mountain several thousand feet high jutted in the right corner of the landscape—solitary, gaunt, stern. We often argued about its distance from the camp and never agreed or found out what it actually was. It was enough for me to let my eyes wander from the smiling, joyous plain to the hills and mountain to pass from one mood into another, from sweet, painful yearning to a severe feeling of claustrophobia.

One morning in May a Spanish couple passed along the crest of the hills across the river—a young man dressed in black and a girl wearing a white dress. They were too far away for us to see their faces, but we could see that they were happy. There were more than a thousand of us outdoors, and we stopped as one and watched them in absolute silence. No obscene remarks, no comments whatever were made. Many of us avoided the other prisoners' eyes when the lovers had disappeared and the spell had been broken, for we felt ashamed of having shown our weakness and longing so openly.

Often I thought about myself. The worst and darkest reflection was to have to admit that I might stay in the camp until the end of the war, then come out to find myself stranded in Spain, without a place in the society of men, without having seen England, and without having tested my physical and moral courage in battle. But I tried to counteract the idea of failure by passing in review my achievements. I knew that my boyhood and adolescence were over, and I summed up what dreams and strivings conceived between the ages of fourteen and eighteen I had realized. I had wanted to see different peoples and countries; I had wanted to be able to speak several languages, English in particular; I had dreamed of dangerous travels. Well, here I was, twenty-four years old; I had seen more of war than Fabrice at Waterloo; I had crossed half of Europe; I was almost fluent in seven languages; I enjoyed reading Pushkin, Tolstoy, and Dostoevsky in Russian, Goethe's *Faust* in German, Flaubert, Stendhal, and Anatole France in French, Mickiewicz in Polish, and Shakespeare, Defoe, Byron, Keats, and Shaw in English; and I knew that I was neither cowardly nor mean.

By now I knew enough of the Polish group to distinguish its component parts and to notice its open and secret conflicts. Of its six hundred members, the officers formed a majority. They were mostly regular officers; the others, the reserve officers, were either professional people, such as engineers, architects, lawyers, and schoolmasters, or former civil servants. Even among these there were no intellectuals in the nineteenth-century Polish conception of the word; that is to say, none of them respected above all the human mind and its creations, or felt responsible toward his less educated fellows because of his own greater knowledge. They had no intellectual curiosity or social conscience. The superficiality of the Polish intellect, which replaces intellectual struggle and heart searching with romantic dreams and the ready-made cosmogony of Catholicism, was obvious in all of them.

A deep and scarcely hidden struggle went on between the older regular officers and the younger reserve lieutenants and second lieutenants. A very high proportion of the former were in their forties and not quite fit for modern warfare; nor were they very far from retiring age. Therefore they were not at all keen on seeing action and were quite convinced that the war would be won without their personal contribution and that after victory had been achieved their years spent in the camp would be counted toward their retirement, their pay being made good in one lump sum.

The reserve officers felt quite differently. Some of them had been volunteers and were still animated by the desire to get even with the Germans; the majority of them realized only too well that Miranda was a blind alley. They all imagined that their lucky colleagues in England were meanwhile either getting promotions or securing sinecures in governmental departments. They found natural allies in the young regular second lieutenants and lieutenants who knew that in peacetime they could not obtain promotion before they were in their late thirties and who considered that the only way of making the Polish and Allied diplomats act on their behalf was to organize a large-scale effort, a hunger strike or mass escape, and demanded that the considerable sums of money in the Polish commandant's hands should be used for these purposes.

The noncommissioned officers, who formed the second largest section of the Polish group, were either regular NCOs or former policemen and gendarmes. They were the most disciplined and least restless section, recognizing without much hesitation the authority of the major and his lieutenants. If they were in their forties, their retirement pensions ranked very high on the list of their preoccupations. The younger ones among them were for action, provided it had the blessing of their superiors.

The soldiers represented the most varied section. Apart from policemen, gendarmes, and low-ranking civil servants, there were among them workers, drivers, sailors, artisans, a few peasants, and quite a sprinkling of students and high school graduates. These, the *intelligenci*, were the unmistakable product of the reborn Poland that had emerged as a result of Russia's October Revolution and Germany's defeat in the West. Born and raised within the parochial horizons of pre-1939 Poland, they lacked even the relatively broader outlook of their parents, who had been subjects of the Russian, German, and Austro-Hungarian Empires. They had been brought up to believe that they were a wonderful generation because they were born in free Poland; that their country was a unique bulwark of civilization in the east of Europe; and that all the other Slav peoples were their inferiors in culture and valor. Because they had been educated on the writings of the Polish Romantic poets, their naturally antirational mentality espoused hero worship and the conviction that action and violence were the most effective means of conducting human affairs. Their belief in their country's might having been denied by the facts, they refused to admit the existence of those facts and grafted upon their irrational Catholic background the racial and anti-Semitic ideas of Hitler and Rosenberg, thus creating for themselves a world outlook very typical of that shared by the majority of the Polish academic youth between 1933 and 1939. They stood in close contact with the young officers and were the moving force opposing the policy of laissez-faire practiced by the command of the Polish group. In the meantime, they did their best to carry on with the fight against the enemy within, the Jews.

There were three Jews—myself included—in the soldiers' company who lived in the Polish barracks and received the same allowances as their "Aryan" compatriots. But there were almost a dozen Polish Jews of various ages who, because they had lived abroad for years and either did not possess Polish passports or had not renewed them, were not recognized as Polish citizens by the Polish command. They lived in the barracks shared by the stateless prisoners and undesirable aliens awaiting deportation, who together represented some thirty nationalities. However, as the Spanish camp authorities still considered them Polish citizens, they were made to queue for their food with the Polish soldiers' company.

This was more than the Polish soldiers could stand. They made the lives of the "unrecognized" Polish citizens as miserable as possible by denying them their fair share of soup, by pushing them out of the queue and, whenever possible, by using violence. Finally, in the summer of 1942, when Hitler's hordes were racing from the Don to the Volga and Rommel's legions were poised at El Alamein, while all the gas chambers and furnaces in the Polish extermination camps were working day and night dispatching the Jews of Europe into the limbo of history, the Poles at Miranda won a victory for all the "Aryans": they forced their Jewish compatriots to stand to their left in a separate queue.

In May 1942, three Poles failed to turn up for the roll call of the Polish group. One soldier, one NCO, and one officer were missing, and on discovering their disappearance the Spaniards went mad. All the prisoners were kept for hours in the parade square and counted time and time again; even the cooks had to abandon their caldrons and join the columns in the square; armed patrols with axes and picks broke into all the barracks, smashed all the cubicles, and ripped the wooden floors to pieces, scaring many rats but not finding any entrance to a tunnel.

At last we were allowed to break ranks, but before we had enough time to eat or get our cabins into some shape, we were ordered to change barracks. While we were busy transporting our belongings from one hut to another, and using the opportunity to get rid of some of the bugs that had ensconced themselves in the wooden frames of our cots, the news came that the Spanish soldiers were confessing by company.

I hurried to the parade square and saw a company of Spanish soldiers drawn up in front of the chapel. I learned from other prisoners, who had arrived there before me, that a priest was actually inside it. We observed the Spanish soldiers enter the chapel one by one and came to the conclusion that the Spanish camp authorities, unable to explain the way the three Poles had escaped, must have decided that one of the Spanish soldiers had accepted a bribe and hoped the culprit would confess his crime to the priest.

Nobody confessed, and another two days passed before the means by which the Poles had escaped was discovered. Heavy rain had been falling for several days; the rain and the passing trains had caused a subsidence that betrayed the existence of an underground passage. The tunnel was found to begin underneath the chapel and continue for a good fifty yards beneath the camp wall, the barbed-wire entanglement, and the railway embankment, which ran almost parallel to the western side of the camp.

The tunnelers had chosen to start at the chapel because it stood only a yard or so away from the wall, but the disadvantages involved were very great, the most serious being that nobody was allowed on the parade square after dark, and consequently they could not approach the chapel during eleven hours out of every twenty-four. For another thing, disposal of the sand and stones was a problem, since neither could be left in the chapel.

The start had apparently been made before Easter, when several Poles had volunteered for the task of decorating the chapel. How they managed to tear the floorboards loose and dig a hole deep enough for two men to hide in while supposedly decorating the altar I fail to imagine. When this had been done, two men concealed themselves under the floorboards just before the Spanish patrol searched the chapel prior to locking it up for the night. They dug and bored during the whole night by the light of an electric bulb, for which they obtained power by tapping the cable that supplied electricity to the powerful arc lamps surrounding the camp.

They deposited the sand and stones in innumerable bags, which were no bigger than the pockets in a man's trousers. These were taken away in the daytime by Poles playing basketball or football around the chapel, then carefully spread throughout the camp, so that the appearance of loose earth should not be noticed by the Spaniards or their informers. Once the tunnelers had burrowed beyond the wall, they worked day and night, hardly able to breathe the foul air, and expected to be buried alive whenever a train passed over their underground passage. But the tunnel held, and they escaped to reach Lisbon.

Following their escape, the camp authorities kept moving us from one barracks to another for several weeks before they became tired of the game. As soon as they relaxed in their vigilance, a new tunnel was started right opposite my cabin. I had not the slightest suspicion of its existence, however, until the moment of its discovery by the Spaniards. The tunnelers had a very long job ahead of them; our barracks stood some fifty yards away from the camp wall, and the tunnel had to pass underneath the row of barracks standing close to it. Secrecy was preserved almost to the end, but when the tunnel was ready, and the builders had only to pierce the last few feet of ground in order to emerge beyond the railway tracks, they found themselves without money.

The major who was the head of the Polish group and his lieutenants refused to give them the necessary funds because, they claimed, the Polish authorities in London opposed all escapes from Miranda. The arguments and discussions lasted a couple of days, during which time quite a few people learned about them. When the difficulty was finally solved and the night of escape came, a score of Poles waited for the tunnelers to get away in order to follow them. As most of them were without any ready food to take with them, they practically invaded the black marketers' barracks at midnight and offered any price for corned beef, sardines, and other tinned food. This action proved fatal to the whole enterprise. The camp authorities were immediately alerted by their informers, patrols cleared the Polish barracks of their inmates, and the entrance to the tunnel was discovered.

All the inmates of the guilty cabin were sent to the *calabozo*. But on the following day their friends "avenged" them. The major, his lieutenants, and all suspects were attacked by a gang who had been trained in the pre-September Polish police force. The younger reserve lieutenants and second lieutenants, who opposed the older regular officers, used the thugs from the soldiers' company in order to get into power. They succeeded, and their leadership resulted many months later in a massive hunger strike.

．　．　．

Preoccupied, fascinated, and awed by the spectacle of the German advance across the steppes of southern Russian and the North African desert, I had less time to think of my own people's fate, but during the summer of 1942 the peculiar nature of the Jewish tragedy could not be dodged, even at Miranda.

It was there, for the first time, I learned about gas chambers. *Gas chambers* has become so much part and parcel of human speech that the phrase hardly stirs a ripple in our consciousness. It has already become a familiar sound, a worn-out coin that we pass on without giving it so much as a glance. Yet, as I am thinking of that summer evening when I learned for the first time of the ultimate degradation of Western civilization, I am again enveloped and submerged by the same feeling of horror, disbelief, and boundless grief.

On that evening a few German Jews—all in their fifties or sixties— arrived in the camp. I wanted to find out where they came from and to learn from them what was happening to the remaining Jews in Germany. But terror was their lord. They did not trust me, they were afraid of the other camp inmates who might overhear their story, and they saw the long claws of the Gestapo reaching for them even inside the camp. I asked them about the fate of German Jewry, and it was then that one of them pronounced the ominous words. I did not believe him; I could not believe him. He told me about a speech by Thomas Mann in which the great German writer gave the name of the camp in which the first gas chambers were known to have operated and the number of victims on whom their efficacy had first been tried. I did not ask for further details and cut short the conversation.

I remember leaving the barracks and stepping into the glory and splendor of a Spanish summer night, a maelstrom of terror, despair, and anguish raging in my soul. My youthful faith and love of life were so shattered by its weight that I could not even share it with my Jewish companions. I felt like howling, tearing my clothes, covering myself with ashes, but I was too far removed from the religious and medieval mind. My intellect never gave up its role of investigator and examiner; despite the absence of human sympathy and understanding, my mind did not crack and I did not go mad. The easy faith of youth suffered, of course; my attitude toward people changed as well. But apart from a temporary loss of appetite and a decrease in patience with my pupils, there were no external signs to show that I felt polluted, outraged, and degraded.

Shortly afterward we all learned from the Swiss newspapers that we used to receive quite regularly about the streamlined liquidation of the Jews imprisoned behind the walls of the Warsaw ghetto. One of the newspapers also reported that the members of the British House of Commons had paid their respects to the memory of some 3 million Jews murdered in Nazi-occupied parts of Europe by rising to their feet and keeping silence. They were commemorating the fate of people who died not because they stood between Germany and world domination but because they presented the easiest offering for a holocaust.

Because the few copies of newspapers the Polish group received could not be read by all its members, and because they were in languages the majority of the Poles did not understand, fortnightly press reviews used to be given in one of the barracks. I attended a press review given by an elderly warrant officer who had commenced his military career in the German Kronprinz's Verdun army and listened to his description of the scene in the House of Commons. When he read out the number of Jews murdered in Europe by the middle of summer 1942, there was widespread applause. There was not a single voice of protest at this expression of solidarity with the aims of Nazism. Not a single Polish officer, NCO, or soldier thought it necessary or had enough courage to cry out "Shame!" Not a single Pole—not even among my pupils—found it necessary afterward to come and express his apologies and sympathies to me.

At the end of August the Spanish newspapers, which we could buy daily in the camp, began to acquaint us with the names of all the factories and works of Stalingrad. I learned that Stalingrad was probably the longest and narrowest city in the world, and I could not see how the Red Army and the workers of Stalingrad could prevent the steel-tempered and inhumanly efficient Nazi columns from reaching the Volga. But September passed and the names of the same works kept appearing in the Nazi communiqués. The Nazi plague even managed to reach and climb the eternal peaks of the Caucasus, but Stalingrad kept recurring in the Wehrmacht's High Command communiqués. A miracle was obviously taking place, but a miracle caused by a determination, by an endurance, by a heroism and willpower such as the world had rarely known. In the face of the Stalingrad epic, even the worst Russophobes among the Miranda Poles had to relent, and they even began to claim credit for Soviet military prowess. They remembered that the Russians were Slavs after all and therefore that they, as Poles, shared the Russians' immortal glory.

The Valhalla was letting its worshipers down or, perhaps, loving them so much as to claim their presence in the hundreds of thousands. Holocausts such as the Aztec gods had never known were offered to propitiate the Teutonic gods, and my people provided the offering. Over a third of Soviet Jewry—more than 1,200,000 men, women, children, and babies— had already been murdered, buried alive, gassed, or burned. Poland became one big death factory, and the best part of 3 million Jews was wiped out scientifically in the same summer. The supply of victims was beginning to run out. But there were still many thousands of them in Vichy France, in the realm of an old man who claimed to represent the noble traditions of a nation that had once stood for faith in man's greatness and intelligence, belief in man's equality and brotherhood. These thousands of refugees, many of whom had been on the run since 1933, were now delivered into Himmler's hands by Laval. Only a few hundred of them managed to avoid being caught by French policemen and gendarmes, by crossing the Pyrenees in search of sanctuary in Franco's Spain. And they found it in a land ruled by a tyrant, in a country where their ancestors had suffered five centuries earlier a catastrophe of such magnitude that it needed all the technical genius of twentieth-century Western civilization harnessed by a paranoiac to surpass it.

I witnessed the arrival of the first group of them. As I learned later, only a few had managed to escape with their families. The majority had left their parents, wives, and children behind or even seen them being taken away in lorries or railway cars. They arrived at Miranda with heavy hearts and numbed or gnawing consciences. And, as they entered the gates of the camp, they found no pity.

Quite a few Poles were waiting for them. Not officers or NCOs, who preferred to stand in the doorways of the barracks or look out through their windows, but keen young soldiers, the product of the same officers' training and the same NCOs' drilling. They received the Jews, many of whom were born in Poland, with a hail of rotten onions, tomatoes, and occasional stones. And then they bawled out in all the languages they knew: "What are you doing here? Go to Palestine! Jews, go to Palestine!"

But the matter did not rest there. A few days later the young Polish *cabo,* who had taken me to my barracks on my arrival, led a Polish delegation to the Spanish camp commandant. They had come, the *cabo* declared, to appeal to the major as Catholics would to Catholics. It was impossible for a Polish Catholic to live together with so many Jews. Something had to be done. The delegation proposed that a special camp should be set up for the Jews inside Miranda de Ebro. It was left to the concentration camp commandant to tell Poles, whose country was being ravaged by German Fascists, that to him all prisoners were equal, Catholics or no Catholics.

When I was ten I read Fenimore Cooper's forest and prairie books in one week at the beginning of the long summer vacation, with the prospect of three months of country life, running barefoot, swimming, fishing, and wandering through the deep Lithuanian forests in front of me. I was full of joy and the elated feeling of freedom. But when I read about the last Mohican's death, such a pall of sadness descended upon me and oppressed my young heart that even the preparations prior to leaving for the country and the actual train journey could not make it depart.

It was the same endless, helpless, and poignant sadness that settled on me in the summer of 1942, when I realized that there would be no Polish and no European Jewry to witness the end of the war—that *victory* was already a meaningless word to me. I could not help asking myself whether my staying alive was just an accident or had some hidden meaning. I felt ashamed of my own ambitions and dreams, which I had gone on cherishing even in the midst of the tragedy of war and my people's agony. A thousand bonds that had made my existence as an individual meaningful only because my family, school friends, and the Jewish community of Wilno had ensured the background and continuity of my life, became suddenly obvious. Here I was, not quite twenty-five, looking more into the past than the future. A terrible feeling of loneliness crept over me.

The Jews at Miranda who were members of national groups—Polish, Czech, Belgian, Dutch, or French—only too often did their best to forget that in Hitler's world they had much more in common with one another as

Jews than with their non-Jewish compatriots. They avoided one another, did not inquire about the fate of their people in one another's countries, even shunned thinking about it. It is possible that they behaved like most other people would in a similar position, but to me they were not like "most other people": they were Jews. This feeling had nothing to do with religious pride, with the belief in being a chosen people; my feeling emerged from the realization that we, Jews, had been made a symbol of all those qualities in human history that Fascism wanted to destroy. Therefore, I felt, having had the burden of being a symbol imposed upon us, we ought to act like people with a mission.

Apart from us Jews with passports, there were others who had none. They were of all origins—German, Austrian, Polish, Czech, Greek, Turkish, Rumanian—with one thing in common: they were stateless. Most had started their wanderings with Hitler's ascent to power but some even earlier. They finally landed at Miranda and had to share a barracks with all the stateless tramps and undesirables of Spain. Before the arrival of Pétain's and Laval's scapegoats, there were perhaps two dozen of them—twenty-four Jews out of Hitler's reach thanks to Franco's mercy.

And yet, to all intents and purposes, it looked as if there were two dozen too many. With all the wealth of British and American Jewry, with all the Jewish statesmen, scientists, and half a million Jewish combatants in the U.S. armed forces alone, they were not even provided with as much money and food as Luxembourg gave its citizens in the camp of Miranda. We all received seven pesetas a day (as much as the average daily wage of a Spanish worker in 1942–43), apart from food parcels and cigarettes. Our pay was so high that many Poles, who had been workers or peasants in their own country, felt like *rentiers* at Miranda, and by selling their cigarettes and some of their food were able to purchase sovereigns and dollars. But the stateless Jews received no parcels at all and, only on rare occasions, eighty pesetas a month. Like the Chinese, Greeks, and Levantines, they took to trading, which consisted of buying cigarettes and food from prisoners who sold them at the beginning of the month in order to get money for wine and reselling them later, when most of us had run out of supplies.

It was they who made me realize how particularly bitter our Jewish fate was; how inefficient the use that we, Jews, made of our talents and resources;

how undramatic and undignified was the expression of our vitality. Wronged and insulted, robbed and murdered, we were not even allowed to have nobility but were made to appear like cheap Shylocks.

During the year of Stalingrad the only people in the camp with whom I could fully share my sorrows and apprehensions, my hopes and faith, were the members of the International Brigade.

When Spanish Fascism won in 1939, several hundred members of the organizations that made up the International Brigade found themselves prisoners in Franco's jails, camps, and hospitals. Those who were British, French, or American were released shortly after the end of the Civil War; the Germans were delivered into the hand of the Gestapo; the Poles, Dutchmen, Yugoslavs, and Balts, deprived of their citizenship by their respective governments, were left to die or languish in Spanish camps.

After the fall of France and the establishment of exile governments in London, new hope was born for those people who had represented European conscience during the terrible years of silence and betrayal. Under the pressure of the 1940 spirit in Britain, the exile governments again recognized these anti-Fascists as citizens and instructed their diplomats in Madrid to intervene on their behalf. In the course of 1941 the surviving prisoners were transferred to Miranda de Ebro. In all there were some fifty of them, the majority being Poles. Had the transfer occurred a year earlier, the number of the Poles alone would have run into a hundred instead of sixteen or eighteen. Even at Miranda the Spanish camp authorities did not treat the International Brigaders in the same way as other prisoners. They made them do all the degrading work connected with keeping the camp clean; they turned them into hewers of wood and drawers of water; and, of course, these prisoners were kept in a separate hut.

The Dutch, Yugoslavs, and Balts, once they were recognized as citizens by their respective governments, had no trouble in obtaining their money and food allowances from the British military attaché's camp representative. But matters were quite different for the Polish Brigaders. In London, General Sikorski declared them to be Polish citizens, but the Polish minister in Madrid refused to carry out the general's orders, which he took for what they were, an expedient with which to placate the anti-Fascist spirit of wartime Britain. As a result of the Polish minister's staunch Fascist loyalties, the Polish International Brigaders received no help in money or food during the first months of their stay at Miranda.

Forced at last to submit to "Judeo-Plutocratic-Communist" pressure, the Polish officers at Miranda had no recourse but to procrastinate. They recognized the survivors of the Polish International Brigades as Polish citizens of a special category, entitled to the money allowance but not to the food. It was not until the end of 1942 that they stopped selling the Brigaders' food rations to the black marketers and began to issue them to their rightful owners. But even then they refused to share the parcels sent by the Polish American Red Cross with the "Reds."

Most of the Polish Brigaders had been taken prisoner in the last great Republican offensive across the Ebro, which the Polish Brigade had spearheaded. The majority were miners, who had rid themselves of chauvinism and learned internationalism in the mines of Belgium and France. A third of the survivors were Jews who, with the exception of two doctors, were all of working-class origin.

Obsessed as I was at that time with doubts as to the martial qualities and physical courage of my people, their very sight was a blessing to me. Through hearing their quiet and modest narratives of personal adventures and war experiences, and witnessing the respect with which they were treated by their non-Jewish comrades, I could reassure myself that centuries of degradation had not destroyed in us the heroic qualities of our ancestors.

At almost the same time as the pitiful trickle of Jewish refugees who had managed to escape Laval's deal with Himmler, the first German deserters arrived at the camp. There were perhaps half a dozen of them, and they posed as Poles or Frenchmen for, had they made their true nationality known, Franco's police would have delivered them into the hands of the Gestapo. Two of them came directly from the eastern front. Back in Germany on their first leave since the beginning of the Russian campaign, they had met some French Communist workers, who had given them their own traveling documents. Once in France they were helped by other French Communists to reach the Spanish border.

The other Germans either deserted their units in France on receiving their marching orders for Russia or took advantage of their units being sent from the eastern front to France to do the same. Kaminski belonged to the latter category of deserters. A very tall, thin man of twenty-seven, with a pale and sad face, he spoke excellent Spanish with a German accent and fluent English with an American one. I learned that he had lived for many years in South America, but as he was unwilling to talk about himself, I never asked him when and why he had returned to Germany. As a "Pole" he had been directed by the Spanish authorities to a Polish barracks, which happened to be mine. He found a cabin whose occupants permitted him to sleep in it, but in return he became their water carrier, dishwasher, and laundryman. Although I never hated the Germans more than in the summer and autumn of 1942, I could not help noticing that he was hungry, insulted, and intellectually far above his tormentors. I began by giving him my Spanish soup and, later on, an occasional tin of sardines and cigarettes. But as I avoided all contact that would establish our relations on a footing of familiarity, it was some time before he learned that I came from Wilno.

He asked me where my family was. I replied that I had left them all in Wilno and that I had had no news from them since the Nazi attack against the Soviet Union. After a short silence he told me that he had spent some time in Wilno in 1941. The Jews had been divided by the Gestapo and SS into two groups: a "productive group," composed of men and women capable of working for the German war effort, and an "unproductive group," composed of the old, the sick, and the children. The two groups had been imprisoned in separate ghettos, and in October 1941 the "unproductive" ghetto had been completely emptied. Where the old and very young Jews of Wilno had been taken he did not know, but they were certainly no longer alive.

When I heard him tell me the fate of my own family, of all my friends and companions, and of the end of one of the oldest and proudest Jewish communities in Eastern Europe, I could think only of the horror faced by those who had had to forsake their flesh and blood in order to live and work for their murderers.

There Is Joy in Our Street at Last

A UTUMN NIGHTS WERE WELCOME at Miranda de Ebro because
their cold kept the bugs in their chinks, thus permitting us to sleep.
The morning mist softened the contours of the hills and trees, and created
shades and shadows where before there had been only hues of almost
Technicolor crudity. The tints and delicate mysteries of northern climes
were with us again and made us violently homesick. The Poles became
moodier and more quarrelsome than ever before. The presence of a whole
bunch of pederasts among the Belgians and the appearance of an extremely
attractive Dutch count who boasted of his successes in London, New York,
and Madrid had their effect upon even the Poles, who are usually quite traditional in their sexual practices.

In the meantime the Polish Legation in Madrid ceased to send its representative to the camp but increased its monthly consignments of food and
cigarettes. The last representative, who arrived shortly after the putsch,
was a priest, but even his cassock did not save him from violent threats and
accusations from the Poles who simply believed that the minister and his
staff were interested only in keeping them interned as long as possible, so
that they could line their pockets with part of the money sent by the Polish
government in London and the American Polish Red Cross. They refused

to believe that Britain and the United States, whose nationals were regularly being released by France, could not obtain the liberation of the six hundred Poles imprisoned at Miranda, and felt that their minister in Madrid was more interested in being on good terms with Franco than in his relations with the British and American ambassadors there.

The Polish minister in Madrid had been one of the signatories of the Riga Treaty, which had concluded the Soviet-Polish War of 1919–20; he was an inveterate enemy of everything Russian and thus opposed to Sikorski's pact with Stalin; he belonged to the Pilsudski clique and was, therefore, on terms of animosity with General Sikorski; and he was a personal friend of Franco. Nor was it any secret that his relations with the British ambassador were very bad. He owed his tenure to the fact that during the Civil War he had granted asylum in the legation to over two hundred enemies of the Republic. Therefore, although Franco refused to recognize the existence of the Polish government in London, he tolerated the semiofficial presence of his personal friend's legation. It was also a fact that before General Sikorski's visit to the Soviet Union and his pact with Stalin, the minister had obtained permission from Franco's government for the departure of Poles in possession of South American visas. Since the conclusion of that pact, no Pole had been released from the camp.

After the priest left, only rare letters arrived from the legation. We were informed that the minister was endeavoring to secure visas for us from the Argentine and Chilean governments, and that the Spanish government would be willing to grant us exit facilities once these had been issued. To make these prospects realistic, a photographer arrived to photograph Poles for their future passports. At the same time, however, the Polish Jews were informed that the Argentine and Chilean Embassies had made it clear that under no circumstances would they grant visas to non-Catholics.

We rejoiced at the news of victory at El Alamein. At last the initiative had been wrenched from Hitler's hands, and for the first time since 1939 a corner of the world was being restored to humanity. This meant that the racial laws established by the Vichy regime were going to be revoked, that at last some of our brothers would be given back their rights as human beings. To all the anti-Fascists at Miranda the day was of special importance, because it was a portent of the approaching liberation of the thousands of Spanish democrats imprisoned in the camps of Morocco by the regime of the senile victor of Verdun.

The day passed full of rumors. Left to our own conjectures by the scarcity and unreliability of the news printed in the Spanish newspapers, we gave free rein to our strategic talents. As a result, a rumor about Allied air landings in the Balearic Islands swept the camp like a prairie fire. But when night came, a rumor of the Germans having crossed the Spanish border in the vicinity of San Sebastián was concocted in the Belgian group. From there it reached the stateless Jews, who had only a few months earlier succeeded in escaping Laval's tender mercies.

Hitler's invasion of Spain sounded only too plausible to all of us to dismiss the alarm among the Belgians and Jews as mere panic. To me, it seemed perfectly logical that Hitler should try to counteract the Allied invasion of North Africa by pushing on toward Gibraltar. In view of the naval superiority of the Anglo-Americans in the Mediterranean, the German High Command could not hope to supply Rommel with sufficient reinforcements or to evacuate his forces by sea. However, if the Wehrmacht succeeded in gaining control over the Strait of Gibraltar, it could hope to turn the tables on the Allies by cutting their sea-lanes, then splitting their expeditionary armies by invading Spanish Morocco.

About midnight we began to calculate the distance between Miranda de Ebro and the French frontier, and we decided that, judging by the average rate of Nazi advances in the first days of their campaigns, the first German motorized troops might appear at the Miranda railway junction the evening of the following day. This prospect was too threatening to be taken lightly, and by two o'clock in the morning everybody in the Polish barracks had packed the few belongings he intended to take in case of a sudden flight. A delegation endeavored in the meantime to see the Spanish camp commandant. It finally succeeded and came back with the news that he had heard nothing of an impending German attack against Spain but promised that if it happened he would throw open the gates of the camp straightaway.

Whether he meant it I do not know, but the effect was reassuring. When the following day passed without German airplanes appearing in the sky but with news of the occupation of Vichy France, I decided that Hitler already had too much with one peninsular war in Yugoslavia to risk another one in Spain. For I was sure that in a German invasion Franco's regime would be swept away and the Republicans, helped by the Allies, would repeat the exploits of the *guerrilleros* and perhaps even surpass Tito's partisans in effectiveness if not in heroism.

The result of the German occupation of Vichy France was a French invasion of the camp. Within a fortnight the first parties of Frenchmen appeared at Miranda, and their flow continued on an ever-increasing scale until, by the end of 1942, they formed the largest national grouping.

The majority of the Frenchmen had been too young to serve with the French armed forces in 1939–40. The remainder were regular officers of the rump French Army, which had survived in Vichy France until November 1942, and a detachment of sailors. Among the officers there was even a general, but in 1942 we had so little respect for French generals at Miranda that I did not even try to find out his name.

Toward the end of November came winter, and the weather, which had been exceptionally mild until then, proved very unfriendly. Sleet and rain turned the camp into a sea of mire, in which most of the Frenchmen had to sleep in old and battered tents that protected them from neither rain nor mud. Their position in the camp was made all the worse because they enjoyed scant sympathy from anyone.

The Polish group—the most influential in the camp—treated them with scorn and even hatred. The Poles especially despised them because the French government had given up the struggle so easily and had betrayed the Allied cause by signing an armistice with Hitler after sitting on the fence until the very last minute; because they felt contempt for their fighting qualities; and because most of them, while serving in France, had had to listen to Frenchmen accuse them of being responsible for the war. In view of the politically primitive sentiments of the majority of the Miranda Poles, it was a waste of time to try to explain to them that French defeatism in 1940 sprang from deep social and political causes.

It did not take much insight to discover that only a minority among the new arrivals were Gaullists intent on joining the fighting French forces. The majority were still unrepentant Pétainists, strongly anti-British, profoundly poisoned by the Nazi "New Order" ideology, and intent on joining General Giraud, in whom they saw the heir of Pétain's policy. Many of them seemed to have taken the radical decision to leave their homes and risk captivity in Spain only because they could no longer stand the hunger reigning in Vichy France.

The Spaniards, whose attitude was of the greatest consequence to the Frenchmen, took an obvious delight in making them suffer; for one thing, there is a standing enmity against Frenchmen among most nationalistic Spaniards and, for another, they considered France's attitude largely responsible for the fall of the Republic and knew about the shameful treatment of Republican refugees in French camps. This explains why the general and several colonels of the French group found no better shelter in the camp of Miranda de Ebro than its new and unused lavatory.

The new year brought us the news of the Stalingrad victory. Every national group in the camp except the Poles received the news with unmitigated joy. When the Swiss papers at last arrived and the magnitude of the Nazi defeat became known to us, a striking number of Polish officers appeared with thoughtful expressions on their faces.

A captain for whom I translated the Soviet communiqués from *Die Neue Zuercher Zeitung* made it perfectly clear to me why so many of his colleagues were in such low spirits. "Thank you, Mr. Ainsztein," he said after I had finished. "These Bolshevik communiqués seem to bear the imprint of truth, I'm afraid. What a victory! After such losses the Germans may not be able to go on fighting for long. And if they are not capable of staging a comeback in the spring and summer, there will be too many Muscovites left alive. Unless many more millions of Muscovites and Germans are killed, there is little hope left for us Poles. Another victory like this one, and the Bolsheviks will be in Poland before the British and Americans can get there, and then," he concluded without the slightest sign of embarrassment, "we shall never see the beautiful Poland you and I have known."

The beautiful Poland he and I had known! In that beautiful Poland, I, as a Jew, could never have become an officer, an airman, or a civil servant, and most of the schools and universities in that beautiful Poland had been closed to me. Yet it did not even occur to him that I might entertain different views from his on the kind of Poland that might be restored if the British and Americans were the first to arrive in Warsaw. It did not occur to him because he had been conditioned by hundreds of years of feudal and

Catholic upbringing into believing a Jew could not be hurt by the same insults or inequalities as a true-born Pole.

I should have known better by then, yet I remember being full of amazement at the fact that it was men of his type who had ruled Poland—a country inhabited by 34 million people at the time of its fall—for almost twenty years. Nor could I help fearing that, in spite of all the carnage in the world, he and men like him might yet stage a comeback and make the sacrifice of millions of lives both senseless and purposeless.

At the end of February a representative of the Chilean Embassy arrived at the camp with visas for seventy Poles. The Polish group spent many stormy hours discussing who should be put on the Chilean list. As it had been made clear long before the arrival of the Chilean official that no Jews would be granted visas by the Chilean government, I felt little interest in the outcome of the discussions. However, immediately on his arrival at Miranda, the Chilean made it known that he was not interested in any lists of suitable emigrants the Polish group might like to present to him. He had his own instructions and standards, which he intended to follow and apply in making the choice of his country's future citizens.

These became obvious when he had visited the camp two or three times. Having watched the Polish group on parade, he took note of all the tall and blond Poles and had them called to his office for interviews. As it happened the majority of these were ex-policemen, gendarmes, or scarcely literate peasants. That did not seem to worry the Chilean. Although he was a dark and rather short man himself, he appeared to think that his country needed, above all, Nordic stock or, as the saying went around the Polish group, stud stallions. This was the proverbial last straw and made even the most procrastinating elements among the Poles decide that action was necessary to convince the Polish minister and the Allied ambassadors in Madrid that we did not intend to spend all the war behind the walls of Miranda and that they owed us as much protection as they gave to escaped British or American airmen or soldiers.

The Frenchmen and Belgians were only too glad to follow the lead and example of the Polish group. The stateless prisoners rallied to the common cause as well. A committee comprising the representatives of all national groups was set up so surreptitiously that, until the very day on which the hunger strike was announced, there were no rumors circulating in the camp to warn the Spanish authorities of the impending event.

Our demands were quite reasonable. We asked that a Red Cross commission be allowed to visit our camp and examine our legal status. We insisted on a commission composed of representatives from a neutral country, because we did not trust one composed of Spaniards. We also demanded the immediate release of all prisoners of nonmilitary age, in other words, under eighteen and over forty-five, and we refused to accept sojourn behind barbed wire for the rest of us because, having arrived in Spain as civilians, we considered ourselves entitled to a life under surveillance in a Spanish village or town provided we did not go beyond the fixed boundaries of our residence. We commenced an immediate hunger strike, which we intended to keep up until concrete steps were taken to satisfy our demands, and placed the responsibility for prisoners dying or becoming ill as a result of the strike on the shoulders of the Spanish authorities.

The news of the strike was received in silence in the Polish barracks. But it was a silence expressing full realization of what lay in front of us, and a dogged determination to continue the strike as long as might be necessary. The decision of the Polish group command was not only to refuse the camp food but also to refrain from eating our own.

The Belgians decided that, since the purpose of the strike was to impress the Spaniards and the Allied governments, there was no need to be too thorough about the business of fasting: as long as nobody went for his food to the Spanish caldrons, it did not matter whether people ate their own food supplies provided they ate in secret. It was a perfectly reasonable solution for the Belgian group command to take, for however brave the average Belgian at Miranda might have been, a 100 percent fast is more than most Belgian stomachs can stand.

The greatest sufferers were the Frenchmen, because they had only recently arrived and thus had had no time to build up their bodies, ravaged by years of starvation in France and the acute hunger suffered in Spanish prisons while in transit. But the majority bravely accepted the decision of their group leaders, while the minority were too frightened of what the Poles might do to them if they were seen taking Spanish food to rebel.

The reaction of the Spanish camp commandant on the first day of the strike was one of skepticism; he obviously did not believe that some four thousand people of various nationalities, ages, and purposes would hold out for long. The meals were prepared as usual, the roll calls took place as usual, and the prisoners filed past the caldrons without taking their bread and soup, while at the evening *bandera* ceremony they were more disciplined than they had ever been before.

At night the Spanish major ordered that caldrons filled with soup and bags filled with loaves should be left outside the cookhouse. He hoped that the weaker prisoners would take advantage of the darkness to sneak out to them and thus destroy the united front presented by his rebellious wards. He failed in his calculation. Only a few Frenchmen crept out to the tantalizing food. They were seen by the Polish and Czech cooks, who informed their compatriots. The Frenchmen were immediately surrounded by a score of Poles, who were on the point of administering a terrible beating when representatives of the strike committee arrived to warn them that violence was precisely what the Spanish camp commandant was hoping for. He could then claim that the strike was the work of only one group terrorizing the remainder of the camp inmates, thus discrediting us in the eyes of the Allied ambassadors in Madrid and obtaining permission from his own superiors to use force against us.

On the second day the usual parades and marches past the caldrons were repeated but, in order to tempt us, the Spanish quartermaster had gone the whole hog: the big caldrons were full of rice and fried fish, and the smaller ones were steaming with *white* and *sugared* coffee! Nobody had seen white coffee at Miranda de Ebro since the first Allied prisoners had arrived in August 1940.

Still, no one succumbed. All the caldrons were left standing in the middle of the square, where they could be much more easily approached by hungry prisoners than if they had been left outside the cooking shed. Nevertheless, I do not think that even a score of prisoners took advantage of the cover of night to snatch something from the heaps of fish and bread.

On the third day the first victims of the strike had to be attended by our camp doctors. It had been made clear by the committee at the beginning of the strike that all prisoners under seventeen and over fifty-five, as well as those with weak lungs, bad hearts, or other serious physical disabilities, were not expected to fast. It so happened that most of the prisoners exempted by age from taking an active part in the fast were Jewish refugees from Vichy France, practically all of whom waived their privilege and refused to eat.

Several prisoners fainted during the evening parade and, as a consequence, the commandant abolished parades for the duration of the hunger strike. The camp command then made an attempt at breaking our spirit by spreading the rumor that our demands had been accepted by the responsible Spanish authorities and that we therefore no longer had cause to continue with our action. The strike committee countered the Spanish move by spreading the news that the whole free world already knew about our fight and that the press and radio of London and New York were full of it. It was only after we had recovered our freedom that we learned this piece of information was without the slightest foundation of truth.

I had stood the first two days of the hunger strike quite easily, but on the third day my stomach ceased to rumble, at night it was difficult to sleep, and my heart began to beat with alarming force. On the fourth and fifth days of the strike, I found myself unable to think of anything but food. I reminded myself of all the good meals I had had in my life, I thought of all the tins of sardines and jam I had under my cot, and I began to hate my neighbor, whom I had heard munching chocolate in the stillness of night.

On the sixth day I felt as if I could go on fasting forever. But at noon an official from the Polish Legation appeared at the gates of the camp with the news that our demands had been accepted and that the first party of prisoners of nonmilitary age would be leaving at the end of March.

A fortnight later the prisoners began to leave the camp; of the Polish group, almost a hundred were released. We saw them depart in silence, and we could read on their faces expressions of joy, happiness, and embarrassment. They knew that we who stayed behind were asking ourselves whether the only result of the strike would be their liberation and whether we would have to recommence fasting in order to gain freedom for ourselves.

It was on the second Sunday in April that the news of our liberation was brought to the camp by our food supplier, who bicycled from the town of Miranda to inform the Polish group commandant of a telephone conversation he had just had with one of the secretaries at the Polish Legation in

Madrid. On the following day the secretary himself appeared at the camp, and we learned that we would be leaving Miranda de Ebro in parties of one hundred a day.

It was decided that the first to have arrived at the camp would be first to leave; thus I, with only fourteen months behind me, would be in the third group. Those in the first group had almost three years' imprisonment behind them—a high price to pay for two days' priority.

The first group left on a Tuesday; the second followed on Wednesday. On Thursday morning we of the third group waited anxiously for the great moment. We did not wait long. A Spanish officer and sergeant went through the list of our names together with a Polish officer before we were surrounded by a detachment of Spanish soldiers armed with rifles and escorted to the first gate. Another roll call took place, and a final examination, before we were allowed to march through the final gate.

At last we were outside the camp. We enjoyed our freedom in hushed tones; we spoke little, but our eyes shone. We arrived in Miranda and followed for a while the bank of the river, but we were in a hurry to get to the cemetery and pay our last respects to the remains of Lieutenant Kowalski, who had been shot while trying to escape from the camp.

From there we went to a restaurant where a meal awaited us. To sit on a chair behind a table, to have food brought to us on plates, and to eat again with a knife and fork was a unique sensation. Somehow it made the feeling of being free tangible to me; it gave freedom meaning and immediate value.

But from the moment I had walked through the last gate of Miranda de Ebro, one triumphant thought filled my mind: I had not failed; I would still reach England and play my own part in the war.

FROM MADRID TO
GREENOCK

THE JOURNEY TO MADRID lasted the better part of a day and night; we arrived in the early hours of the morning and were dispersed in small groups through the hotels and boardinghouses of the capital. I found myself in a boardinghouse facing the headquarters of the Spanish police. To be away from my compatriots and the atmosphere of envy, hate, drunkenness, and megalomania they created was happiness itself.

The result of fourteen months' imprisonment was a constant restlessness, an inability to concentrate, and a hunger for feminine company. I found that I could not sit through a single film show, that a feeling of claustrophobia pursued me even in cafés, and that I couldn't read anything except newspapers. The only advantage of my restlessness was a constant urge to stay outdoors and to be on the move, so I explored Madrid and its surroundings in detail for the five weeks that I spent there.

In the first place I was struck by the modern character of the capital, which compared very favorably with Brussels or Paris. After all the sad, gloomy, and empty cities I had seen in Nazi-occupied Europe, I could not help being impressed by the well-lit streets, the opulent shop windows, the food in the fashionable groceries, the smart young men and beautifully dressed women who lounged on the terraces of the cafés in the Alcola. However, I could not help noticing the various kinds of police on my first day in Madrid: the civil guards, who always made me think of ravens; the *policía armada*, parading in German field gray, armed with guns and looking like Mexican bandits; and the municipal police, in charge of city traffic but well supplied with pistols and rifles. Nor could I miss the Moors of Franco's bodyguard, tall and powerful figures with ginger beards and in many cases, to my surprise, blue eyes, who walked the streets of the Spanish capital as if they owned it.

As I was still too young, too moral, too inhibited, or simply too frightened of catching venereal disease, I refused to act like most of my companions and take recourse in the facilities offered by Madrid's numerous brothels. So I began to look for a woman in the cafés and taverns of the city. And there was no lack of them; as a matter of fact, these places seemed to be frequented only by girls and young women, who, with very few exceptions, were modestly dressed and polite. It was therefore quite a shock for me to find out that they were all to be had for a price that a common London prostitute would refuse to consider.

I became acquainted with several of them before I found one whom I wanted to become my mistress. They were all surprisingly courteous, very often charming, and, in spite of their way of life, never obscene: there is a romantic and puritanic strain in Spanish women that makes them passionate without seeming salacious. Most of them had a child to support; many were married, but their husbands either had been killed during the Civil War or were languishing behind the bars of Franco's prisons; others again had borne children to fathers who had died in battle or by the slaves of Franco's execution squads. Afraid or ashamed of their unmarried motherhood, they had left their small towns and villages, and come to Madrid to look for work.

But in Madrid there had been no work for them. In a country full of unemployed men, with factories idle for lack of raw materials and fuel, in a land ruled by the blackest sort of clerical reaction, there was room for them only at home or in brothels. They fought against the final degradation of entering a brothel and spent their days over single cups of coffee, hoping to find a man who would provide them with enough money to pay for their child's and their own board and lodging.

About them there was nothing of that hard, money-grabbing mentality that characterizes the real harlot. Judging by the experiences of those of my companions who were frequent visitors to brothels, the same lack of mercenary motives and a romantic generosity also characterized the pensioners of those establishments. It is a fact that many of those brothel ladies came to the railway station when the Poles left Madrid and behaved much more like women seeing off their lovers than like prostitutes bidding farewell to their customers.

Most of them were politically ignorant, although they were the worst sufferers under a system based on shameless privilege, sanctified by an immoral church, which aimed at the permanent social and economic slavery of women. Made into pariahs by the semifeudal society of Franco's Spain, they took their revenge—however unconsciously—by spreading venereal diseases. How efficient they were in this task can be judged from the fact that of the five hundred Poles who spent a little over a month in Madrid, more than one hundred became infected with gonorrhea and more than thirty with syphilis.

My stay in Madrid was not, of course, all gloom and erotic pursuit. In the first place, there was the buoyant feeling of freedom, which prevented me from falling into a mood of excessive introspection. In the second place, I made friends with several Spaniards and an Englishman. The friendship of the Spaniards made me realize that human hatred is self-destructive and of a temporary nature, and gave me the hope that the Nazi blight would also pass and become as little comprehensible to future generations as Torquemada's autos-da-fé had proved.

Horace, my English friend, was also a great comfort to me in those days. He came from Birmingham and worked at one of the Anglo-Iberian banks in Madrid. He had been in Spain less time than myself, but his Castilian was excellent: fluent, correct, and colloquial. He had learned Spanish in London from Spanish refugees. Although born clubfooted, he was always gay, cheerful, without any visible self-pity, and very keen on walking. His temperament was the best possible counterweight to my own. We got on well together, and he found me very helpful in dealing with awkward Spaniards who, having found out his nationality, would let him know their views on Britain and Germany. These views were generally to the effect that Britain was the successful aggressor, defending the plunder she had accumulated over centuries, while Germany was the pretender to Britain's position. In view of the continuous occupation of Gibraltar by his country, they refused to believe that Britain was fighting the war solely to restore Poland's and Czechoslovakia's freedom. Poor Horace, who had never thought while living in England that the British Empire needed any justification, would in such cases call on me. Being a foreigner in love with England, I knew most of the arguments the Spaniards might advance and almost all the justifications for the existence of the British Empire. But, although very convincing in my arguments as to humanity's interest in the preservation of the British Commonwealth, I could never think of a moral argument that could settle the problem of Gibraltar.

In the first half of May I left Madrid in the company of over a hundred Poles. I was happy to leave because, after almost five weeks in the city, many of us had begun to doubt whether the usual *mañana* policy was not being pursued by the Spanish authorities and whether we might not have to spend the rest of the war in Spain after all. Our apprehensions became all the more acute as we discovered that Goebbels's *Das Reich* was devoting some editorial space to our holiday in the capital of Germany's reluctant ally.

We boarded our train in the afternoon of a very warm and sunny day and set off, as far as we knew, toward Lisbon, but as soon as we left Madrid I thought of Horace, my Spanish friends, and my mistress from Málaga, to whom I had lied about the date of my departure, and I felt sad and depressed to be leaving.

Late at night the train stopped where we had to undergo a perfunctory examination. While I was waiting for my turn, I realized that I was standing next to Leslie Howard. I had known about his visit to Madrid, where he had lectured on Shakespeare, but to stand next to a very great actor, whose *Pygmalion* had been the first English film of which I had understood the complete dialogue, was the greatest of joys. I wanted to speak to him and express my appreciation, but I dared not interfere in the comical attempt at a conversation he and his English companion were having with the customs officers, who were admiring stills of his films they had found in his luggage.

After the customs and passport examinations, our train moved on at a leisurely pace. At last we were in Portugal, and breakfast awaited us at the first border station. The station restaurant was a low building, all white, covered with exotic creepers and surrounded by beds of flowers. We sat down at little tables that stood outside the restaurant, and I maneuvered myself nearest to the table that Leslie Howard and his companion shared.

From what I overheard of their conversation, I realized they were puzzled by the presence of so many fit young men, the majority of whom had fair skin, fair hair, and blue eyes, in the heart of the Iberian Peninsula. I explained who those strange-looking young men were, at which Howard invited me to his table. I found him the same as he appeared on the screen: modest, gentle, quizzical, with an indefinable charm, and felt that I was facing the foremost product of English civilization: a perfect English gentleman. (It came as a great surprise to me to learn after his death that he was born a Hungarian Jew.) I explained to him our presence on the border of Portugal, and our conversation then turned to his visit to Spain. He told me that he had been treated with great friendliness by the representatives of the Spanish film industry but, although he thought that Spain had all the factors needed for the establishment of a flourishing film industry, he had refused offers to stay there and direct films because he could never see himself working under a regime such as Franco's.

During our conversation he noticed that my pipe was unlit and asked me to try his tobacco. When I accepted eagerly, and explained that I had not smoked any English pipe tobacco since 1940, he emptied his pouch on the table and made me put his tobacco into my own pouch.

We parted just before the train steamed off and met again at noon, having lunch at another gay and whitewashed station. Howard offered wine to the odd hundred of us and refused to accept our thanks.

All day we traveled westward. When we were quite near Lisbon, our railcars were detached and, after a good deal of shunting, attached to a goods train, which made south. We had now left severe grandeur behind us and were crossing a plain dotted with trees, orchards, and meadows. Our train seemed to avoid all towns and villages, but we could see little gaily painted houses dispersed all over the countryside. The people who inhabited them must have been a merry lot, for they painted nonexistent windows on the walls of their houses, and even on their chimney stacks. The idyllic and slightly absurd landscape, decked out in May blossoms, appeared to our northern eyes as the nearest thing to our childish dreams of Paradise, and its effect was all the greater because at the back of our minds there was the thought that we were leaving the security of a neutral land, and that very soon we would be braving the dangers of submarines and bombers.

We spent another night aboard our train, and on the following day, after having crossed half of Portugal, we arrived at Villa Real de San Antonio, an agglomeration of white houses covered with red or green tiles dozing in an afternoon sun as gentle as good old wine. The mild ocean breezes had carried the sand from the beach to every street and alley of the little town so that all the houses stood in a carpet of gold, their interiors shut off from the radiant daylight by curtains of beads that crackled in the gentle breeze.

Nobody appeared to stir in this little collection of colors—nobody apart from urchins who surrounded and followed us like a pack of faithful dogs and endeavored to make us give them cigarettes in exchange for chameleons they carried in their pockets or in their hands. We hardly had time to have a meal and send our last mail to people living in the Nazi-occupied parts of the Continent before the hour of departure arrived.

A launch manned by Britons as sunburned as the Portuguese urchins took us all aboard and sailed out of the little harbor. We were beginning to wonder whether we would travel all the way to Gibraltar in this boat when a destroyer emerged on the skyline and approached us at a terrific speed. We boarded her just outside Portuguese territorial waters and headed for Gibraltar.

The sailors took care of us as if being hosts to Poles was the only purpose of their training and service. We were shown to our quarters, given mugs of strong, sweet tea, and offered cigarettes and tobacco. I was struck by the absence of all shouting or barking of orders and by the grinning faces of the men. To be among naval or military people who issued commands in conversational tones was an uncanny experience to all of us brought up in Poland and acquainted with a German kind of discipline. We immediately felt that there was something about the way these people ran their naval affairs that made them different from all other nations we had known. Their self-assured behavior impressed even the most stupid and arrogant among my companions.

From the way night suddenly descended on us, I realized how far south we were. With a few other Poles I gazed at the winking lights of the Spanish coast and talked to the sailors on watch about the days of submarines, about England and the stars above us. We could not see one another's faces and remained only disembodied voices.

We landed at Gibraltar in pitch darkness and scrambled up interminable stairs to find ourselves at last in a lighted room. To the constant accompaniment of explosions caused by depth charges, we gave our names and ranks and filed singly into what was a former school hall, where we could rest on mattresses. But, although I was very tired, sleep would not come easily. I felt like Joseph Conrad at the end of his first long voyage to the Far East, which he described in *Youth*. There had been so many adventures and experiences to test my character, to rid me of complexes, and to make the ultimate triumph of arrival all the sweeter.

On that night I felt as if adventure was only beginning. To have met Leslie Howard, to have entered the English world aboard a Royal Navy destroyer, and to be looking forward to sailing for Britain from Gibraltar—in none of my boyhood dreams had I ever envisaged such events.

We embarked on an American liner of some fifteen thousand tons, which had cruised in peacetime between New York and South America, and was now sailing back to the States, having transported several thousand American soldiers for the North African invasion.

We spent several days aboard her in the Bay of Gibraltar, basking in the sun and admiring the blue sea, before sailing. General Sikorski happened to pass through on his way to the Middle East and came aboard to review us. We drew up in two lines for the inspection, the small group of Czechoslovaks joining our contingent at the very end of the Polish line. The general walked slowly along the front of the detachment, talking to some and asking questions of the escorting officer, and finally reached my place in the line. He had a slightly bloated face with lines that showed suffering and many disappointments, while his eyes were of a cold, blazing blue and of frightening penetration. He stopped almost opposite me, our eyes met for a fraction of a second, and then he spoke to the commander of the Czechoslovak detachment. "Misfortune has united us," he said in Polish. "If fortune divides us again, then woe to us."

A few days later we sailed out of the strait in the early hours of the morning. When at breakfast time we looked at the waters around us, we already saw the difference between the glittering gray of the Atlantic and the blue of the Mediterranean we had left behind. But on the first and second days of our voyage, the skies were still warm and the ocean peaceful enough not to make us shiver and think with yearning of the South we were leaving behind.

We were sailing west to get out of the reach of German land-based aircraft, so on the fourth day of our voyage we were for a time nearer to the American continent than we were to Europe. Our convoy consisted of some thirty ships escorted by several corvettes and two Woolworth carriers. The presence of aircraft made me quite confident of reaching Britain without any serious mishaps. As it turned out, my optimism was justified, because apart from running into bad weather and gales, which made me seasick, our seven-day passage proved to be uneventful.

The week at sea was a priceless experience and made us realize some of the implications of sea power. Seen from our deck, the whole of the ocean appeared covered by ships: fast passenger ships like ours, tearing the seas at half their wonted speed; new American Victory ships; old cargoes and tramps plowing along with determination although at the cost of great effort—one armada of the many sailing the oceans of the world under British and American flags, yet larger than the whole merchant marine Poland possessed before the war.

Our existence aboard shattered many other ideas about life held by our Polish soldiers, NCOs, policemen, gendarmes, and petty officials. In the Polish Army a soldier used to receive sufficient but coarse food and eight groshes a day, less than a penny; here, after dinner, which included ice cream, he was given a packet of American cigarettes as he walked out of the dining hall. In Poland even the regular NCOs could not afford to go to the cinema more than, perhaps, a dozen times a year; aboard the SM we were given free film shows every night. We all felt that in some magic way we had been transported to a different plane of existence, on which our persons had somehow acquired a much higher price without having changed in any noticeable way.

On the fourth day we ran into gales. The overcast skies, the rain coming in squalls, the restricted horizon, the heaving and dropping ships, the general air of grayness and gloom made us, accustomed as we were to Spanish skies and colors, feel deeply miserable. Some two thousand German prisoners, carried in the hold of an old French cargo boat that seemed to advance only by sheer obstinacy, were made desperate enough by their prolonged misery to threaten mutiny unless their position were improved. When they were told that if they did not behave Poles would be brought aboard to act as their guards, the spirit of revolt speedily left them.

We approached Scotland from the northwest, having given Ireland a wide berth. In the early morning of our seventh day at sea, our convoy broke up and we entered the calm waters of the Firth of Clyde. Hundreds of seagulls swooped over our ship and accompanied us insistently and effortlessly. A mist covered the horizon on either side of our ship, and we felt a new kind of dampness penetrate our flesh and reach the very marrow of our bones; it was with a pang that we thought of sun-scorched Spain and smiling Portugal. It was the beginning of June; at this time of the year in Poland people leave for the wooden bungalows in the countryside to escape the oppressive heat of the towns, and all young people throw away their coats to walk throughout the summer in their shirtsleeves. But as we stood on the decks of the SM dressed in greatcoats and sweaters, we felt as if we had reached a land where sun never shines and rain never ceases.

We sailed up the Clyde and cast anchor in a gray, opaque world in which our ship seemed to be the only vessel afloat. But early in the morning the Poles on fire watch came running belowdecks to awaken their comrades so that they, too, would witness a unique sight. In the paleness of breaking day we saw our ship surrounded by a majestic and stupendous array of steel. Battleships, cruisers, destroyers, frigates, and corvettes were anchored all around us. It looked as if the river was too small to hold them all. Yet somehow I felt as if I had always expected such sights to greet me on approaching the island vastness of Britain.

I had arrived at last, but the fight was by no means over. I was intent on severing all bonds with the country of my birth; I could not admit for one moment the possibility of fighting in the war alongside Poles, who logically should have been in the same camp as the Nazis. Aboard the ship I had heard all sorts of rumors to the effect that the Poles in Britain enjoyed legal autonomy. But, come what might, I decided not to serve with people who promised to use their first bullets against their Jewish comrades, and their last against the Jews whom they might find still alive when they entered Poland as "liberators."

AMONG THE FREE
AT LAST

A CERTAIN NUMBER of tall, middle-aged gentlemen smoking pipes, at whom we looked with admiration and dread because they represented the mythical British Intelligence Service, came aboard and screened us with great speed and efficiency. Having been vain enough to announce my knowledge of English, I had to work as hard as they while helping them compile the sets of cards that heralded the arrival of every alien in the British Isles, then rush like mad in order to board the tender that took us ashore.

A train was waiting for us in a gloomy and dirty railway station. To us, used to the hard seats of the continental trains, it appeared to consist of first-class carriages. We had expected nothing of the kind, for soldiers in Poland used to travel in the same way as French soldiers: in goods trucks, which they often had to share with their horses. This accommodation immediately intensified our feeling, acquired aboard the American ship, of having stepped onto a different plane, on which our poor soldier-persons had somehow become more valuable. As for me, I felt as if I had been finally admitted to a club whose members enjoyed all sorts of privileges denied to the rest of mankind. It was pleasant to be admitted to it, although slightly demoralizing when one came to realize that it was only the accident of birth or war, and not one's intrinsic value, that made one a member.

We arrived at Cowdenbeath, a small mining town in West Fife, after which we were told we would be sent to our respective services: army, air force, or navy. The dance hall where we were put up had no windows and was illuminated day and night by a few dirty bulbs. We slept on palliasses spread on an unswept floor and covered ourselves with blankets that had served many people before us without having been disinfected. Even the plumbing of the lavatories was not much better than in similar places on the Continent, and very few washing facilities existed. As a result of the darkness, lack of water, and absence of elementary hygiene, many of us caught scabies.

I spent almost a fortnight at Cowdenbeath. Thanks to my English I made immediate friends with several Scotsmen, including a publican, a Home Guard captain, and a miner. The publican's wife asked me why my compatriots hated Jews. "Don't they know that the Jews are the chosen people?" she asked me. "Don't they ever read the Bible?"

I replied quite truthfully that they never read the Bible, but I did not dare to tell her that I felt rather embarrassed to be regarded by anybody as a member of a chosen people. The Home Guard captain invited me to come trout fishing with him, and the miner befriended me to such a degree as to invite me to his home. Their friendship made my loneliness, springing from my determination to refuse service with the Polish forces, easier to bear during those days in the dark dance hall, when my companions were uttering hardly veiled threats against "all those traitors and Communists who preferred the easy life of a British mercenary to the heroic and hard road of a Polish soldier."

At last a British official appeared to issue us the final documents that would permit us to join the Polish armed forces in Britain. I refused to sign my document and had to answer the irritated official's question: "Why have you come to Britain?" After having taken note of my explanation and Wing Commander Davies's letter of recommendation, he arranged for me to be sent to London together with a group of Poles wanted for further interrogation. Of the dozen Jews who were at the Cowdenbeath dance hall at the same time as myself, only one dared to follow my example. The others, too cowed by threats, faltered when their chance to make their choice known turned up and had to suffer another year in the Polish Army. When their lives were made absolutely unbearable by the Afrika Korps Poles, who were released from German POW camps by the British and allowed to swell the ranks of the Polish Army, they deserted en masse and caused Parliament to take up their case in 1944. They were then given the opportunity of either joining the British armed forces or becoming miners.

We left by train for London escorted by several plainclothes policemen. Living in Scotland had taught me a number of facts about Britain, the most important being that "British" and "English" are not synonymous. Like most foreigners, I had thought that "British" was a word mostly used by poets, writers, and politicians, and that its purpose was mainly to avoid repetition of the word "English," and until my arrival at Cowdenbeath I had imagined that nothing could gratify a Scot or Welshman more than being called English. It was therefore with some surprise that I discovered that the sturdy Scottish lads, who had made friends with us before we even had enough time to find out where cigarettes and beer could be bought, resented being called Englishmen but consented to be known as Britons. It was quite a revelation to hear them tell me that they disliked the English because they had killed Bruce. These little miners' children were not even afraid to declare their dislike of Mr. Churchill, although, when pressed, they would admit that they preferred him to Goering.

We traveled overnight from Edinburgh to London. It was the end of June, and it was with a feeling of very real joy that I greeted the London skies, with their particular kind of blue, with their clouds of light brick color, and the silvery barrage balloons that had become a part of them. We were taken to Royal Victoria Patriotic School in Wandsworth, a massive pile of brick buildings in pseudo-Gothic style standing in vast grounds. Southern England had been having several weeks of sunshine, and the grass looked almost like grass on the Continent: jaded and yellowish. But how good it was to lie down in it and gaze at the sky.

I spent a fortnight at the Patriotic School answering all kinds of questions and waiting for something to happen. The colonel in command of the place treated us with as much consideration as if he were in charge of a sanatorium and not a place of internment. Nevertheless, boredom and unexpended energy made time appear endless. I was finally taken to the Air Ministry and introduced to a squadron leader who told me that the Royal Air Force would be prepared to see me in its ranks. I would be released as soon as the Wandsworth Borough Council had found accommodation for me.

I found it wonderful and extraordinary that, in the midst of a war involving the mobilization of all the manpower and a great deal of the womanpower of Great Britain, there should still be time left for some authorities to think of my comfort and welfare during the short period between my exit from the Patriotic School and my entry into the RAF. It struck me as a sign of typically British preoccupation with each individual's fate and a proof of great organizational ability.

Mr. Collins, the billeting officer of the Wandsworth Borough Council, took me to my boardinghouse in Streatham, made sure I had enough money for fares, cigarettes, and the cinema, introduced me to his wife, and on the first Sunday took me to Streatham Common to acquaint me with the English idea of free speech. And free it was. I heard a number of cranks ranting on about religion, but I also heard an Independent Labour Party speaker attack the war and Churchill. It was an almost uncanny feeling to be able to watch scenes of idyllic quietude in the summer of 1943, at the time of the Battle of Kursk-Orel and so near a continent befouled by Buchenwald and other factories of death. I was torn between a feeling of admiration that these people remained a race apart and a feeling of exasperation, envy, and almost hatred at their good luck, their contentment, and their apparent inability to realize what was happening beyond their shores.

Yet the overwhelming impression I have retained from those first days in London is one of amazing abundance. To see bread and potatoes sold freely and meals in restaurants available without the surrender of ration cards in the fourth year of war was, to me, nothing short of miraculous. Had I needed any other proof than the changed tide of events in Russia and Africa to know that Nazi Germany could never win the war, the unrationed potatoes and bread and crowded restaurants of London would have been sufficient to convince me.

I had left the Patriotic School in the second week of July, in what turned out to be a good month. In Russia, in the Battle of Kursk-Orel, the Red Army proved that it could now stop German offensives in their tracks; in Italy, Fascism was overthrown and Mussolini interned. When I presented myself in a building near Euston to pass my medical examination, I felt nervous not only because I might be rejected on medical grounds but also because I was afraid the war might be over before I joined a squadron.

I passed my medical examination and expressed my desire to become an air gunner. As I had not tried to join up as a pilot, navigator, or even bomb aimer, I was immediately called up, for there were always vacancies for gunners. And on July 27, 1943, having reported to Lords and seen its mythical lawns, I was marched off to a block of flats facing Regent's Park. I was, at last, one of those whom millions of men, women, and children throughout occupied Europe had endowed with almost legendary qualities.

But even at the very moment of tasting the sweet feeling of achievement, I was reminded of the fundamental failure of my life. When I put on the RAF uniform for the first time and asked one of my roommates what I looked like in it, he replied: "Your mother will be proud when she sees you." An elegiac chord was struck as I remembered my mother, standing on the stairs of the rail station in Wilno, saying only, "I shall never see you again."

During my first three months in the Royal Air Force in London, Yorkshire, and Shropshire, I just about managed to absorb all the new impressions, values, technical knowledge, injections, and vaccinations. The time for classification and generalizations came later, but when it did come it only confirmed most of my first impressions.

In the first place, there was the impact of the RAF organization itself. As an air cadet, I came into contact with its most efficient side, and it made me gasp. The attention paid to my health was astonishing. In spite of the inoculations I had suffered in Spain, I had to go through them all again. My chest was X-rayed and found sound, my sight proved to be excellent, but my teeth were in a deplorable state. They had been my main pride as a boy, but the years of undernourishment as a student in Belgium had impaired them, and the year and a half spent in occupied Belgium and Vichy France on a diet deficient in most things a normal young man needs had finished the work of decay. After I reached Miranda de Ebro, all the Spanish dentist could do when I finally got to him was to pull five of my teeth. They were now seen to in record time and the breaches in them camouflaged.

The issue of uniforms and personal kits surprised me by its abundance. Familiar with the scant issue of a Polish, Soviet, or even German soldier, I felt the way an English serviceman would if suddenly transferred to the U.S. Army. Indeed, for a very large percentage of men and women in the British armed forces, the state managed to make military service more attractive financially than civilian life. And I was struck for the first time by the realization that the Anglo-Saxon powers could afford to have armies with a semimercenary outlook even when undergoing total mobilization. It occurred to me that the first result of such a state of affairs was the absence of necessity on the average serviceman's part to worry about the reasons for the war in which he was taking part.

I met few officers during my first three months in the RAF, but I came to respect the NCOs immediately. Those I met as a cadet were hardworking, conscientious, well-acquainted with their duties, and in constant touch with their men. The junior officers I came in contact with as a cadet knew nothing about their men and had no specialized knowledge of any sort. This state of affairs was, of course, due to the surviving feudal spirit, which made it possible for a man to become an officer not because he had some special knowledge or had passed some special tests but because he had applied for a commission.

The patience and absence of sneers and sarcasm on the part of our teachers struck me as extraordinary. Our instructors were not brilliant and not in the least intellectual; yet, because they were neither, they understood and sympathized with the difficulties of the slowest among their pupils.

During the initial stages of my training, I had many opportunities to test the RAF instructors' patience. I was far from a good pupil although, on the whole, not a bad cadet. During the first three months I was behind most of my comrades for several reasons. The first was my inability to concentrate, which was the result of the fourteen-month confinement in Spain. To sit for hours in airless huts and listen to technical descriptions numbed my powers of perception. The second reason lay in the linguistic difficulties I encountered. For although I could read Shakespeare much more easily than could most of my fellow cadets, they beat me without any apparent trouble in simple and essential matters such as the names of tools and elementary mechanical terms such as *clutch* or *stoppage*. Obviously, without knowing what these terms stood for, I could hardly follow the description of the Browning machine gun given by my instructors. I was therefore forced to ask many questions, which won me the reputation of being rather dense.

I later discovered, however, that my initial backwardness was not altogether due to my unmechanical mind. The majority of my fellow cadets were between the ages of nineteen and twenty-two, and had gone through a complete course of gunnery and aircraft recognition with the Air Training Corps, of which they had all been members before joining the RAF. As well, many of the cadets who were my age or even older had already served as ground staff and knew as much about the .303 Browning and the hydraulic systems of turrets as our instructors.

By the end of my first three months in the RAF, I had become sufficiently used to my new life to be able to devote increasing attention to the wider issues of our conflict and to adopt a more critical view of my comrades. Because they were Britons, I had been conditioned to regard them as a human type apart; because they had chosen to wear the RAF uniform, I was prepared to see them as heroes. But to my surprise and painful disappointment I discovered that, although they were worthy of admiration for their determination and doggedness, their gallantry was not always the outcome of a conscious appreciation of the dangers they would be facing as airmen and their choice of flying duties had only rarely been dictated by ideological reasons.

I found that most of them had joined as air gunners because it was the most glamorous role they could ever hope to play in their lives. Mostly engineers, mechanics, or clerks, they were reasonably intelligent, had a smattering of mathematics and more imagination and love of adventure than most of their friends in civilian life. The RAF promised them easy promotion to the rank of warrant officer if they remained alive for two years and a salary that, although ridiculously low and unfair as compared with those of other members of a bomber's crew, appeared quite attractive. Moved by this combination of incentives, they joined as air gunners and during their initial training period behaved very much like overgrown Boy Scouts. When we were issued our uniforms, boots, shoes, and badges, they spent literally hours polishing them without ever being quite satisfied with their work. They brought with them their Air Training Corps mentality, which somehow gave them faith in their future immunity in the air provided they shaved closely, cleaned their badges, and polished their footwear several times a day.

These future airmen, whom I had expected to be preoccupied with the causes and aims of the war more than any other servicemen, knew very little indeed about its origins and evinced even less interest in learning about them. In Spain I had not shared my sorrows with my Polish fellow prisoners because they actually took pleasure in hearing about them. With most of my British comrades I could not speak of what the war meant to me because I felt that they were neither interested nor capable of understanding.

Many of them had only a vague idea of the extent of Nazi cruelties, while even those who came from the bombed cities generally knew nothing about the nature of Fascism and Nazism and almost nothing about the Munich betrayal; they claimed that their country was at war in order to liberate Poland and other "small nations"; that Britain was bearing the brunt of the fighting; and that the Russians did not know how to fight but held out only because they had millions of soldiers. Many of them actually believed that the Germans had tried to land in England and had been defeated in some mysterious circumstance while crossing the Channel.

They did not remain quite so naïve and insular throughout their air force careers. As they reached the fighting stage, they matured very quickly and lost most of their Boy Scout ideas. But, much more than the average British soldier who came into daily contact with the liberated peoples and his German enemies after the invasion of Europe, they managed to preserve their insular illusions and naïveté.

The longer I stayed in the RAF, the more I learned to admire the unostentatious courage and unflinching devotion to duty of British aircrews. But even after I had met the other members of a bomber's crew, I still had to admit to myself that as a body they did not represent the heroic type I had searched for: the hero combines a conscious, intellectual life with physical courage. Nevertheless, individual representatives of my heroic model were perhaps more common among them than among any other body of British fighting men.

IN UNIFORM AT LAST

IN OCTOBER 1943 I was posted to the Elementary Gunnery School on the Isle of Man and offered the opportunity of seeing another example of the English genius for preserving multiplicity and diversity within the framework of a single commonwealth. My reasoning, grown rigid under the impact of the political and economic conceptions of Europe, had some trouble in accepting the fact that this island, so much part of the economic and political life of the mainland, was yet allowed to have a different system of taxation and even different call-up regulations in the middle of the greatest war in human history. It was on the Isle of Man that the idea began to dawn on me that perhaps the lack of a single logical system in the government and laws of Britain was not the result of mental haziness and indolence but rather a state of affairs consciously willed by a people highly civilized yet aware of the dangers lurking in excessive uniformity.

It was my first autumn under English skies. Because there were no washing facilities on our camp site, we had to get up half an hour earlier than was usual for cadets in the RAF, dress, form up in squadrons, and march off to the main camp. There we would have to undress again, wash, and shave in crowded washhouses, dress again, queue up for breakfast, swallow the ample but unappetizing food, fall in again in squadrons, and march off to the cold or overheated Nissen huts in which our lectures were given. These were interrupted for an hour of physical training, but as we had to dress again after it without being able to wash, that diversion was of the most unpleasant nature.

We marched again to dinner in squadrons and returned in the same manner to our classrooms. The only time during which we could breathe and enjoy the gray daylight was the morning tea break, when the Navy, Army, and Air Force Institutes van would visit us with tea and buns; we drank the tea and threw the buns to the seagulls swooping into our midst. When the day's work was over, night was already covering the island, and since we had risen while darkness still shrouded it, we missed most of the daylight for five days of the week.

I am essentially a land animal; the sea engenders within me a quiet melancholy. The English landscape satisfies my aesthetic sense perhaps more than any other I have seen but fails to absorb me in admiration, wonder, or curiosity. Only mountains—among which I was not born—and forests—among which I spent my childhood and boyhood—can make me forget the affairs of men, can dwarf their importance. The green, treeless meadows of the Isle of Man washed by constant rain caused me to feel utterly alone.

My unease deepened upon my realization of the utter indifference the many hundreds of airmen in my RAF station felt about the fate of millions of people who happened to be my own. I had suggested to the education officer at our station—a powerless replica of the Soviet political commissar—that I give a talk on my experiences in occupied Europe and Spain because they might be of interest to airmen, some of whom were likely to be shot down over enemy occupied territory. The education officer willingly accepted my proposal and gave it all the publicity he could, including the use of the public address system. The response was enthusiastic, and I had an audience that included aircrew, ground staff, and WAAFs. Encouraged by my success, I proposed to the education officer that I should give a talk on the end of the Warsaw ghetto. Would it not be better, he suggested, to call the talk "German Terror in Poland"? I insisted on my original title. The education officer did not pursue the argument; however, he had his way, for he did not use any of the means at his disposal to make it known that such a lecture was to be given, so my audience consisted of three persons, one of whom was a Canadian Jew.

A few days after this incident I received a letter from Mr. Collins of Streatham, in which he suggested that I ought to apply for a post in the Intelligence Branch of the RAF, where use could be made of my linguistic accomplishments. I could serve the war effort, he pointed out, quite as well by doing useful intelligence work as by firing machine guns. Besides, he insisted, there were many more people capable of becoming air gunners than good intelligence officers.

The fact that the letter came from an Englishman made it all the more difficult for me to refute its arguments and withstand its temptation. After all, one of the main reasons why I had chosen the air gunner's job was the anti-Semitic accusation I had heard so often that Jews in the armed forces always aimed at finding safe niches. Yet here was an Englishman who advised me to obtain a safe post and leave the dangerous duties of an air gunner to one of his countrymen.

I overcame the temptation because, in the first place, I knew that if I accepted my own arguments and those of Mr. Collins I should never be sure whether I had given up my air gunner's job out of cowardice, taking advantage of plausible excuses, or because I was really convinced that I could be more useful as an intelligence officer than an aircrew. The other reason was my feeling that I had no right to a safe existence when my aged parents must have gone through the greatest horrors and terror human imagination can conjure. The third reason was my conviction that I should never lay aside the ghosts of doubt about myself, raised during my childhood and adolescence by my anti-Semitic Polish environment, unless I went through with my fighting job. Luckily for my torn soul, the theoretical part of my air gunnery training ended at the time of my greatest doubts, and flying began. For the first time in my life I was leaving the familiar earth in a machine that I profoundly distrusted. Until the time I would become accustomed to the new sensations flying brought, all other doubts and anxieties had to recede into the background.

As a boy, Joseph Conrad fell in love with England through the medium of Captain Marryat's portraits of English naval officers of Nelson's time. When he arrived in late Victorian England and found a people that had very little in common with his childhood heroes of the Napoleonic era, he acted like a very typical Polish romantic: he refused to accept reality and

went on creating English heroes of the Lord Jim type, who had many more
of the features of romantic Polish squires than of romantic English sea
rovers.

No doubt my first love for England and the English had sprung from
romantic illusions no more justified than those of Joseph Conrad, since to a
large degree they had come to me as a result of reading his books. Yet, dif-
fering from Conrad in my romantic boyhood dream of the world, I had
constantly striven to adapt my vision of England to my changing world
outlook. Admittedly, the Englishman I had chosen as my model was a synthesis of Victorian virtues, and the Englishman of my own era differed
greatly from his Victorian predecessor; yet, on my arrival in Britain, I
found that as an individual the modern Englishman still remained very
near my boyhood's ideal.

It is possible that being at war had a great deal to do with the fact that I
found Britain and her people almost as I had imagined them to be in distant
Wilno and not-so-distant Brussels. I found that, of all the Western peoples
I knew, the British were the only ones to have become completely civilized
without losing the more primitive virtues that lie in the love of danger and
adventure. The ideal hero I had dreamed of as a boy in Wilno—the man
in whom action and thought were harmoniously combined—seemed to
occur very frequently in the ruling class of Britain. I also discovered new
traits in the British character that I had never even suspected. I was struck
by the degree of trust and confidence governing the relations between
individuals. I also discovered the extraordinary decency, kindness, and
humanity of the English. I did not meet any Conradesque heroes, but I
did encounter possible Pickwicks, Livingstones, and General Gordons.
The modest and determined courage of my British comrades impressed me
increasingly as we progressed together through training toward battle. I
was very disappointed to find how frightened the average Englishman is of
appearing individualistic and different from others, but I also discovered
how tolerant he can be of the existence of those who are out of the ordinary.

But there was one feature in British life that I found utterly sordid. I
found the relations between the sexes lacking in grace, fun, and interest. I
was revolted by the sentimental hypocrisy of some of my comrades when
dealing with matters of sex and the coarse, unimaginative attitude of the

others. I may have largely succeeded in accepting the illogicality of English spelling, but I never managed to accept the perverse and unnatural love-making in doorways and dark passages. The sight of thousands of couples lying in broad daylight on the worn grass of Hyde Park, engaged in every possible caress short of actual copulation, made me understand why D. H. Lawrence could have been born only in these isles!

BECOMING AN AIRMAN

O UR LAST THREE WEEKS on the Isle of Man were mainly devoted
to flying. We used Ansons, two-engined aircraft that almost flew
themselves and were as safe as an airplane can be. To my landlubber's eyes,
however, they looked very small and extremely fragile. Before we ever left
the ground in them, we had been instructed in how to abandon them in case
of emergency over land or sea. I refused to admit to myself how alarmed I
was at the prospect of having to walk onto one of the aircraft's wings, then
slide down it with my parachute still unopened and pull its cord only when
out of danger of having it caught by the Anson's tail. The feeling that from
now on my life would depend, while flying, on soulless engines and con-
traptions such as parachutes and dinghies was a new one.

My courage hardly knew how to deal with the new sensations of danger
and anxiety. It was put to an even more severe test when, for the first time, I
squeezed myself into the Bristol turret, a clumsy and primitive affair that
needed both my hands to rotate and whose machine-gun cradle persistently hit my chin. I now understood, for the first time, why an air gunner's
trade was considered such a hopeless one. Not only is he isolated from his
mates but a gunner is often conscious of the fact that if anything happens to
his aircraft he is unlikely to be able to get out of it quickly. There is so little
room in the turret that he cannot even keep his parachute strapped on and

has to leave it outside. No wonder, therefore, that when off guard most gunners look deeply preoccupied, while when on guard they affect an attitude of absolute daredevilry.

There is much comfort for even an experienced airman in flying overland, but any airman training in the British Isles will probably, on his first flight, fly over land and sea. Being trained on the Isle of Man, I saw during my first flights more water than land, more clouds than open skies. I had to adjust myself immediately, without any transition whatsoever, to all possible dangers. I did it, as I suppose most people do, by refusing to let my imagination run freely.

Finally, just before the end of 1943, a giant in the uniform of an air commodore handed me the single wing of an air gunner and the three stripes of a sergeant.

I was given a week's leave, and I spent it in London with relatives, whom I had at last traced there. A great-uncle of mine, on my mother's side, had come to the hospitable shores of Great Britain some sixty years earlier to escape serving in the czar's army at the height of the pogrom wave in Russia. He was no longer alive, but his wife, a tiny, indomitable, half-blind old lady, was still there to speak Yiddish to me and to talk of Wilno and Russia as if they were her real home. Their six children had all been born in the East End of London but had moved to the suburbs and South Kensington. One of the sons had died in the First World War for the country that had granted his father asylum. Two sons had married Christians, and their children neither were Jews nor looked Jewish. However, the lesson of the fall of German Jewry and the possibility of a Nazi invasion had made the first generation born in England more Jewish and more imaginative than they might otherwise have been, so when I turned up they gave me a very warm welcome. But even though they still knew a few words of Yiddish and their childhood in the East End of London acted as a link with a pattern of Jewish life long abandoned, I found very few points of contact. For instance, I was introduced to one who, having made it clear to me that there was as much difference between a British Jew and a non-British Jew as there was between Englishmen and all the other races, proceeded to tell me that all the evils of Europe were due to the French Revolution.

She certainly caught me unaware. Of course, I knew that there were people in France and elsewhere who held a similar view of European history. For one thing, all educated Polish anti-Semites professed to believe it. But that a Jew or Jewess, in the midst of Hitler's war, should have a quarrel with a revolution that gave his or her ancestors equal rights as human beings and citizens after some fifteen centuries of semislavery and debasement hurt me deeply.

She, however, found me without a sense of humor and incapable of understanding the fundamentally different nature of English Jewry. I found her views so unexpected that I did not even think of contradicting them. And so, instead of wasting my time trying to explain to her that we lived in the year 1943 and not in the early nineteenth century, I devoted my time to seeing London. And London at the end of 1943 provided in some ways the most stimulating company in the world. The bombs, and the invasion by innumerable foreign governments, newspapers, publishing houses, and aliens in uniform and civilian clothes, had turned London into a true cosmopolis. The bookshops and newspaper kiosks were full of publications discussing the origins of the war, condemning the pre-1939 world that had led to it, and outlining the shape of the brave new world that was to emerge after the defeat of Nazism. The streets were full of young men and women from every part of the globe, all of them apparently prepared to give their lives for the same cause. An amazing spectacle.

I reported to an Operational Training Unit in Yorkshire and discovered within the first few hours of my arrival that the three stripes on my sleeves had made an immense difference in my service life. In the first place, I was no longer marched about from one place to another but was allowed to walk at my own pace and almost in my own time. I no longer had to carry my own knife, spoon, and fork about and queue up for my food. Most important, I did not have to turn my lights out at ten o'clock just when I felt like reading and perhaps thinking a little, and was not even obliged to return to the camp by a certain hour. As well, the OTU was full of different nationalities: Canadians, Norwegians, Poles. And they got on together, thanks to the unobtrusive English genius for mixing people with actual fighting experience in with those who had none; the atmosphere of the

place was no longer that of a Boy Scout camp. All this made me feel that I
was in the finest fighting organization in the world.

After a few days came the teaming up. The idea—quite typical of the
RAF—was to allow the aircrew to choose their own mates. I had not
teamed up with another air gunner while I had been at the Air Gunnery
School and therefore had to wait for the last bomber crew to be constituted.
However, I found myself liking my mates as much as if I had selected them
myself.

The skipper was a short, fair Londoner, thirty-six years old, married
and a father of two children. He had several thousand hours of flying time
to his credit because he had been serving for some three years as a flying
instructor. My fellow gunner was an absolutely self-reliant, perky little fellow, and a very thoughtful husband. Having got together as a crew, we left
the OTU for a satellite station in Lincolnshire.

The prospect of flying produced in me a state of mental and physical tense-
ness. With my mind full of doubts and distrust, I was introduced to the
Wellington aboard which I was to become acquainted with the type of turret that I would use when flying Lancasters. Dispersed over a flying plain
swept by sleet, rain, and a northeast wind stood the inanimate bodies of
Wellingtons, looking like huge and brainless prehistoric mastodons. One
of them was having its engine tested. Vibrating and yet unable to leave the
earth, the bomber appeared to me a soulless monster provided with titanic
strength by man's brain and threatening to become its maker's master. On
that late winter afternoon I felt an irrational hatred for the plane.

A few days later we began to fly these aircraft. My turret was no longer
a ludicrous contraption reminding me of a Heath Robinson machine.
Moved by hydraulic power and electricity, it rotated and swung up and
down together with its four machine guns at the slightest pressure of my
fingers. However, the feeling of being trapped inside it was much stronger
than when I was flying in the semimanually operated turret of the Anson,
and I had an increased sensation of isolation. The Anson's turret was in the
center of the aircraft, almost within arm's reach of the rest of the crew. To
reach the rear turret of the Wellington one had to walk the length of the
airplane until, near its tail, one could advance only in a huddled posture.
Once in position, the rear gunner was some forty feet away from his near-

est companion, the wireless operator. Inside the turret, with an open per-
spective and without any protective armor, I felt at first like a bird in a cage:
exposed to every missile that came my way. Needless to say, this feeling of
nakedness was purely psychological. The crew inside the Wellington were
just as likely to get hit by bullets and shrapnel as the air gunner, for the geo-
detic structure of the bomber was simply covered with canvas.

We flew mostly in clouds during our training flights, rarely seeing the
sun, the earth, or the sea. My guns were worn-out Brownings, jamming
constantly and firing wide of the mark. They were, of course, veterans of
many operational flights and were given to us in order to cause as much
trouble as possible, so that we should learn to cope with them. However, as
I blamed my own lack of skill for their capricious behavior, I did not feel
very confident of my ability to defend my companions in case of an enemy
attack. This feeling of unworthiness, combined with a tautness of mind and
body, made those first flights unpleasant experiences.

Finally, we reached our night-flying stage. We began as was usual with
"circuits and bumps"—the practice of takeoffs and landings that were to
make our pilot accustomed to the surrealist aspect of the airfield and its
runways at night. The routine was to take on these flights only one gunner,
whose job was to keep a very close and necessary lookout for other aircraft
taking off, landing, or circling the aerodrome.

On the second or third night, when it was my turn to fly, my gunner
mate offered to take my place in order to have the following night free,
because he expected his wife's visit. Naturally I agreed and went off in
the early evening to the nearby town. When I returned at midnight to the
camp, I learned that one of the engines of the aircraft had cut out on the
takeoff as the Wellington was hardly five hundred feet above the ground.
The bomber crashed, and not a single member of the crew of five escaped
alive.

I went back to the parent station and waited for another crew to be
formed. After a demoralizing fortnight of inactivity, I was teamed up
again. But this new team as well was not to be, and I again spent a few
weeks doing nothing, sleeping late, and endeavoring without much success
to find relaxation in the feminine company afforded by the pubs of Don-
caster. Spring came in the meantime, and I began to feel as if the RAF had
completely forgotten my existence.

But it had not. It actually had a great surprise in store for me: I was posted to an Australian OTU in Derbyshire.

It was a wartime station but a very different affair from the Lincolnshire satellite. The Nissen huts stood in a meadow dotted with elms, oaks, and chestnut trees. The hedges were full of blackbirds and whitethorn. In the fields around the camp lazy cows lay in the shade of trees that seemed to have come out of a Constable painting.

I met a skipper who was the flight sergeant, and he introduced me to the other members of the crew. Clarence, the skipper, was in his early thirties, about six feet tall, blue-eyed, with fair hair receding from his forehead, and he spoke the kind of Australian English that makes one wonder whether the speaker's father was a Cockney and his mother a native of Birmingham. He came from Queensland, from a town famous for its rum, and in civilian life he was a garage proprietor. He was married and had two children.

Ben, the navigator, was of Irish descent, with brown eyes and black hair, of the same height as the pilot, and very slim. He was lively, quick-tempered, and friendly. A schoolteacher by profession, he held the rank of flying officer and was in his late twenties.

Cram, the bomb aimer, was not quite so slim as the navigator. Of remote Savoyard descent, he was probably the most Australian of the crew. Taciturn when sober, argumentative and noisy when drunk, he spoke the kind of educated Australian that betrays a slight American influence. By profession a chemist, he held the same rank as the navigator and was also in his late twenties.

Ron, the wireless operator, was the youngest of the crew—scarcely twenty years old. He was an inch or two short of six feet, slim as a girl, brown-eyed and black-haired, soft-spoken and reserved at first sight. He was a flight sergeant.

Arthur, my gunner mate, was of Irish descent and a Queenslander. About five feet eight, powerfully built, with too much of a stomach for his twenty-seven years, he had jet black hair, very dark eyes, and swarthy skin. He scowled at me as I was introduced to him and showed his displeasure at having me as his mate by avoiding any conversation with me for several weeks. I didn't miss much due to this initial animosity, for he spoke a very broad dialect, which occasionally I found unintelligible. He was also, I soon discovered, a heavy drinker, a Homeric blasphemer, and as big-hearted as a large, slightly fat, flap-eared gundog.

It was with admiration for the English genius for dealing with different people and the most opposed temperaments that I observed our English station commander. His rank was wing commander; he was in his early thirties, with a hundred operational flights to his credit; his face was adorned with a walrus mustache; he spoke with a definite Oxford accent; his peaked cap had lost its original shape and color; and he rode a bicycle.

He was never in anybody's way, and when occasionally he addressed us his short speeches usually ran as follows: "I saw the old man with the scrambled eggs yesterday. I did not visit him uninvited, as you may well have guessed. The group captain is not a very inquisitive individual, but his adjutant is a rather nosy type, and he keeps him unusually well informed of the doings of all his flock. As you know, you happen to be part of his flock, and he seems to know more about you than I do. Apparently two young and innocent damsels at Lichfield have been put in the family way by two very careless Aussies from this station. At the Hare & Hounds a couple of Yanks were beaten up by some unknown Australian aviators two nights ago. The SP's at Derby no longer have any fun in putting Australian aircrews on charges for being drunk, disorderly, and improperly dressed. The MO also tells me that you have been very stingy in your use of French letters, and that I may have to fly our Wimpeys myself for lack of aircrews if the VD rate continues to increase. Well, I think it is teatime now, so all I want to say is that, unless you want the Pommies at Group HQ to talk of 'those colonials, you know,' you had better be more careful. That's all."

We did our last training flight at the Australian OTU on the night of the invasion. We took off as the sun was setting and flew westward through the summer night over the Irish Sea, as if in its pursuit. As we turned back for our base, the sun was rising to greet us. To me in the rear turret it seemed as if the sun had never left us. At six o'clock in the morning, as we were having a breakfast of eggs and bacon, a WAAF waitress announced to us that the Allies' return to the Continent had begun.

We left friendly Derbyshire and traveled by train to Lincolnshire Conversion Unit, where the aircrews slept in overcrowded huts and ate in a

barnlike mess, while the ground crew senior NCOs lived in comfortable
billets and ate off snow-white tablecloths in their mess. Here our pilot was
to learn how to fly four-engined bombers, while our crew was to receive its
final member, the flight engineer.

The four-engined bombers were Halifaxes. They appeared very solid
and efficient when compared with the Wellingtons we had left at the OTU,
yet none of them inspired us with much confidence. The fact that every
time we took off and landed the gunners and the navigator had to leave
their positions and take up crash-landing stations in the center of the
bomber was not conducive to a tranquil state of mind. Yet Arthur and I had
grown sufficiently confident in the pilot's flying and fatalistic as to have had
to be reminded that we ought to be out of our turrets when taking off and
touching down.

Our flight engineer finally arrived, and after a few weeks of intensive
flying we left the Halifax Conversion Unit for a Lancaster finishing school.
The new station was also in Lincolnshire and far away from any towns.
Our living quarters were no longer overcrowded, and the aircrew person-
nel were not treated as wartime nuisances by resentful ground crew NCOs.
We recaptured a little of the happy atmosphere of the Australian OTU on
arrival at the new place, and our morale improved tremendously as soon as
we took off in our first Lancaster for the so-called familiarization flight. I
remember that flight because it was one of the few when I enjoyed being
among clouds and felt proud of man's ability to tear himself away from the
earth. From the midupper turret I could see the runway flee as soon as the
aircraft was allowed to race toward the horizon. The Lancaster gained
height quickly, and the pilot instructor then began to display the aero-
dynamic perfection of his aircraft. He feathered one engine, and I was
astounded and rather anxious about the immobile propeller. He then feathered the second, and finally the third, and we were flying on just a single
port engine. While I was tensely sitting in my turret and thinking that I
ought to be standing close to the escape hatch with my parachute on, the
instructor cheerfully talked of the inevitable loss of height involved in flying on one engine only. He then restarted the engines, and I breathed freely
again. After fooling about in the clouds, we landed almost as gracefully as
if flying an Anson.

While the British and American armies were preparing to break out of Normandy, we were flying day and night, becoming more and more a team, learning to use the latest radar devices, to land and take off at night, to shake off fighter aircraft by corkscrew maneuvers that made us all airsick, to use our turrets, and to be more cunning than the air that threatened us with insidious icing.

In the meantime, the great Soviet spring offensive had freed the remaining Soviet lands of all Nazi armies. A Red Army led by a Jew, General Chernyakhovsky, captured Wilno and struck at the citadel of German expansionism, against East Prussia itself. I read the news of Wilno's liberation in one of the morning papers while attending a lecture on the hydraulic systems of Fraser-Nash turrets. The lecturer saw me neglect the diagrams he had drawn on the blackboard and had me brought before the commanding officer on a charge of disrespect. I explained to the CO that I had waited to read news of Wilno's liberation for three very long years, and that I did not intend to be disrespectful to the flying officer, but of course I did not add that I felt I had waited in vain, that the liberation had come too late, much too late. He listened to my explanation in silence and told me that in the future I should not read newspapers when I was expected to pay attention to what the lecturer had to say. I saluted and left his office.

Our training was completed. Each of us had cost the British taxpayers some ten thousand pounds, "enough to send ten men to Oxford or Cambridge for three years," in the words of Sir Arthur Harris, commander in chief of Bomber Command. We had the conviction that we were the best-trained airmen in the world, yet in anticipation of the ultimate test, and with death in many shapes stalking at our side, we did not feel like bragging or defying chance.

BEING PUT TO THE TEST

WITHOUT ANY SPEECHES, seeing-off parades, or even an ordinary drinking bout to celebrate the great moment, we left the Lancaster finishing school and drove across the level countryside of Little Holland to our squadron at Elsham Wolds.

Once we arrived, we were separated: the pilot, navigator, and bomb aimer, being commissioned officers, were taken to their hut on a different site. In our own huts, having chosen our beds and emptied some of our kit bags, we had a wash; then we trundled off to the mess.

It was there that I realized for the first time the essentially different atmosphere of an operational station. Yes, in the dining hall the food was a little more copious than in other dining halls I had gone through, but the difference was not there; it was created by the subdued, almost monastic behavior of the aircrews. In that dining hall I discovered that living constantly in the company of death has a chastening effect. There was a certain gentleness in the voices and gestures of my companions; very little aggressiveness when speaking or queuing; a constant concentration on a few things, which resulted in absentmindedness; a taciturnity, which was broken only occasionally when discussing matters connected with flying; an attitude of surprising consideration for others; and a thoughtful way of doing the everyday things of life that might have made an outsider pause.

Almost as soon as we arrived at the squadron, its atmosphere got hold of us, and after a few days I no longer noticed the idiosyncrasies of my new companions and took for granted the long silences, unuttered hopes, clumsy curses, and swearwords that were meant to replace terms such as *death, terror, determination,* and *hope.*

We were given our Lancaster. Complete with its radar equipment, the bomber was worth some fifty thousand pounds—enough to make us reflect on how much this country at war was ready to trust us. We became familiar with it by carrying out cross-country flights, takeoffs, landings, and bombing runs, as well as by testing its turrets and brand-new Browning machine guns over the sea. We finally decided that Arthur would be the rear gunner and I the midupper. Then, within a week of our arrival, we saw a battle order on the notice board in our mess containing our names.

On September 8, 1944, the loudspeaker in our hut awoke us in the early hours of the morning. We dressed and left the hut without speaking, our sleepiness gone but not yet fully awake. Outside it was still dark, and the stars twinkled in a sky that awaited the dawn. We took a shortcut across a wood and fields, scaring some sleepy ponies, who raced away as far as the hedges would allow them.

The mess was full of lights and smells. The cooks were ready to serve us with tremendous mugs of tea, platefuls of porridge, and generous helpings of bacon and eggs. They had had much less sleep than we but waited on us like loving and doting mothers. We ate our food and drank cups of tea, watched the hands of the clock hanging over the door and, when the time came, scrambled into buses waiting outside to convey us to the airfield.

The briefings were held in a specially designed hut, which was, barring the hangars, the biggest construction on our station. We had to show our identity cards to an RAF policeman at its entrance, which was completely covered by a map of the British Isles and the European Continent as far east as Poland. We could see two ribbons stretching over the map from a point indicating our squadron's route, somewhere deep in the heart of Nazi Europe. One ribbon marked the outward course and the other the return. It looked as if our operation would have Berlin as its target.

The ribbons were not meant to reach so far into Hitler's fortress; it was somebody's idea of a joke to make the newcomers and pessimists quake on entering the briefing hall by stretching the ribbons as far as they would go. Before we found our seats, they were considerably shortened, to the relief of all.

There were sufficient chairs in the room to seat thirty crews. The custom was for a crew on their first "op" to sit in the front row. As a crew's number of ops increased, the distance between their seats and the map grew accordingly until, on their thirtieth operation, they occupied the back row. Being on our first operational flight, we walked up the narrow passage between the chairs and sat down in front of the dais that touched the map-covered wall.

Somebody shouted "Attention!" We got up and waited for the procession, consisting of our group captain, wing commander, and several other officers, to take their seats on the dais. When they had sat down, we were allowed to follow their example, and without any preliminaries the meteorological officer unrolled his chart and began to speak about pressures, cyclones, anticyclones, and depressions. When he finished I still did not know if the weather on our route was expected to be favorable or not.

The ribbons connected our station with Le Havre. The intelligence officer followed the weatherman and told us why we were flying there. By denying the Channel harbors to the Allies, the Germans hoped to stop the drive of our armies toward Germany's borders. To capture the ports in the traditional way, by using infantry and artillery, would cost us much time and much blood. It was therefore left to Bomber Command to prove its ability to reduce fortresses by precision bombing. We had to bomb visually and from very low altitudes in order not to hit the Canadians, who were frightfully close to the target area. On no account were we to get rid of our bombs without having managed to identify our targets by sight.

The flying control officer followed and explained how he expected thirty-three Lancasters, carrying five tons of bombs apiece, to take off within a minute of one another. As he finished our wing commander got up and said, "Your all-up weight—sixty thousand and so many pounds. You carry so many gallons of fuel; that gives you so many flying hours. You ought to be all right should the weather close in and you have to be diverted. Good luck."

He had to his credit 130 operations, and it was only his rank that prevented him from flying on every operation his squadron was engaged in. It was said of him that he refused promotion to the rank of group captain because that would mean having to abandon his squadron.

The last man to speak was the group captain, who used the language of a scoutmaster addressing a gathering of Cubs, and its very silliness made me hesitate for a while in my judgment of the man. Perhaps, I told myself, there was some secret significance in his words, hidden to my un-English eyes and ears. He finally concluded by wishing us "Good hunting, gentlemen."

We quickly left the briefing hall and made for the dressing hut. On the way there I began to learn in earnest why an air gunner's lot was considered the least enviable of all flying duties. While the navigator and wireless operator, sitting in sheltered and heated compartments, did not even bother to wear flying boots, and the pilot, bomb aimer, and flight engineer had to put on only their heavy sweaters, socks, and flying boots, we, the air gunners, had to wear so many clothes that we needed almost as much time to get into them as a medieval knight to don his armor. The time, however, was rarely available, because each crew tried to be first in the scramble for transport to the planes, so as to have more time for testing the aircraft before taking off.

From the drying room Arthur and I obtained our flying suits, harnesses, and parachutes; out of the lockers we fished vests, long pants, socks, sweaters, and stockings. We put on two or three pairs of socks, a pair of long hand-knitted stockings, our everyday shirt, pullover, and battle dress, a hand-knitted sweater, an electrically heated suit, a windproof canvas overall, and a pair of sheepskin-lined flying boots. On top of all these layers of wool and cotton we strapped our parachute harnesses and Mae West jackets, since we were as likely to come down over the sea as over land. Later on, when seated in our turrets, we finished dressing by encasing our hands in two pairs of white silk gloves, woolen gloves, a pair of woolen mittens, a pair of black electrically wired gloves, and an elbow-length pair of leather gauntlets.

No doubt we had dressed too warmly on our first operational flight. We could have done with fewer pants and vests because we were flying by day and never higher than ten thousand feet. But there were operations later on—mostly night flights—when, despite all the weight of clothes and heat provided by electricity, we still felt uncomfortably cold in our turrets.

Once in the Lancaster we had to place the machine guns in their cradles, load them, and then test the sights and turrets as soon as the pilot was ready to start the engines. This was never an easy piece of work in the cramped conditions of the turret for people as heavily dressed as we were. When we had finished, we were bathed in sweat and felt the weight of our clothing as if it were made of lead. In the meantime, the engines, the compass, and the intercommunication telephone had been checked and found to be in order, and a quarter of an hour remained before takeoff. We clambered out of the bomber, smoked our last cigarettes, relieved our bladders, and spoke about everything except the flight ahead of us. When some officers stopped to ask us whether we had any trouble with our aircraft, we replied jokingly, stamped our unfinished cigarettes into the grass, and climbed back into the plane.

My own thoughts did not reach far beyond the immediate present, which consisted of the fact that I was sitting on five tons of bombs, and that it was the first time in his life that our pilot was going to take off in an aircraft so heavily and dangerously laden.

Finally came our turn to taxi out of our bay to the runway. I could see the WAAFs on the roof of the sick-quarters building wave to the roaring monsters that became so graceful and maneuverable once they left the earth. Then a green light beckoned us, the brakes were off, the engines roared at full throttle, the boost was all in the engineer's hands, and the runway disappeared as quickly as if it were a ribbon rolled up by some gigantic machine. We were off and free of the earth.

We climbed through clouds to open blue skies. I was surprised that only now and then could I catch sight of another Lancaster, although more than two hundred four-engined bombers had already taken off or were taking off, all of them bound on the same mission. I began to grasp the highly complicated and scientific process of getting hundreds of aircraft into the air at almost the same time over a country so small as England. Slowly the four-dimensional world was becoming a reality to my earthbound and unmathematical mind.

We flew over wide banks of clouds that completely excluded any glimpse of the earth. Above us a cerulean sky was illuminated by a dazzling sun. Between ten and twenty thousand feet over us, silvery Flying Fortresses and Liberators were maneuvering to gain height and combine into box formations. Several times we ran into the slipstream of some invisible aircraft, and for moments that seemed like minutes our Lancaster behaved as if the only force it obeyed was gravitation. Our pilot had not yet learned to deal with the effects of slipstream, and instead of putting the aircraft's nose down and getting clear of it by gaining extra speed, he tried to fight it. We, in our two turrets, had not learned to follow the plane's movements. Instead of letting ourselves go, we tried to cheat the effects of the bomber's fall in the void left by another aircraft's wake by swinging our turrets in the opposite direction. The result was that we experienced the effects of the slipstream twice; once when our Lancaster actually encountered it, and again when our skipper regained control of the aircraft. Those split seconds when the Lancaster appeared to be controlled only by physical laws threw me into a cold sweat. There was no other noise aboard the bomber except the roar of the engines and the few words uttered by the navigator as he was giving the course to be followed together with the pilot's plaintive falsetto asking us, the gunners, whether we were all right.

Suddenly the bomb aimer's voice announced that we were over the Channel. I looked out, but the cloud banks below us allowed no glimpse of the sea. Then the noise of our engines grew into a mighty roar and, as if by magic, we found ourselves in the company of some two hundred Lancasters, filling the skies as far as the horizon, progressing like a disordered and undisciplined horde at varying heights and speeds, but actually making for the same point without having to follow a leading aircraft.

We were over the target area before I fully realized the significance of the bomb aimer's announcement, "Bomb doors open." I had no time to think about the target, because our whole fleet of bombers had become engulfed in clouds, and the security of our Lancaster depended on whether we, the two gunners, could warn the pilot in time of any aircraft that might cross our track. We came down to six thousand feet—almost within reach of the enemy's machine guns—but all we could see wherever a break in the clouds occurred were other Lancasters. We circled the target three times before the bomb aimer chanted out, "Bomb doors closed," and in a matter of seconds we were out of the terrible melee without having dropped our load.

For the first time, I realized the eerie nature of a bomber crew's psychological experiences. A few seconds earlier we had been threatened by dangers as great as a man can find in war, and now we were flying through a quiet, peaceful sky, with England's shores almost in view and nothing but our memories to remind us of what we had felt and seen.

We landed at our airfield in time for lunch. The ground crew received us with almost as big a show of joy as a dog would on the return of his master. They had not slept since the night before, having worked around the clock to make our bomber ready for the operation, but they were all there even before the propellers of our Lancaster stopped rotation.

A bus collected us and took us to the briefing hut, now turned into an interrogation center, where coffee and rum were waiting. Having finished with the intelligence officers, we undressed, talking little about the flight; only Ben, our flight navigator, became involved in a hot argument on some obtuse point of navigation with a Canadian colleague. We then made for the mess, ate our lunch, criticized the pudding, and decided what we would do in the evening, after which we hurried into the bar, made for the armchairs nearest to the fireplace, and dozed for an hour or more.

Such was the end of our first op. Two days later, on September 10, we returned to Le Havre, in daylight again, to bomb the Germans who still held out there. This time we dropped our bombs and left the unlucky harbor under a mushroom of fire and smoke. But only after Bomber Command had carried out seven raids in one week, and dropped 9,850 tons of bombs on the unfortunate port, did the Germans surrender Le Havre. We then flew by day against Sangatte, and when that town fell into the hands of the Canadians, we turned to Cape Gris-Nez and Calais.

Calais fell only after repeated air assaults. Our squadron took part in two of them, and we managed to get rid of our bombs only after a great deal of trouble. As in the case of Le Havre, our troops were just fifteen hundred yards away from the target area, so the bomb aimers had to identify their targets with their naked eyes before engaging on their bombing runs. During both raids there were low clouds. The absence of an antiair-craft barrage made some crews forget that they were flying four-engined bombers and, in their eagerness to get rid of their bomb loads, some skip-pers brought their aircraft down to three thousand feet, where the Lancas-ters met with heavy machine-gun fire. A Canadian midupper gunner, an old pal of Arthur's, was hit by several bullets while in his turret and died a few days later in the hospital. When a few months after this raid we happened to land on a U.S. Air Force airfield, we told our American colleagues of the height from which we had bombed Calais. We could tell by their silence that they took us for shameless liars, which was understandable consider-ing that their own bombing height was usually between twenty-five and thirty-five thousand feet.

In RAF jargon the first six operations were "pieces of cake." Carried out in daytime against Channel harbors that had practically no antiaircraft artillery, they were as safe as bombing raids could be. There was no threat from fighters, so that we, the air gunners, felt like superfluous passengers, and we must all have been secretly happy at the prospect of doing most of our early flights against such easy targets.

Yet, though my own instinct of self-preservation was healthy enough to have gone through so much in order to join the RAF Bomber Command, to spend my operational tour as a passenger in an uncomfortable turret appeared to be a supreme piece of irony. It also struck me as trickery, because it would allow me to falsely claim the credit for having risked my life at a time when my own family had known every possible terror and death itself. Luckily, these conflicts between one's sense of duty and one's instinct for self-preservation are in wartime settled by other forces beyond one's control.

The Channel harbors either surrendered or were left alone, and our squadron soon found itself engaged in the bomber offensive against Ger-many's synthetic oil refineries.

On September 23, 1944, we experienced our first night operation. Neuss was an important industrial and railway center lying less than ten miles west of Düsseldorf, and our goal was the local synthetic oil plant, defended by guns and an artificial smoke screen and the constant industrial haze that covers the Ruhr. Some three hundred Lancasters and Halifaxes had been detailed.

The briefing followed the usual pattern. The meteorological officer forecast cloudy skies with occasional breaks, strong winds, and the danger of icing. The gunnery leader told us to look out for enemy fighters, both single- and twin-engined. He also warned us that there would be a few twin-engined Mosquitoes in our bombers' stream so that we should make quite sure of what we saw before we opened fire.

We were among the last aircraft to take off and could see the Lancasters becoming airborne against an ominous background of blood-colored clouds that concealed the sinking sun. One after the other, at minute intervals, they rose like some winged antediluvian monsters long extinct on this globe, to disappear into the limbo from which they had momentarily emerged.

Our turn came. I experienced the usual moments of tension as we took off, although by now I had become quite used to the idea of sitting on our load of bombs, and my confidence in the skipper had grown as strong as faith in another man's skill and self-control can grow. As soon as we had left the earth, we plugged our masks to the oxygen supply, for we were to fly at over twenty thousand feet. The setting sun illuminated the western horizon and gave it a baleful and threatening appearance; darkness gathered all around us; the regular rhythm of the engines was like the collective beat of all our single hearts. The pilot switched on the red and green navigation lights to warn the other aircraft turning like ourselves to gain height, but not one was in view.

Inside the aircraft the roar of the engines was our common pulse, the intercom our only means of contact. Occasionally the navigator's voice gave the pilot the course to be followed, and the skipper's voice repeated his words. Then silence would fall again; we, the gunners, without rudders to handle, dials to watch, radar screens to decipher, radio signals to listen to, with the sky and clouds all around us, were left mercilessly exposed to our thoughts and imaginations.

We were no longer quite alone in the skies, and we could see an ever-increasing number of green and red lights betraying the whereabouts of our companions. We were glad to have company, yet were afraid of it, and every free pair of eyes was on the lookout to warn our skippers of any bomber that appeared to fly as if its pilot had not noticed us. Unused to darkness, we saw danger everywhere, because there were always a few pilots unable to keep a level course. Instead of flying straight and at a determined height, they zigzagged through the sky, to appear from the most unexpected quarters.

At the meeting point over Reading, the clouds were many thousands of feet below us. In the deceptive dusk of the open sky, hundreds of green and red lights appeared suddenly as if by some feat of magic. Within sight of one another we flew across the Channel and northern France. This progress in visible company was the most cheerful part of any night operation. Then Ben's snappy voice announced the end of the lights. Like some cosmic catastrophe, the whole constellation suddenly disappeared from the vastness of the sky, and a feeling of frightening solitude gripped our hearts. For some time after the sudden extinction of lights I would feel as wretched and sad as when my first adolescent love affair had come to an end—utterly alone and forsaken.

Now came the time to concentrate on only one thing: the darkness outside the transparent cupola of my turret. I repeated in my mind again and again the fact that my right was the bomber's port and my left its starboard, for I was afraid that if I suddenly had to warn the skipper of the presence of an enemy fighter, I might fall into the lifelong reflex of saying the opposite. I worried about my ability to tell one aircraft from another and even to recognize the enemy in the opaqueness of cloud and night. At the same time I realized that I was in a much more fortunate position than the gunners who had flown in bombers only a few months earlier, before the invasion of Western Europe by our armies, who had had to fly in darkness almost all the time from the moment of takeoff; as soon as they had crossed Britain's coast they had been in hostile skies, and their approach had been known to the enemy for hours, thanks to radar warning systems. Tonight, with the German radar defenses dislocated, the Luftwaffe would probably not learn of our approach until our arrival over the target.

The bomb aimer, helped by the engineer, began to throw out packets of long, metal-covered strips of paper, which the RAF knew as window. Each of these strips had the same effect on the enemy's radar screens as if it were an aircraft; three hundred Lancasters and Halifaxes showering window in their flight created almost insuperable difficulties for the enemy's disorganized antiaircraft and night-fighter defenses.

As a result of relentless staring into the night, I began to see things. On several occasions I imagined that I saw aircraft dangerously close and was on the point of ordering the skipper to take evasive action. However, I was afraid of being considered panicky and delayed giving the order long enough to lose sight of what I'd thought to be an aircraft. We were already over Germany when, against the background of a cloud, I saw on our port astern the silhouette of an aircraft that I took to be twin-engined. I was going to chant out, "Midupper to skipper: enemy aircraft port quarter up: corkscrew port go!" when I lost sight of it.

I decided that another pair of eyes would be helpful and asked Ronnie, the wireless operator, to look out as well. When, sometime later, I got a glimpse of the same suspect silhouette, he saw it too. I could see the shadow a little more clearly now, and I was not at all sure whether it was not a four-engined aircraft after all. But when it came too close, I decided to take no chances and told the pilot to do a corkscrew to port.

He performed a model corkscrew in spite of the aircraft's load, dived the bomber some eight hundred feet to the port, changed course, climbed eight hundred feet to the port, rolled, climbed eight hundred feet to the starboard, changed course, dived eight hundred feet to the starboard, rolled, and brought us back to our track. There was no sight of the suspect aircraft, and no more evasive action had to be taken.

The bomb aimer had meanwhile left the business of dropping window completely in the hands of the flight engineer and returned to his bomb sights. I knew now that we were approaching the target. Then I heard the navigator give the bomb aimer his final directions, including the latest "gen" on the winds in the area.

There were no searchlights or explosions to announce the target, but we could see the extraordinary brilliance of the target markers, dropped by our Pathfinder squadrons, several minutes before engaging on our bombing run. I barely glimpsed the fantastic sky illumination, despite the vantage point afforded me by my turret, because I now had to scan the darkness for possible fighters, and for our own bombers, which might fly above us and unload their cargo of death in our path.

The moment of supreme excitement came: the bomb aimer was now directing the aircraft's flight. Cram, lying on his stomach and peering through his bomb sights, was a very different man from the lackadaisical and sleepy individual we knew on the ground. His voice absolutely clear and firm, he instructed the pilot in almost coaxing terms: "Right-right . . . that's fine . . . a little to the left . . . keep level—keep level! That's fine, Clary. . . . A little to the right. . . . Bomb doors open!"

"Bomb doors open," Clary's plaintive voice confirmed the order.

"Bombs going—going—going . . ." the bomb aimer chanted in his clear voice. "Bombs gone! Close bomb doors!" And in a very different tone of voice Cram concluded, "Get out of here!"

Our skipper did. He put the bomber's nose down and cleared out. As he turned the aircraft on its homeward course, I could see a mushroom of fire and smoke rise over Neuss. Yet the sight of devastation was less striking than the wonderful brilliance of the green and red target markers.

I was more bewildered than actually frightened, for it needed an effort of imagination to realize that we were in mortal danger. The night hid the explosions of shells aimed at us; the trace of the light antiaircraft guns stopped several thousand feet below us and looked like elaborate fireworks; a conscious exertion was necessary on my part to translate this cacophony of lights into a concert of death, for somehow it was difficult to imagine the fury of war without sound.

The worst thing about night operations was the fact that the bombing was only an anticlimax. After we had released our bomb load, we still had to fly through the frightening shadows of night and expect the worst.

With a favorable tailwind to help us, we traveled at more than three hundred miles an hour and were soon crossing the coast of Flanders. With solicitude for us and defiance to our adversaries in the air, England was greeting us with several pillars of light formed by massed batteries of searchlights, which pointed at a slight angle into the emptiness of the nocturnal sky and invited those whose aircraft had been damaged to crash-land on the gigantic runways of Manston. We could see those columns of light when still over the Continent, and I, for one, felt at their sight what a very patriotic Englishman returning from a long absence abroad is supposed to feel at the sight of the cliffs of Dover.

· · ·

Thus passed the month of September. Operations now became numbers in my logbook, but I dared not yet subtract them from the total I had to fly. After the fright and excitement of the first operations, I now experienced the resignation that came with the knowledge of what I had to face. From odd words, remarks, and reflections made by comrades, I understood that their feelings resembled mine.

Because of frequent flying we rarely left the station in the evenings. Apart from a solitary pub some four miles away from our airfield, there was nowhere to go. We spent most of our free evenings at the mess, the local YMCA club, or the station cinema. The result was that at times a certain conscious effort of imagination was required in order to realize where one was—at a bomber station engaged in the task of "emasculating" German cities and killing German men, women, and children inhabiting them, and not a peacetime RAF establishment with its routine training flights and routine amusements.

Absurdities and incongruities struck me as being the most important characteristics of a bomber crew's existence. While flying there was a sudden transition from being alone in the sky to being shot at, dazed by searchlights, and calculating how to cause as much death and destruction as one's load of bombs could wreak. When safely back at the base, the sensations one experienced in the air became inexpressible and unreal in the face of the orderliness and safety that prevailed. Within the space of hours we were hurled from safety and comfort into hideous dangers, then brought down to safety again without any stage in between. We were given no time and no chance to adapt ourselves to whatever state we happened to be in. Those among us endowed with some imagination suffered the most. Our only defense was not to think.

HALFWAY THROUGH

D URING OCTOBER 1944 the First Bomber Group, to which our squadron belonged, took part in the greatest day raids the RAF undertook in the Second World War. With the western approaches to the Reich itself in the hands of the Allies, the German radar system still largely ineffective, and the Luftwaffe fighter squadrons deprived of experienced pilots, aircraft, and, above all, fuel, Air Chief Marshal Harris threw his Bomber Command into daylight operations over Hitler's empire. The target of the first great diurnal operation was Emmerich, on the right bank of the Rhine.

It was chosen as target for more than five hundred Lancasters and Halifaxes because of its importance as a railway junction. As the Arnhem tragedy was approaching its end and the army unable to help the encircled paratroopers, the Royal Air Force was called on to try to stop the flow of German reinforcements to the Nijmegen bridges. Harris's response was generous and wholehearted.

On October 7 our group captain told us that he would fly with us on the mission and that he expected his two squadrons to "put on a bang-on show." Then the intelligence officer took over and told us that our bombing height would be between 8,500 and 9,500 feet; that concentration in attack would be our main defense; that 250 Spitfires would cover our unwieldy stream on the way to the target; and that another 250 Mustangs, including a famous Polish fighter wing, would be waiting for our 500-odd bombers over the target itself.

We left the briefing hall all very much aware that Harris had taken to daylight operations with a vengeance. The Americans, provided with an armament at least twice as effective as ours in striking power and range, flew by day at heights varying between 25,000 and 30,000 feet. We, when flying at night, kept to altitudes ranging between 19,000 and 24,000 feet. Armed with machine guns whose maximum range was 600 yards, and flying in an unwieldy stream some two miles wide and five miles long, we certainly felt that we were taking off to face the unknown. Yet our apprehensions were balanced by our pride in doing what no other heavy bombers had done, and by our conviction that we were the men to do it.

We had clouds above and below us all the way across the North Sea. I looked out keenly for our fighters but never saw one. They flew many thousand feet above us watching for any Messerschmitts and Focke-Wulfs that might try to swoop down through the cover of cloud banks. We never had a glimpse of the sea, and the first sign that we had flown over it was the navigator's announcement: "The Hague is to our port."

"Antiaircraft barrage ahead," Cram sang out. I swung my turret 180 degrees and had a good look at the horizon toward which we were flying. It reminded me of old wallpaper seen in Polish provincial houses: so stained that you could not recognize its original color and pattern. It was the first heavy antiaircraft barrage we had seen so far during our operations, for at night we could sight only tracer fired by light ack-ack guns. From the distance it seemed to me that we could never penetrate the barrage without being hit. I remembered the German bomber diving to meet the shell that turned it into a ball of fire over Boulogne. I swung the turret back again and decided not to look. It was my business to scan not the horizon toward which we were flying but the skies nearby.

The barrage did not look quite so bad as we came closer to it. It had a few gaps, and our skipper took advantage of one, so that again we flew between a ceiling and floor of clouds, Lancasters and Halifaxes filling the air as far as the horizon, an uncanny silence accompanying the puffs of smoke in the sky. The clouds suddenly disappeared, giving way to the most amazing aerial view of the earth that I was to see as an airman.

Astern of our aircraft the earth rose at almost right angles to the horizon, above which a gray wall blended imperceptibly with the pale blue sky. That the sea should be higher than the earth was astonishing; I felt as if I were watching the emergence of the dry parts of our globe at the time when the waters had first receded, and I repeated aloud to myself the word "Netherlands" as if I had never pronounced it before. At each repetition of the name, the view of the rivers running up to the sky to meet the gray wall of sea became more comprehensible.

We were again in overcast skies, sandwiched between two layers of cloud many thousands of feet apart. Excitement rose; I could see the turrets and their guns on all the aircraft within sight revolve in the same tense manner as my own. Then the shapeless stream of bombers, wide as the mightiest river, suddenly began to narrow, contract, and shorten; all the Lancasters and Halifaxes appeared to be making for the same spot. The target was ahead, but now was the time for me, as midupper gunner, to watch the skies above and nothing else.

I could hear the pilot tell the navigator that he was going to climb an extra thousand feet, which meant that we would bomb from a height of 9,500 feet. I heard the navigator's dissatisfied reply and the bomb aimer taking command. We were on our bombing run.

Cram's voice was as clear as usual. I heard him say, "Steady, steady . . . right, right . . . keep it up . . . lovely," and then our aircraft dived violently and the pilot screamed, "Blast that bastard!" I later learned that a Lancaster had opened its bomb doors on top of us and the skipper had noticed it only just in time to avoid a shower of incendiary bombs. The bomb aimer's voice resounded again as steadily as if we were on a training flight: "We'll have to orbit."

That meant circling the target and coming back to our original bombing course. Clary's reply was an angry "Hell, we won't!" and he swung the bomber as if it were a fighter and not a heavy monster carrying five tons of bombs in its capacious belly. Next I heard the bomb aimer sing out, "Bomb doors open!" and the Lancaster leapt in the air to Cram's chant: "Bombs going, going, going . . . bombs gone! Close the bomb doors! Bomb doors closed. Get out of here, Clary!"

The rear gunner yelled at that moment: "Port quarter up one Lancaster on fire one, two, three, four bailing out!"

The navigator entered the time and position of the unknown Lancaster's end and the number of survivors.

I kept looking up for possible fighters. I saw none, but I perceived a lonely parachute descend through the clouds on our starboard quarter.

The retinas of our eyes still preserved the images of explosions and our ears still resounded with the words of battle, but we were already in peaceful skies. As we turned westward, I could see the Rhine, a forest on one of its banks, and a pitiful little town with a reversed pyramid of smoke rising above it. A few minutes later even this reminder of the battle disappeared and we were over Belgium.

The sky was again clear, and from our height we could gaze at almost the whole of Belgian Flanders. A slight mist covered the cities and villages; the belfries and steeples of the Flemish cathedrals stood out in that plain like solitary mountains. We very clearly saw the belfry of Malines Cathedral and, in the distant mist, the cupola of the Palais de Justice of Brussels, while to our port we could admire the fjordlike estuaries of the Schelde, and Antwerp trying to defeat German flying bombs with an antiaircraft barrage.

We could not land at our own base because of fog and instead were directed to the Lancaster Finishing School airfield, which we had left not so many months ago and where we were treated like heroes by the WAAF waitresses in the mess. We packed the local pub as soon as it opened, and drank and sang till closing time with the gusto of men who had to loosen their taut nerves and in some way show their joy at having stayed alive.

Despite unfavorable weather, "Bomber" Harris continued all through October to throw his squadrons against the already ravaged Reich in support of the Allied ground forces. We revisited the Ruhr by day to bomb the ruins of Essen and by night to spread the devastation of Cologne. Our force was never below five hundred bombers and occasionally amounted to one thousand. Our squadron was also assigned the task of breaching the seawalls of Walcheren, the Dutch island whose continued German occupation denied the use of Antwerp to our needy armies.

To revisit the "Happy Valley" by day at the cost of losses that amounted to one percent of the total bomber force engaged was an occasion to make one think of the lads and men who had flown over this hazy industrial landscape a year or two earlier and who, in their thousands, had been burned alive, torn to pieces by shells, reduced to atoms by their exploding aircraft, or hurled through space to destruction. Whenever I felt frightened in the face of a barrage, I thought of my family's fate and of my predecessors in the air assaults against the Ruhr, and I refused to give ground to my fears.

The raids that fall, directed at built-up areas, could not but make one reflect on their justification. My own thoughts, however, were without pity and remorse. I did not think that our so-called strategic bombing was militarily justified, nor did I believe that bombing built-up areas was as fair a way of warfare as that in which the Red Army was engaged in the East. But I believed that the Germans as a nation did not deserve the slightest pity, because they could never be sufficiently punished for the crimes committed by so many of them or in their name. The majority of them followed Hitler's leadership obediently and enthusiastically, because during the first two years of the war he had managed to convince them that by the judicious use of air terror and panzer divisions he could win the world for them at a ridiculously low cost in German blood. I did not believe it possible to make Hitler's followers see that a war of conquest was an unpardonable crime, but I thought it a feasible proposition to make the Germans realize that war does not pay. To achieve this aim, ever-present monuments of horror and destruction had to be piled up throughout the Reich to make the average German man and woman see the price of wanting to "live dangerously" at the expense of others. Even the carnage of millions of German fighting men on the Russian front could not teach the German people as a whole that lesson, because soldiers who fall in foreign lands easily appear as heroes, and not the dupes or murderers they actually are.

Above all I saw in the indiscriminate bombing of German cities the only means of making certain that Germany would not win the war. I feared that when the last shot had been fired and the Allied flags had been hoisted over the Brandenburg Gate in Berlin, it would be found that for every dead German there were ten dead non-Germans, so that recovery would come sooner to the predatory race than to its victims. I doubted whether the Soviet Union would be permitted to mete out punishment to all the Nazi and aggressive elements in the German people in the name of

Hitler's victims; I was dubious about the very ability of the British and American people to understand the enormity of Germany's crimes, and about their determination to prevent a repetition of them. I therefore saw in the ravaged cities of Germany the only guarantee that another aggressive Reich would not be building yet another formidable war machine within the period of my own liability to further military service.

The consciences of the men flying British and American bombers could have easily been set at rest had they known the harvest of their work. At the cost of some 80,000 aircrew killed, some 350,000 German women, children, and men were killed, according to German sources. At the cost of only a few hundred criminals and paranoiacs, Nazi Germany murdered half a million innocent human beings in the ghetto of Warsaw alone.

THE ULTIMATE TEST

B Y THE END OF 1944 we had to our credit an average of twenty-one
operational flights. We were now seated in the last rows when we
attended a briefing, and had lost our defiant attitude to the dangers of our
calling; we were filled with superstitious fears and premonitions, which of
course we rarely, if ever, disclosed to one another.

Having begun our operational tour against easy targets, we now found
ourselves detailed for raids whose average duration was eight hours. The
Germans had in the meantime managed to reorganize their radar-warning
system to some extent, and their night fighters became somewhat of a
problem again. For eight or even ten hours at a stretch there was no rest, no
possible letup for the gunners in their turrets scanning the night around
them in search of aircraft and trying to guess whether the sudden patches of
lights might be fighter flares.

At that advanced stage of our tour, Cram, the bomb aimer, began to ask
me before each raid for my opinion on the dangers we were likely to
encounter. He somehow imagined that, because of my knowledge of Germany's geography, I could foretell to some definite degree the movements
of Hitler's night fighters, although it is also possible that he simply wanted
to hear the expression of another man's optimism. Whatever his motives, I

felt flattered by his confidence and responded by being moderately confident in my calculations.

Whatever his inner anxieties, Cram certainly did not show any sign of
them while flying. On our twenty-second raid, with Nuremberg as our target, our starboard outer engine began to spill sparks while we were still
more than an hour's flying time from our destination. The flight engineer
decided to feather the propeller in order to prevent the engine from catching fire, and we continued our flight on three engines. We progressed quite
well without the fourth engine but were unable to climb above fifteen thousand feet.

To make matters worse, we arrived over Nuremberg a minute too early.
Our Pathfinder squadrons had not yet dropped their markers, so if our
bomb aimer got rid of his bombs, the explosions and conflagration caused
by them might be taken by the main force for the work of the Pathfinders
and be bombed accordingly. An error of that kind could, of course, lead to
the operation being a total failure.

For some obscure reason—possibly because military transport was
crossing the city—Nuremberg was not blacked out. There were no searchlights and antiaircraft guns to greet our early arrival. The navigator stated
peevishly that we were a minute too early, and the bomb aimer calmly
announced that the skipper would have to orbit the target.

Without a word of protest the pilot circled the city. As we were hurrying back to our bombing course, the Pathfinder squadrons dropped their
fireworks and the witches' Sabbath opened up. The enemy's light antiaircraft guns, reaching to about a thousand feet beneath us, turned the sky
directly below us into a carpet of tracer explosions. The Germans' heavy
antiaircraft guns, firing shells that exploded some five thousand feet above,
where we should have been, did not bother us. But from my midupper turret position, I could see all too well our own bombers, many right on top of
us, getting rid of their loads of high explosives and hundreds of incendiary
bombs.

Some twenty minutes after leaving the target area, our bomb aimer discovered that one of his five-hundred-pounders had refused to follow its
companions on their fall over Nuremberg. It was, of course, unfused and
therefore only moderately dangerous, yet the prospect of keeping it in our

Lancaster's hold did not appeal to a single member of our crew. The skipper made this feeling clear by telling Cram to get rid of it on the spot.

"But you can't drop it anywhere," the bomb aimer replied. "It might fall on some town or village and hit some poor sleeping buggers." He consulted the navigator as to the kind of country we were flying over and only then got rid of the awkward bomb.

Flying on three engines, we could not keep up with the main stream. That spelled increased danger, because our isolated position in the sky allowed the enemy's radar stations to plot our course much more easily than would have been the case if our aircraft had been part of a pack of five hundred. Flying on three engines also signified that, in case of attack by night fighters, we would not have recourse to our main weapon of defense: evasive action in the form of corkscrews.

No wonder that I saw the friendly pillars of light over Manston with a feeling of profound relief.

On approaching our base we saw a bright conflagration on the ground accompanied by continuous small explosions. Our pilot was already speaking to our airfield's flying control and asking for landing priority on account of our dead engine, and when he was told to fly over the blaze so that our navigator could get the exact position, Clary carried out the order without a murmur, then landed almost as perfectly as if he had four propellers to give him equilibrium and braking power.

We learned that we had landed half an hour behind the last straggler, and that we had already been regarded as missing. We also learned that the conflagration was due to two Lancasters having collided in the air. Both belonged to different bases—neither to our own squadron—and had been circling their respective airfields waiting for their turn to land when the disaster occurred.

To have been lucky enough to reach one's target, to bomb it, and then to make one's way safely back to the sky over one's own airfield only to meet one's end in such a manner appeared to us particularly cruel and senseless.

The Nuremberg raid, carried out on January 1, ushered in the new year. Only two more operational flights of importance remain to be described.

My twenty-fourth raid was against Merseburg again and lasted over
eight hours. We bombed the fires, which had been started by the preceding
waves of bombers, from our maximum height of a little over 22,000 feet.
On our return flight the night was starless, cloudy, but not too dark. That
made the work of the skipper and gunners less strenuous, for we could see
far enough not to take every shadow for a possible aircraft.

I was gazing into the night when I heard the pilot asking the bomb
aimer to have a look in the direction in which we were flying. I could
understand from the short exchange of words between the two that some
firing was going on ahead of our Lancaster, but I controlled my curiosity
and continued to rotate the turret to cover the areas I was expected to watch
from my midupper gunner's position. The skipper called on me to have a
look over the aircraft's bows.

I swung my turret and saw over the port wing, well ahead of our Lancaster, a ribbon of tracer bullets obviously coming from an invisible
bomber, and then a streak of light looking like the tail of a comet. It sped in
our direction, but I suddenly lost sight of it because, as it approached our
aircraft, it disappeared under the port wing. It struck me that a German
night fighter, having attacked one of our bombers and failed, would be
forced to swing a tremendous semicircle in order to rejoin our bomber
stream.

As this thought raced through my mind, an enemy plane appeared from
under our port wing. It flew on a course parallel to our Lancaster but in the
opposite direction. I held the luminous circle of my gun sight on the streak
of light as soon as it became visible again, calculated its size, and made the
necessary firing allowances by setting my sight three radii ahead of the
night fighter. Then I pressed the triggers, saw my two Brownings shoot out
a pattern of tracer, and heard the pilot shout out in a frightened voice,
"Who's firing? Stop firing!"

I remember answering rather peevishly, "All right! Stop shouting! Any-
way, he is breaking up," I added as an afterthought.

I stopped firing almost as soon as the pilot's voice reached me; the night
fighter exploded simultaneously with the appearance of my last tracer bullets in the sky. It broke up into three irregular pieces of fire, which kept
falling for quite some time before reaching the ground, where they continued to burn fiercely. The silence that followed my last words was then bro-

ken by Arthur, who could see the burning debris of the German aircraft from his rear turret after it was lost to the sight of all the other members of the crew. He complimented me on my shooting.

Then Cram spoke in his precise and unhurried voice: "Bomb aimer to navigator: one enemy jet shot down by the midupper gunner."

There was no reply from the navigator. Only then did it strike me that I had been the cause of the enemy aircraft's sudden end—that I had actually shot down a German night fighter—and I felt an unexpected weakness in my knees. Had I not been sitting I might have slumped to the floor.

During the two or three hours of flying that followed the air engagement, not a word was said aboard our bomber regarding the incident. When we landed, the navigator asked me how I had done it. "It was an accident," I replied, but I doubt whether Ben realized how sincere I was when I uttered those words.

Under the date of January 14, 1945, the last entry in my diary, I wrote:

Shot down a jet-propelled plane. Take it very coolly. Everybody else seems to be very thrilled. I feel a little frightened—there is a feeling deep in us, which tells us that blood calls for blood, that shooting down an airplane may mean being shot down oneself.

I am a great deal more moved by the news in today's newspapers that the British Government is against the execution of Hitler and co., but for sending them to some sort of St. Helena. If that is the case, they are clearly thinking of the time when they may need them.

On the following night our squadron was detailed for a night operation against the synthetic oil plant at Zeitz, one of the few remaining oil-producing plants in Hitler's Germany. It was the twenty-fifth operational flight for the majority of our crew. And, strangely, I do believe that we all felt a sense of foreboding upon our departure.

We flew through clouds over England, the Channel, and the breadth of France, crossed into Germany not very far from the Swiss border, and were greeted over the front line by massed batteries of German searchlights.

They were the first enemy searchlights we had seen during our operational tour. Numerous and very powerful, they penetrated the clouds below us and seemed to turn the night into a succession of cold and visible patches of nakedness. One of them must have concentrated on us, for its luminous finger twice touched our stern. It blinded me for a good while and made me fear that, if there were German night fighters around, my eyes, deprived of all night vision, would not detect them in time.

We saw one of our bombers caught in the cone of light sent by several searchlights and corkscrew violently to escape. Our skipper took advantage of the other fellows' predicament and dived our plane through the ruthless and silent javelins of light.

About half an hour later our port-outer engine began to emit a shower of sparks. A little later the engineer feathered the propeller, and I could see it, looking like a dead branch of a living tree, every time I swung my turret forward. But this time the dead engine did not worry me too much, for the Nuremberg raid had convinced me that we could get anywhere on the three remaining ones.

We flew some forty miles north of Frankfurt and could see fires started in that city by another wave of RAF bombers. We saw explosions and searchlights, and the pilot suggested to the bomb aimer that in view of our missing engine we should bomb Frankfurt instead of Zeitz and make for home. Cram replied that we might as well continue on our course for Zeitz, which was "not too far."

We had hardly left Zeitz when the port-inner engine began to shower sparks. It must have been hit by the intense flak we had encountered over the target area. There was nothing else to do but to feather this propeller as well. Yet, despite the matter-of-fact tone in which the flight engineer announced to the skipper what he was going to do, I felt for a moment like leaving the turret and getting hold of my parachute. Of course, I did nothing of the sort, because nobody else seemed to worry, but I swung my midupper turret forward only to see the second port propeller go dead and useless. Nothing seemed to follow the sudden death of more than a thousand horsepower, nothing except the pilot's plaintive voice: "Cram, for Christ's sake, I can't hold the rudders any longer!"

Then Cram's clear voice: "Clary, it's all right, I'm holding them."

He had to use all the weight of his body in order to hold the rudder pedals against the terrific drag of the dead engines until Ron, the flight engineer, having cut off the rope attached to the dinghy, managed to lash the rudders to some solid part of the aircraft.

Ben, busy working out our homeward course, had taken off his ear-phones not to be disturbed by the conversation of the other members of the crew and therefore knew nothing of what was happening. But the port-inner engine provided the electric power for his radar equipment, and its stoppage caused his instruments to cease functioning. It was the first inti-mation he had of trouble aboard the aircraft, and he now suddenly chimed in querulously to announce that his hydraulics had gone, and that we were a quarter of an hour behind the last stragglers in the bomber stream. I do not remember who enlightened him on our changed circumstances.

We dropped to some eleven thousand feet, far below where we should have been. The night became dangerously clear.

Our homeward course was not the shortest way out of Germany. On that particular night, in order to mislead the German night-fighter squadrons, the return course of our bomber force was set to run northwest of Zeitz, between Münster and the Ruhr, and then suddenly to turn west over Holland and the North Sea straight for our bases in Lincolnshire. The last leg of the course was an absolute innovation, for usually the return track ran over the Channel, so as to give limping aircraft a good chance of not having to come down in the sea.

We were alone in the clear night sky, right in the heart of Germany, and almost defenseless. The pilot was hardly able to keep an even course, much less take any evasive action, and was constantly losing height, his speed affected by the slightest wind. The navigator scarcely knew where we were. We were flying in a general northwesterly direction, hoping that we would not stray too far west and thus get caught by the Ruhr antiaircraft defenses.

Not a single unnecessary word was spoken aboard the bomber. Each of us was left alone with his own thoughts and the roar of the engines. I was in a state of mind in which excitement and fear are inextricably linked, but I was not terror-struck. As an air gunner I considered my own and the rear gunner's chances of bailing out in case of emergency: neither of us had his parachute strapped onto his harness nor were our parachutes readily at hand. All I could do to increase my chances of survival was take my para-chute from where it lay outside and put it inside between my legs. As a Jew I could not help wondering what would be my chances of survival should I manage to land in Germany. I was the only one of the crew to carry a revolver, and I was glad to have it. I decided that, if I landed on German soil, I would try to hide so as not to be taken prisoner, and then endeavor to reach Switzerland.

Finally we saw on our starboard a large city lit up by searchlights. Again I could not help wondering why we had never seen a single searchlight during all our previous flights over Germany, and why we were now seeing so many. The navigator and bomb aimer decided after a short discussion that the city was Münster. So we now knew where we were—and that we had not strayed over the Ruhr.

We were down to nine thousand feet. The navigator gave the pilot a new course to follow, and the skipper did his best to enable us to fly it. He needed great skill and tremendous physical energy to steer the wounded Lancaster, for he could not leave the rudders for a single moment. Nor could he get any relief by using the automatic pilot, because that gadget had ceased functioning, as it, too, ran on the electricity supplied by the now dead second engine. The bomb aimer, who had had some training as a pilot, could have replaced him for a while, but such was his sense of duty as skipper that he never left his seat.

As we flew west, my hopes rose. My confidence in the remaining two engines of the bomber being capable of flying us to England grew, but I began to wonder whether Clary would ever be able to land the aircraft in her present disabled condition. I had heard of Flying Fortresses landing on only two engines, but I had never heard of any Lancaster achieving it. It was therefore likely that we should have to bail out at the end of our flight. The prospect of having to use my parachute frightened me so much that I hoped our pilot would try a crash landing. But before I could become seriously preoccupied I realized that after all we were still over Germany and that the very act of thinking about our journey's end was in the nature of a challenge to fate.

As we approached Holland we flew into overcast skies and no longer felt quite so exposed. Our chances of escaping German night fighters increased, but we needed all the luck in the world not to pass over enemy antiaircraft defenses, to which we would have fallen an easy prey. Time always appeared the most relative of sensations while flying; minutes often seemed as long as hours, while hours slipped away never to be recalled. That night my mental registration of time never corresponded in the slightest to the mechanical registration of my watch. Hours elapsed between Münster and Amsterdam, yet nothing remains in my memory to mark their passage. The next registered point in the flow of time was the navigator's voice announcing that we were probably near Amsterdam.

There things began to happen again. I could hear the skipper exchange only half-understood words with the flight engineer, and then it became clear to me that we were losing height too rapidly. Finally I heard the pilot say that our height was only two thousand feet. In spite of the nearness of the earth, we were still wrapped up in clouds, but the fact that we were flying over a country as flat as a pancake eliminated all danger of collision with a hill or building. Our position looked hopeless, and yet with a kind of fierce despair I refused to accept it.

Even at that moment of acute danger our pilot did not forget his crew. He called each of us over the intercom and asked us how we were doing. When he called the rear gunner, no voice replied from the rear turret position. Finally he told me to go find out what had happened to Arthur.

I got out of my turret and debated for a moment with myself whether I should strap the parachute onto my harness or leave it in the turret. After all, in the case of a sudden explosion occurring while I was groping my way in darkness to the Lancaster's rear, it was only too likely that I might not manage to get back to where the parachute lay. But somehow it seemed to me that to strap on my parachute would be a sign of faintheartedness on my part, a kind of abdication to fate, and an expression of distrust.

I made my way to the tail of the aircraft without my parachute and found Arthur standing in front of the entrance hatch, his parachute strapped on, without his helmet and consequently deprived of his earphones and intercom connections. I shouted until he could understand that I, and above all the skipper, wanted him to plug in his intercom and, having seen him do it, returned to my turret.

A day later I heard Arthur tell the wireless operator that when he saw me walking up to him without my parachute on, as if all the engines of the Lancaster were throbbing and roaring, he felt that no disaster could ever happen to our plane.

I plugged in my own intercom just in time to hear the flight engineer tell the pilot that he would risk restarting the feathered engines. Obviously we could not stay even at the height of two thousand feet without their power.

I heard the two dead engines begin to sputter in an unhealthy bout of activity, and then I saw the two feathered propellers begin to rotate, but even before the port-inner propeller acquired sufficient momentum to become invisible to the human eye, pieces of the port-inner nacelle flew loose and hit the fuselage. Fortunately, they had broken loose as a result of vibration and not explosion, for otherwise they would certainly have penetrated the fuselage, and the navigator's cabin would have suffered as if a German shell had hit it.

The port-outer engine worked; a shower of sparks formed its trail and quickly changed into a nice little flame. I could feel the bomber become more certain in its flight even without hearing the navigator announce that we were climbing. At the same time I wondered, with my hands nervously grasping the turret control, whether we could climb high enough before the nice little flame became an uncontrollable blaze. At the height of some eight thousand feet, the flight engineer cut out the port-outer engine, and the propeller again became dead.

The pilot had meanwhile set the aircraft's course for Belgium, because to endeavor a sea crossing on our tired remaining engines would have been sheer madness. Although our navigator had a general idea of where we were, he was unable to pinpoint our position. It now became the wireless operator's task to help by obtaining a fix.

The silence weighed as heavily as lead; time became a slow process measured by one's heartbeat and the tired rhythm of the two remaining engines. At last the navigator's voice resounded again over the intercom. He was telling the skipper our position and giving him a course to follow. The pilot repeated the course to make sure that he had understood correctly, then gave us the order to prepare for bailing out.

I took off my helmet and left it in the turret: to parachute while wearing it was a most dangerous thing to do, as the long intercom leads were known to have strangled several careless airmen. Picking up my parachute, I strapped it onto my harness and walked forward to the passage outside the wireless operator's and navigator's cabins.

I stopped at the bulkhead separating the two cabins. Ronnie, a nervous grin on his face, was sending in Morse to our base headquarters the news that we were abandoning our flight. Ben, all the mysterious lights of his radar apparatus gone, was busily filling in a large sheet in his logbook, looking as unruffled as if he were a chartered accountant examining a ledger. I had caught a glimpse of the flight engineer on first entering the passage but when, from outside the navigator's cabin, I looked for him again, he was no longer at the entrance of the pilot's cockpit.

Ever since my first flight, I had considered with horror the probability of having to jump into space. Whenever I thought that such an emergency might arise, I had hoped that our skipper would avoid it by carrying out a crash landing. I must therefore have reached the passage outside the wireless operator's and navigator's cabins in a state of unbearable tension. Yet I remember perfectly well that, on seeing first Ronnie's grin and then Ben's calmness and businesslike activity, I experienced a sudden sensation of admiration for both and began to feel that our situation was quite an ordinary one and that dangling through space at the end of a parachute was an occurrence to be taken in one's stride as casually as any other everyday event.

It was soon my turn to bail out. I stood in the nose of the aircraft. The escape hatch was gone, and through its opening I saw nothing but the yawning darkness of the night. I dreaded getting my parachute entangled in some part of the bomber and decided to count to five before pulling its rip cord. I sat down on the floor and clumsily put my legs into the gaping void. The slipstream pushed them in, I bent forward, as if I were going to dive, and the same slipstream sucked me smoothly out of the bomber.

My next impression was of elemental silence rent by the plaintive howling of the wind. After the roar of the engines, which had been deafening during my last minutes aboard the bomber due to my no longer having a helmet to protect my ears, the sudden silence of nature was like the work of magic. I pulled the rip cord without counting and, before I even had time to think that my parachute might not open, a sudden and unpleasant jerk reassured me. A wave of elation and grateful joy swept over me at the realization that I was not going to die, and that the land below me was not Germany.

I tried to remember the little parachute-landing drill I had learned, but I was soon out of the cloud that had enveloped me since the moment I had abandoned the Lancaster and could see the earth covered by snow. It appeared to be some distance away even when I hit it.

IN BELGIUM AGAIN

A SEARING PAIN in my right foot was my first intimation of having reached the earth. I remained lying on the snow-covered ground, thinking that it was just my luck to escape great danger, land of all places in Belgium, and yet manage to sprain my ankle at the very last moment. When the pain subsided a little, I got up and tried to walk, but after a few steps the agony became unbearable, and I lay down again and endeavored to think things through.

My wristwatch showed me the time was a quarter past one in the morning. We had thus been airborne for a little over seven hours. I had abandoned the bomber at some six thousand feet in altitude and landed in a narrow country road. Had I landed a few feet to the right or left, in the deep snow covering the fields, I should have most likely escaped all injury. As it was, it was pretty obvious that I could not use my right leg as a means of locomotion, but I consoled myself with the thought that Belgium was a very small and thickly populated country, so I must encounter some house nearby.

I got up again and with some difficulty began to hop on my good left leg and, when I got tired of hopping, I crawled. Finally, I reached what looked like a narrow-gauge railway embankment. I slid down it, crossed the

single-track line, and proceeded to climb the opposite bank. Although it
was neither high nor steep, the snow had made it very slippery. With a
single leg as support, I found it impossible to reach the top. I hopped along
the embankment looking for some means of support until I found a section
of it covered with bushes. I used the bushes to pull myself up, frequently
lost my grip, slid a few times right to the bottom when almost within reach,
and finally made it.

I had to rest for some time before being able to undertake anything further. When I succeeded in standing up again, I could see at some distance
the black outline of a house. At the cost of much energy and even more
determination, I finally reached it, only to discover that it was roofless and
uninhabited. My disappointment was great and my fatigue even greater;
my foot hurt very badly, and I lay down in the snow with the intention of
spending the night where I was.

As I rested, however, my energy came back. I heard the noise of a
motorcar in the distance and then saw its lights sweep the night on its passage. I decided to make for the road along which the car must have traveled
and to wait there for somebody to pass so that I might learn where I was
and possibly find help.

I reached the road after an eternity of effort and hopped along the pavement until I saw a house on the other side of the road. Not a living soul was
abroad, and not the slightest noise of life disturbed the wintry night as I
began to knock at the door.

After a very long while a window and shutter were opened on the first
floor, a man's head appeared, and a frightened voice inquired, *"Qui est la?
Qui est la?"*

I replied in French, "An airman of the RAF. Let me in; I am wounded."

The man answered in an even more frightened voice, "I am all alone
with my children. My wife is not here."

His reply made me frantic, and I pulled out my revolver and threatened
to shoot him if he would not let me in.

He shut the window and was gone long enough to make me wonder
whether I should not fire once through the door. Finally he came out—a
big, bulky man, towering over me but shaking like a leaf.

I asked him where I was and whether there were any Germans about.
He informed me that I was at the outskirts of Jodoigne and that the Ger-

mans were many kilometers away, but he was plainly suspicious, because he asked me again who I was.

"*Un aviateur de la RAF,*" I replied. "*Nom de Dieu, vous ne savez pas dire la différence entre un uniforme anglais et boche?*"

He apologized and repeated that he was alone at home, that his wife was absent, and that I should be better off at the house opposite, for the daughter of the old lady who owned it was a trained nurse. I accepted his advice and hopped across the road holding on to his arm. Following a path through a leafless garden, we reached an old-fashioned *maison de campagne.*

My trembling companion knocked rudely at the door of the silent house. After a short while a little old lady opened the door; the man helped me into the sitting room, said good night to the old lady, and left us. I learned a little later from my hostess that his wife was in prison for having been an enthusiastic collaborator.

Jodoigne had no electricity, so it took me a good while to take in the old-fashioned room, in which the old lady received me by the light of a paraffin lamp. She had a kindly face and gray hair, and looked well over sixty. She told me to sit down in an armchair and to be patient, because her daughter, who was a nurse, would be with us presently. As I sat down I looked at my wristwatch and realized that it was a quarter past four in the morning. It had taken me almost three hours to reach her house.

Madame Servais's daughter appeared after a short while, gazed at me with an embarrassing intensity, and then asked me whether I was not a German *parachutiste* parading in a British uniform. When I had reassured her she told me to take the flying boot off my right foot, examined it, and said that it looked as if I had a fractured ankle. The little old lady asked me whether I was a Jew, and when I nodded she told me that she had three Jews in her house who would certainly be very happy to see me.

Mademoiselle Servais left the room to fetch them. There were two young lads in their twenties and an old man, their father, bearded and with lovelocks, who looked as if he had never left the Galician town or village in which he had been born. The old man shook my hand and stood speechless with incredulity. After a while, having discovered that I knew Yiddish, he told me in the unpleasant Yiddish dialect of Galicia how he and his sons had come to be saved by Madame and Mademoiselle Servais.

Madame Servais had made the acquaintance of one of his boys in 1940, and when in 1941 the Germans began to round up all foreign-born Jews living in Belgium, she sent her daughter to Antwerp to offer him and his sons refuge in her house. She kept the three of them in the attic, risking, of course, her own and her daughter's life. Although by no means a rich woman, she spent quite a fortune on buying the necessary food for them at black market prices. From 1942 until the invasion she also had a German officer billeted in her house and occupying a ground-floor room. His presence saved her from the attention of the local Gestapo and their Belgian aides but did not make life very easy for those living there. Not content with sheltering three Jews, the old lady had also turned her house into a transit point for escaped British prisoners of war, of whom some forty had enjoyed her hospitality. In 1944, in expectation of the invasion and fearing that her house might be suddenly taken over by German troops, Madame Servais had the local Belgian underground organization build a secret chamber in her cellar and connect it through a thirty-yard tunnel with an abandoned shed in her garden, so that her Jewish wards would have a chance of escape if worse came to worst.

So that was how, in a manner that I might have been justified in regarding as symbolic, I met the first people of my race who had survived Hitler's implacable hatred. Yet our greetings were as restrained and almost casual as if we were Britons of a certain class. We said so little not only because our hearts were brimful with sorrow but mainly because we had lost the ability of our ancestors to express feelings in great words, tears, and gestures of pathos.

I was too overwhelmed by my own experience and sheer physical pain to appreciate fully the heroism and nobility of the little old lady and her daughter. Still, I had enough sense to tell them, when they expressed their admiration for what we had to bear as airmen, that there was nothing they could learn from us in regard to bravery. To return to the abattoir and charnel house that the Continent had become and to encounter immediately three Jews, who survived because there were still good and brave people about, was something for which I felt deeply thankful.

I discovered that there were British troops stationed at some distance from my hostesses' house, and I sent one of the young Jews with a note giving my name, number, and the probable nature of my injury. He returned with a towering Welsh Guardsman and Ronnie, the wireless operator, whom they had met on the road. Ronnie looked slightly shaken by his experiences. He had landed on the roof of an old barn and gone right through up to his armpits. He had felt "so disgusted" at his position that he spent half an hour smoking cigarettes before bothering to extricate himself. He was the last but one to bail out, and he did not think that our skipper was likely to have escaped, because our plane had been shuddering as if it were about to blow up at any moment when he rushed past Clary to the escape hatch. His own escape had been delayed because Arthur, whose turn to bail out came after mine, had discovered at the very last moment that his harness was twisted and certain to come off in midair. Ronnie helped him to straighten it out, but this cost them several precious minutes.

I said good-bye to the two Belgian ladies and the three men who owed them their lives, and left their house on the Welsh Guardsman's back. On the way to the school where his detachment was billeted, the Guardsman made me an offer of several thousand Belgian francs for my flying boots and revolver. I did not think my boots would ever fit his feet, but I felt I owed him something for the patient manner in which he carried me on his back, so I told him that he could have them both without payment, provided he supply me with some other kind of footwear. As soon as we reached the school, he gave me his pair of gym shoes, which were of a size that even a giant would have found comfortable.

Inside the school, by the dim light of hurricane lamps, fully dressed men wrapped in blankets were fast asleep on the floors of classrooms and what appeared to be the main hall. Ron, the flight engineer, was there too, tearing up his parachute into strips of nylon for his girlfriend's use, and at about six o'clock in the morning Arthur was led into the school by a returning patrol.

It was still dark when the ambulance drove up and carried me off to Brussels. Arthur and the two Rons came along with me and waited in the reception room of the hospital, which I had known as a student, until I was finally accepted and conveyed to bed. By then I was very tired and only half aware of what was happening around me. Yet despite the physical agony I suffered, I felt very happy indeed when, having been washed and shaved by an efficient and friendly orderly, I finally landed between two white sheets. I could not relax, however, until I had a young hospital aide telephone my Belgian friends and bring back the news that they were in good health in Brussels.

An X ray of my right foot showed a broken ankle and three fractured metatarsi. I was wheeled into the operating theater late in the evening, and I woke up in my own bed feeling relieved and hungry. I slept through the night without any dreams and on the following morning had the joy of seeing all my flying companions, including the skipper, by my bedside.

I learned from Arthur that when Clary had made his dash for the escape hatch, without the automatic pilot to keep the Lancaster on an even keel, the plane had been only a thousand feet above sea level. The pilot was scarcely outside the bomber when it blew up. Altogether we were one of the luckiest crews to fly on that January night through the skies of Western Europe. But that visit to my bedside was the last time we were all to be together.

The kind and honest Minnes arrived in the afternoon. They kissed me and greeted me like a son who had made good, and left me a huge Flemish tart that must have cost a fortune. They were followed by Madame and Monsieur Caprasse, who greeted me with no less affection and showered me with such fruit and pastry as I had not seen—let alone tasted—since 1940. I had hardly any time and opportunity to enjoy their company, however, for at least half a dozen people whom I scarcely knew turned up to give me a hero's welcome. Although they prevented me from tasting fully the delight of my best friends' company, I could not but feel touched and proud at their presence.

On the following day I had even more visitors. There were only two Jews among them, one of whom, a middle-aged man born in Odessa, was a friend of mine. He owed his life to the Minnes and another Belgian. The striking thing about his escape was that neither the Minnes, who provided him with food for almost two years, nor the Belgian jeweler who hid him in a little attic over his business had been his friends at the time they offered to save him. The Minnes knew him only as my friend, while the jeweler had only once had business dealings with him. To them and his own ability to stay in the attic without making the slightest noise in daytime, so that his presence would remain unknown to the jeweler's partner for twenty months or so, he owed his survival.

From my visitors I learned all I wanted about the people I had known in Brussels during my years of hunger, humiliation, and dreams. Of my Jewish acquaintances, more than half were dead, and not even their bones remained. Even my aunt in Antwerp, a woman in her late sixties, failed to escape the gas chambers. She had been bedridden since 1940, when she had been knocked down by a car. The Gestapo came to her flat in 1943 and carried her on a stretcher to a train that took her to one of the death factories in Poland. As for my cousin and her husband, they had spent the years between the fall of France and the Allies' return to the Continent in Vichy France, where their money and Belgian nationality saved them from becoming victims of Laval's exchange deals with Hitler. They were already back in Brussels and getting richer every day.

There was much sweetness, but even more bitterness, in my return to Brussels. In the first place, it made me realize that this was the nearest thing to a homecoming I could ever hope to achieve. To think of the pride and joy my parents would have felt at seeing me in the uniform of the country to which they ascribed almost legendary virtues only served to bring home the completeness of the tragedy and catastrophe brought about by the evil genius of a man and a sick nation.

As an aircrew I was given priority in the allocation of berths aboard the fleet of ambulance planes engaged in evacuating wounded and sick servicemen to Britain. Consequently I had only four days of pampering and affection at the Brussels hospital before being taken in an ambulance to Evere Airport, from where a Dakota was to fly me over to England. But as I arrived at the airport, a blizzard broke out and all flights for England were canceled. Bad weather over Belgium and England delayed my flight for six days, which I spent fully dressed on a stretcher in what was formerly the waiting hall of the airport. However uncomfortable and disappointing those days were after the four full days at the hospital, they were far from boring. My Belgian friends visited me daily and enjoyed the atmosphere of cheerful expectancy and suffering, the strong cups of tea, and the occasional film shows that the makeshift sick quarters offered to its few visitors. Therefore, although I was unable to have a real wash or change my shirt, and my foot hurt enough to keep me awake often until the early hours of the morning, I did not feel too impatient. The news that the Soviet Army had reached the Oder was enough to keep my thoughts away from my injury.

Finally the weather cleared and I was loaded aboard a Dakota in the company of a large batch of soldiers. My recent experience had not made me more than reasonably apprehensive of flying for, although I did not even have a parachute, I spent the flight reading and enjoying a volume of short stories by O. Henry.

THE BEGINNING
OF THE END

I LANDED IN ONE of the largest RAF hospitals in the country and dis-covered that life there had two disadvantages: I was not allowed suffi-cient sleep and I did not get enough food. Unable to fall asleep before midnight, I found it very hard to have to wake up at five o'clock in the morning, only in order to wet my face and hands with hot water, and found it even more difficult to understand why my fellow inmates and myself should be given much less, and much worse, food at the hospital than we had been used to getting when perfectly healthy and able to visit cafés and restaurants.

Lack of sleep and food are not, of course, the only memories I have car-ried away from the hospital and, if the other impressions come second to my mind, the reason is obvious. Having escaped death by a miracle and being therefore supremely aware of the joy of being alive, I subconsciously fought against the horror and tragedy surrounding me by clinging to the prosaic facts of life with more selfishness than I should have done under different circumstances.

There was enough misery around me to make me often embarrassed, if not ashamed, at the elemental, animal joy I experienced at being alive. But even in this refuge of mortified flesh and broken limbs, human nature refused to be beaten. Several aircrew patients, who because of the nature of their wounds had had to stay in the hospital for years, undergoing repeated operations, had married their nurses. As for the others who, like myself, were not seriously wounded or injured, they were soon flirting with the nurses and buxom WAAF ambulance drivers. The atmosphere of the place was not unlike that of a wartime dance hall. The presence of WAAFs and VAD nurses, the combination of the surreal cinema world and the not entirely real hospital world, charged the very air with a current of eroticism.

After a fortnight or so spent in bed, I was allowed to walk about the hospital with the aid of crutches. By then I had begun to chafe in earnest under the routine of hospital life, to miss my crewmates, and to feel increasingly lost and lonely without the comradeship and purpose of squadron life. So it was with an end-of-term feeling that I received the news of having been granted a month's leave—a period deemed sufficient by my surgeon for the broken bones in my foot to set.

I went to London to stay with my distant cousin Sarah and her cousin Sam. At the hospital they had not been able to find a boot big enough to encase my broken foot, so I now hopped about London with my right foot in a woolen stocking. It did not take me long to learn the art of walking on crutches, although a little deftness was required when boarding a bus or getting off the Underground escalators. Women could rarely hide their anxiety as they saw me approach the moment when I would have to get off the moving staircase. Often they offered to help me, which I refused not out of pride but because I could do it much better on my own.

On the whole, although my broken foot often hurt and the use of crutches turned walking into real work, I enjoyed being an invalid, for London was no longer politely indifferent to my existence. I could see people taking notice of me, and on several occasions I experienced their kindness. At times, when I wanted to pay my bill at restaurants, I was told that it had been settled by some anonymous diner. Once, as I was waiting in a long queue outside a West End cinema, the manager ushered me inside ahead of everybody else and told me that my seat had been paid for by a young lady. However, my most cherished memory of that month in London had nothing to do with pecuniary generosity.

The incident happened just after I had visited the Soviet Consulate in Kensington in the vain hope that I might be able to find out what had happened to my family. The official, whose distrustful peasant face and way of speaking Russian showed that he owed his position to the effects of the October Revolution, told me quite rightly that millions of Soviet people had been killed and dispersed, and that I would have to wait for the war to end before I could discover the fate of my parents and sisters. Although I had expected very little when I decided to visit the consulate, I could not help feeling deeply depressed. I hopped along to the nearest bus stop and had taken my place in a short and disciplined queue of servicemen, house-wives, and officials of several exiled governments when a little elderly woman, pinched and worried, appeared from nowhere and said to me, "Thank you, thank you very much." I had enough presence of mind to ask, "What for?" She pointed to my foot, replied, "For what you have done for us," and she and her shopping bag were gone.

After a fortnight in London, however, I again began to miss my crew-mates badly. I took a train north and arrived at Fogdrome, hoping to meet them there and to experience again the comradeship of squadron life. I found only Ron, our flight engineer, who on returning from Belgium had immediately volunteered for another operational tour. I learned from him that the others were on indefinite leave, and that our crew was no longer a family—even worse, had ceased to be a band of friends.

"Gongs" were the cause. Our skipper had been awarded a Distin-guished Flying Cross immediately after the crew's return to base, while the wireless operator and flight engineer received Distinguished Flying Medals a few weeks later. Neither the navigator nor the bomb aimer, who throughout the tour displayed unfailing skill and determination, and who on the last trip had done so much to make it possible for our pilot to bring us as far as Belgium, was awarded a decoration. When it later transpired that both Ron and Ronnie owed their DFMs to the recommendations of their section leaders and not of our own skipper, the other members of the crew began to ask questions and discovered that our captain had given no credit in his report on our last flight to anybody but himself. When we later saw the citation of his award, it read as if he had been the only man aboard the Lancaster.

I returned to London a sadder man than when I had set out for Lin-colnshire. With the end of the war in sight and the comradeship of squadron life gone forever, the thought of what my life would be like when peace came and the gnawing doubt as to whether living would make any sense at all with the world that had created me forever gone became the constant companions of my waking hours. I was therefore glad when my month's leave ended and I had to go back to the discipline and collective existence of a convalescence center. The center, at Hoylake in Cheshire, was in a requisitioned boarding school whose grounds adjoined one of the most famous golf courses in England. I arrived there to find the sweet smells and noises of spring wafted by breezes from the Irish Sea.

The place was run with that maximum of informality and freedom, yet with that minimum of discipline and efficiency that only the English seem capable of contriving. We got up at eight and spent the morning doing physical exercises suitable to the nature of our injuries, receiving physio-therapeutic treatment, taking long bicycle rides along the sea, or swimming in the school's covered pool. On certain afternoons we danced with a bevy of local maidens specially vetted by a formidable-looking local matron. After four in the afternoon we were free to do what we liked.

There was very little one could do with one's spare time apart from going to the local cinema, visiting the nightly dance in the town hall attended by the types of ingenuous teenagers of whom American service-men are so fond, or crawling from one dismal pub to another. Liverpool was very near, but the city depressed me by its ugliness and could offer a stranger in uniform only overcrowded service clubs and pubs full of drunken sailors, slovenly prostitutes, and hard-faced good-time girls.

Of course, the fault was not with my surroundings but with myself. This was the time when the American and British Armies, having crossed the Rhine, were racing across Germany to the Elbe and the mountain vast-ness of Bavaria, where what remained of the Fuehrer's Reich was expected to make its last stand. In their advances the British had come upon Belsen and the Americans upon Dachau and Buchenwald. The newspapers were suddenly full of pictures of naked heaps of skin-covered skeletons being bulldozed into gaping ditches, or others dressed in striped pajamas crawl-ing about with expressions of pariah dogs. Any one of them, of course, could have been my mother, father, or one of my three sisters; my nephew, my niece, or any of the many relatives and friends I had left behind in Wilno and Brussels.

There was not much in those pictures that truly surpassed the horrors I had lived with since that day at Miranda de Ebro when I had learned for the first time from a German Jew of the existence of the gas chambers. Nevertheless, the contrast between the fate of those who had remained on the Continent and my own, which I was once again compelled to realize as I watched the newsreels in the local cinema, was too great to allow me to preserve even the subdued mood of joie de vivre that had been mine since my last flight. It was not so much pity for my people as helpless anger that corroded my mind and feelings. Anger at the reactions of the people around me, who now for the first time appeared to be convinced that Nazi Germany had committed unimaginable horrors. It had been necessary for British soldiers to see and smell the typhus-ridden inside of Belsen before the great British public would at last really believe what the newspapers and numerous refugees in its midst had been telling it for years. There was anger in me because I felt that if British people as a whole had believed earlier in the reality of Hitler's crimes, they would have forced their government to do at least as much to save the Jews as it had done to help the Poles.

In such a state of mind, inactivity became quite unbearable. I also felt a growing urge to return to the Continent and, above all, to step on German soil. I wanted to get to Germany in the hope of finding out what had happened to my family, but I was also driven by a devouring curiosity to see with my own eyes the men and women who had proved themselves capable of betraying every decent and rational element in European civilization.

Toward the end of April I traveled to London. I could now wear a shoe on my injured foot and walk with a cane, and I was absolutely determined to cut my convalescence and get back to active service.

Once in London I did something that I feel could never have been done in any other country but England. Although my rank was only that of a flight sergeant and I knew nobody in Whitehall, I simply went to the Air Ministry and asked to see somebody who could make use of my linguistic qualifications. I may have been exceptionally lucky, but the fact is that I was immediately told where to go and whom to see. The man I wanted to meet turned out to be a studious-looking squadron leader who asked me a few questions and listened attentively to what I had to say about myself. He told me to return a few days later, and I was then examined in German by a wing commander and in Russian by a hefty woman of the ancien régime, who told me to read and translate a *Pravda* article on the progress of spring sowings in Kazakhstan. I did sufficiently well in both examinations to be told that my posting to the RAF Intelligence Branch would follow.

In expectation of the posting, I spent my time watching the mallards and ducklings in Regent's Park, examining lists of Jewish survivors compiled by Jewish welfare organizations and, above all, worrying over the progress of the battle for Berlin.

But, for once, my apprehension proved unfounded. Zhukov's and Rokossovsky's armies broke the last desperate resistance of the Nazi war machine and ended the war in Berlin. Had the Americans and British occupied Berlin instead of the Red Army, it would have been easy for German nationalists to create another myth of German invincibility—to claim that they had not really lost their capital in battle but had surrendered it for the sake of Europe's future or to spare good Nordic blood. But to have suffered the fullness of defeat at the hands of despised Slavs and Asiatics after a titanic struggle disposed forever of the myth of German racial superiority and made it hard even for a people as gullible as the Germans to go on believing that they were invincible.

My elation at the news of the fall of Berlin did not last very long. VE-Day came and found me at my relatives' home. Had I been born, like them, in England, this would have been for me, too, a day of elated rejoicing. But I never felt more lonely, never more part and parcel of the millions of Jews for whom victory had come much too late, than on that day in London. I had shared their life, their hopes, some of their sufferings, the long road they had traveled from medievalism, spiritual and physical degradation, and religious fatalism to mental and physical health. They had survived for two thousand years to see at last the beginning of their emancipation as a nation and now, in less than five years, they had been wiped off the face of the earth. My survival seemed senseless and undeserved.

A signal from the Air Ministry posting me to the Intelligence Branch followed shortly afterward. But an unexpected obstacle to my plans suddenly appeared in the person of an Air Ministry doctor whose duty it was to find out whether I was fit for overseas service. He examined my foot and decided that, although I might be able to return to duty in the United Kingdom, I was unfit for overseas service. It took all my powers of persuasion to make him see that my duties abroad would be no more strenuous than if I were posted to an office job in London, but it was my final confession that

I wanted to get to the Continent because I hoped to find out what had happened to my family that made him relent.

I reported to an address in Kensington and found myself one of a company of German, Russian, and French interpreters presided over by a tall and slouching English squadron leader who had learned his languages before the war in the export business and was now permanently on the brink of a nervous breakdown. My colleagues were either Russian-born Scotsmen or Englishmen, politically more obtuse than the most reactionary White Guards, or Austrian, German, and Czech Jews, several of them ex-aircrew like myself. I made friends with one of them, an RAF observer by the name of Harry, whose faith in mankind and the future despite the gassing of his mother was utopian enough to make him support Sir Richard Acland's Common Wealth Party.

I found it extremely difficult to have to stay for eight hours every day within the four walls of an office, exposed to the choleric temper and fussiness of the squadron leader: it was too much like going back to school after the free and unfettered life I had known as an aircrew. It is true, though, that on a few occasions the monotony of our office life was broken by such forms of entertainment as full dress rehearsals of imaginary intelligence interrogations and shows of captured German newsreels. The interrogations consisted of one of our army officers dressing up as a German general and being interrogated by another officer, with one of us acting as an interpreter. The major who specialized in playing the part of a German general was extremely good: he had the presence of a Hindenburg and wore a monocle in real life. Of the film shows the most remarkable was a film of the execution of the officers who took part in the July 1944 attempt to save Germany from her day of reckoning by blowing up their Fuehrer with a bomb. We saw them being garroted and then strung up from butcher's hooks; I can still hear their frightful, degrading, inhuman screams.

After a fortnight spent under the watchful eyes of our temperamental squadron leader, I was posted to the Supreme Headquarters of the Allied Expeditionary Forces at Versailles. A few days later I boarded an early train at Victoria Station in the company of Harry and another RAF navigator, who looked very much like a younger edition of Anthony Eden and was one of those Hungarians who have the charm and debonair manners of a Viennese count. He later improved his worldly prospects by refusing to deny that he was a count after he had been persistently addressed as one by a very large number of Germans and not a few Britons, who had been greatly impressed by his looks and grand manner.

We embarked at Newhaven and after an uneventful passage sailed into the shattered harbor of Dieppe. I stepped ashore troubled by conflicting feelings. I was back on the continent of Europe. As I walked from the ship to the waiting train, I felt as if I were treading unclean soil soaked with Jewish blood—the hateful, indifferent, hostile yet beloved soil of a continent to which I would always belong.

ABOUT THE AUTHOR

REUBEN AINSZTEIN was born in Wilno, Poland. After serving as a turret gunner for the RAF during World War II, he worked as a writer and researcher for the BBC and Reuters, specializing in Eastern European affairs. He was the author of two critically acclaimed studies on the Jewish Resistance: *Jewish Resistance in Nazi-Occupied Eastern Europe* and *The Warsaw Ghetto Revolt*. Married in 1941 to Pat Kearey, Reuben Ainsztein died in 1981.

ABOUT THE TYPE

This book is set in Fournier, a typeface named for Pierre Simon Fournier, the youngest son of a French printing family. He started out engraving woodblocks and large capitals, then moved on to fonts of type. In 1736 he began his own foundry and made several important contributions in the field of type design; he is said to have cut 147 alphabets of his own creation. Fournier is probably best remembered as the designer of St. Augustine Ordinaire, a face that served as the model for Monotype's Fournier, which was released in 1925.